Hands-On Design Patterns with Java

Learn design patterns that enable the building of large-scale software architectures

Dr. Edward Lavieri

BIRMINGHAM - MUMBAI

Hands-On Design Patterns with Java

Commissioning Editor: Richa Tripathi
Acquisition Editor: Denim Pinto
Content Development Editor: Tiksha Sarang
Technical Editor: Royce John
Copy Editor: Safis Editing
Project Coordinator: Prajakta Naik
Proofreader: Safis Editing
Indexer: Rekha Nair
Graphics: Jisha Chirayil
Production Coordinator: Arvindkumar Gupta

First published: April 2019

Production reference: 1250419

Published by Packt Publishing Ltd.
Livery Place
35 Livery Street
Birmingham
B3 2PB, UK.

ISBN 978-1-78980-977-0

www.packtpub.com

To IBB, my ride or die, and our eternal puppies, Muzz and Java.

– Ed

`mapt.io`

Mapt is an online digital library that gives you full access to over 5,000 books and videos, as well as industry leading tools to help you plan your personal development and advance your career. For more information, please visit our website.

Why subscribe?

- Spend less time learning and more time coding with practical eBooks and Videos from over 4,000 industry professionals

- Improve your learning with Skill Plans built especially for you

- Get a free eBook or video every month

- Mapt is fully searchable

- Copy and paste, print, and bookmark content

Packt.com

Did you know that Packt offers eBook versions of every book published, with PDF and ePub files available? You can upgrade to the eBook version at `www.packt.com` and as a print book customer, you are entitled to a discount on the eBook copy. Get in touch with us at `customercare@packtpub.com` for more details.

At `www.packt.com`, you can also read a collection of free technical articles, sign up for a range of free newsletters, and receive exclusive discounts and offers on Packt books and eBooks.

Contributors

About the author

Dr. Edward Lavieri is a veteran software engineer and developer with a strong academic background. He earned a Doctorate of Computer Science from Colorado Technical University, an MS in Management Information Systems (Bowie State University), an MS in Education (Capella University), and an MS in Operations Management (University of Arkansas). He has been creating and teaching computer science courses since 2002. Edward retired from the U.S. Navy as a Command Master Chief after 25 years of active service. He is the founder and creative director of three19, a software design and development studio. Edward has authored more than a dozen technology books, including several on Java.

About the reviewer

Aristides Villarreal Bravo is a Java developer, a member of the NetBeans Dream Team, and a Java User Groups leader. He lives in Panama. He has organized and participated in various conferences and seminars related to Java, JavaEE, NetBeans, the NetBeans platform, free software, and mobile devices. He is the author of jmoordb framework, and tutorials and blogs about Java, NetBeans, and web development. He has participated in several interviews about topics such as NetBeans, NetBeans DZone, and JavaHispano. He is a developer of plugins for NetBeans.

Packt is searching for authors like you

If you're interested in becoming an author for Packt, please visit authors.packtpub.com and apply today. We have worked with thousands of developers and tech professionals, just like you, to help them share their insight with the global tech community. You can make a general application, apply for a specific hot topic that we are recruiting an author for, or submit your own idea.

Table of Contents

Section 2: Original Design Patterns

Preface

This book was written to provide software engineers, system architects, and software developers a timeless reference and guide on over 60 design patterns. While the examples are provided in Java, the explanations and examples are programming language-agnostic.

In addition to covering behavioral, creational, structural, architectural, functional, and reactive design patterns, this book provides the reader with an introduction to the **Unified Modeling Language** (**UML**) and **Object-Oriented Programming** (**OOP**). UML is covered with specific focus on behavioral and structural diagrams, as they are used throughout the book to provide a deeper understanding of the featured design-pattern implementations. OOP is covered to provide the reader with an overview or refresher, depending on their experience. Understanding OOP principles is key to understanding how to program in Java.

Who this book is for

This book is for software engineers, system architects, and software developers that want to understand the different design patterns and how they can be used to create more efficient and resilient systems. Familiarity with the fundamentals of the Java programming language is expected.

What this book covers

Chapter 1, *Unified Modeling Language Primer*, provides an introduction to UML and explains how it is used to help communicate class structures, objects, and interactions. Four behavioral diagrams and six structural diagrams are explained, along with examples to help solidify your understanding of these important components in systems design, and their applicability to the design patterns featured in this book.

Chapter 2, *Object-Oriented Design Patterns*, explores fundamental, intermediate, and advanced concepts and approaches to OOP and their applicability to design patterns. OOP approaches are examined and a complete OOP class serves as an example of how to implement OOP concepts. The principles of design patterns are explored, which will prime you to dive into the design patterns featured in the rest of the book.

Chapter 3, *Behavioral Design Patterns*, explores behavioral design patterns with a specific focus on the chain of responsibility, command, interpreter, iterator, mediator, memento, null object, observer, state, strategy, template method, and visitor design patterns. This chapter demonstrates how behavioral design patterns focus on how system components interact to form a system.

Chapter 4, *Creational Design Patterns*, takes a thorough look at the abstract factory, builder, factory method, prototype, simple factory, and singleton design patterns. The exploration of these six creational design patterns demonstrates how they are used to manage objects as they are instantiated.

Chapter 5, *Structural Design Patterns*, provides detailed information on the adapter, bridge, composite, decorator, facade, flyweight, and proxy structural design patterns. These patterns have either an object scope or class scope and relate to how objects and classes are combined to form a system.

Chapter 6, *Architectural Design Patterns – Part I*, examines the blackboard, broker, client-server, event-driven, extract-transform-load, layered, master-slave, and microkernel architectural design patterns. These design patterns are explained, as is their applicability to system-level design.

Chapter 7, *Architectural Design Patterns – Part II*, continues our coverage of architectural design patterns with a specific look at the microservices, model-view-controller, naked objects, peer-to-peer, pipe-filter, serverless, service-oriented, and space-based design patterns.

Chapter 8, *Functional Design Patterns*, takes a look at functional design and functional programming. The execute around, lambda, loan, MapReduce, memoization, streams, and tail call patterns are examined. The chapter also reviews how functional design patterns use functional programming to solve computational problems and system design challenges.

Chapter 9, *Reactive Design Patterns*, examines the responsive, resilient, elastic, and message-driven characteristics of reactive design patterns. Specific design patterns covered in this chapter include asynchronous communication, autoscaling, bounded queue, bulkhead, caching, circuit breaker, event-driven communication, fail fast, failure handling, fan-out and quickest reply, idempotency, monitoring, publisher-subscriber, self-containment, and stateless patterns.

To get the most out of this book

The reader should have a familiarity with Java and be capable of writing, compiling, and executing Java applications. In order to execute the examples in this book, the reader should have access to a 64-bit version of Windows 7 (SP1), 8, or 10; a Mac with macOS 10.11 or higher; or a computer running Linux GNOME or KDE desktop.

Download the example code files

You can download the example code files for this book from your account at www.packt.com. If you purchased this book elsewhere, you can visit www.packt.com/support and register to have the files emailed directly to you.

You can download the code files by following these steps:

1. Log in or register at www.packt.com.
2. Select the **SUPPORT** tab.
3. Click on **Code Downloads & Errata**.
4. Enter the name of the book in the **Search** box and follow the onscreen instructions.

Once the file is downloaded, please make sure that you unzip or extract the folder using the latest version of:

- WinRAR/7-Zip for Windows
- Zipeg/iZip/UnRarX for Mac
- 7-Zip/PeaZip for Linux

The code bundle for the book is also hosted on GitHub at https://github.com/PacktPublishing/Hands-On-Design-Patterns-with-Java. In case there's an update to the code, it will be updated on the existing GitHub repository.

We also have other code bundles from our rich catalog of books and videos available at https://github.com/PacktPublishing/. Check them out!

Download the color images

We also provide a PDF file that has color images of the screenshots/diagrams used in this book. You can download it here: https://www.packtpub.com/sites/default/files/downloads/9781789809770_ColorImages.pdf.

Conventions used

There are a number of text conventions used throughout this book.

`CodeInText`: Indicates code words in text, database table names, folder names, filenames, file extensions, pathnames, dummy URLs, user input, and Twitter handles. Here is an example: "Next, we have the `Mother` class, which extends `Grandmother` and has its own constructor method."

A block of code is set as follows:

```
Mother() {
    System.out.println("Mother constructor executed.");
}
}
```

When we wish to draw your attention to a particular part of a code block, the relevant lines or items are set in bold:

```
public abstract class MotorHomeAbstractFactory {
    public abstract Frame createFrame();
    public abstract Style createStyle();
    public abstract Engine createEngine();
    public abstract Kitchen createKitchen();
}
```

Bold: Indicates a new term, an important word, or words that you see onscreen. For example, words in menus or dialog boxes appear in the text like this. Here is an example: "Beneath the **Receive Order** node is a horizontal black bar referred to as a **fork**."

Warnings or important notes appear like this.

Tips and tricks appear like this.

Get in touch

Feedback from our readers is always welcome.

General feedback: If you have questions about any aspect of this book, mention the book title in the subject of your message and email us at customercare@packtpub.com.

Errata: Although we have taken every care to ensure the accuracy of our content, mistakes do happen. If you have found a mistake in this book, we would be grateful if you would report this to us. Please visit www.packt.com/submit-errata, selecting your book, clicking on the Errata Submission Form link, and entering the details.

Piracy: If you come across any illegal copies of our works in any form on the Internet, we would be grateful if you would provide us with the location address or website name. Please contact us at copyright@packt.com with a link to the material.

If you are interested in becoming an author: If there is a topic that you have expertise in and you are interested in either writing or contributing to a book, please visit authors.packtpub.com.

Reviews

Please leave a review. Once you have read and used this book, why not leave a review on the site that you purchased it from? Potential readers can then see and use your unbiased opinion to make purchase decisions, we at Packt can understand what you think about our products, and our authors can see your feedback on their book. Thank you!

For more information about Packt, please visit packt.com.

Section 1: Introducing Design Patterns

In this section, you will gain an understanding of the concept and significance of design patterns, learn necessary unified modeling language constructs, and learn how design patterns are classified into a comprehensive library.

The following chapters will be covered:

- Chapter 1, *Unified Modeling Language Primer*
- Chapter 2, *Object-Oriented Design Patterns*

1
Unified Modeling Language Primer

This book features several design patterns and covers their implementation using Java. We can use **Unified Modeling Language (UML)** to help communicate class structures, objects, and interactions. This chapter provides an overview of UML, with a specific focus on diagrams applicable to the hands-on activities in this book.

The following topics will be covered in this chapter:

- Introducing UML
- Behavior diagrams
- Structural diagrams

Technical requirements

This chapter does not have any technical requirements. In order to create UML diagrams, the following open source software tool is recommended:

- Modelio, which is available at `https://www.modelio.org`

Modelio can be run on systems with any of the following operating systems:

- Debian/Ubuntu
- macOS X
- RedHat/CentOS
- Windows 7
- Windows 8
- Windows 10

Introducing UML

UML was developed in 1994 to document object-oriented systems. Since that time, UML has become a standard tool for software engineers, software developers, and businesses. UML is used to design software and, after programming, also provides a visual record for the system which can be included as part of formal software documentation.

There are two types of UML diagrams—behavioral and structural. Both are described in the sections that follow.

Understanding behavioral UML diagrams

Behavioral diagrams illustrate how system components interact to form a system. The four diagrams listed here are behavioral, and are briefly described in the subsections that follow:

- Activity diagrams
- Interaction diagrams
- State machine diagrams
- Use case diagrams

Activity diagrams

Activity diagrams illustrate the flow of processes in a system. This type of diagram is used to visually document activities within a system, also referred to as a system's procedures or dynamic components.

The following activity diagram shows the activities involved when a coffee shop customer places an order. The starting point is the top black circle. From there, an order is received. Beneath the **Receive Order** node is a horizontal black bar referred to as a **fork**. There are three activities that take place in parallel after the fork—**Make Drink**, **Get Bakery**, and **Collect Payment**. All of those activities take place in parallel. Each of those activities feed into a second black bar, this time referred to as a **join**, which has multiple activities linked to it. Once all three activities are completed, the order can be completed and ends with the bottom black circle:

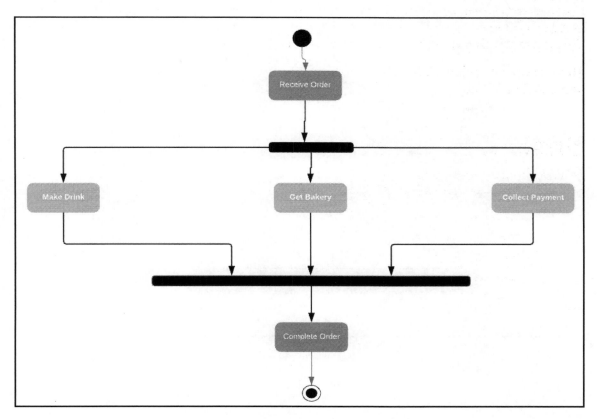

An activity diagram for a coffee shop order process

Interaction diagrams

Interaction diagrams visually document how system components interact with each other.

In the following interaction diagram, you can see that the flow starts with a decision on whether the customer is a new, or already existing, customer. In both cases, the interaction between the **Customer** object and **Customer Database** object is documented:

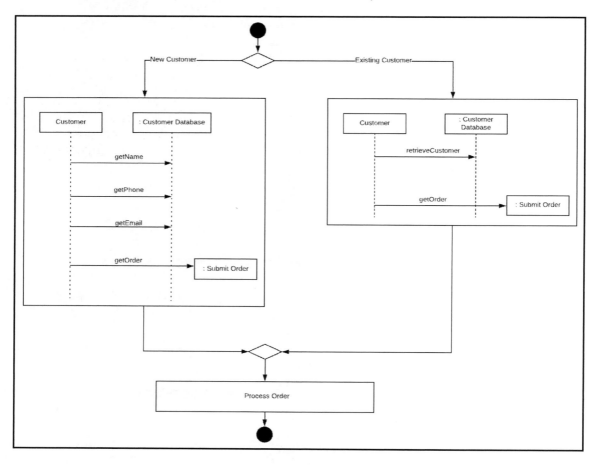

An interaction diagram for a coffee shop order

Interaction UML diagrams are robust and come in several different types. The interaction UML diagram types are listed here and will be covered in the subsequent sections:

- Sequence diagram
- Communication diagram
- Timing diagram

Sequence diagrams

Sequence diagrams are used to show a specific use case scenario. So, these diagrams are representative of a typical behavior based on the given use case.

The following sequence diagram example visually documents the use case where a student logs on to an online book order system and enters their course code. The online system calculates a price and provides this total to the student. The student is then able to submit their payment, which goes through the online bookstore and informs the fulfillment center, which ships the books to the student:

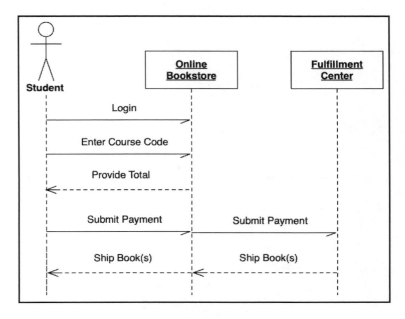

An example sequence diagram

Communication diagrams

Communication diagrams are a special type of interaction diagrams. They focus on how system participants are linked to one another.

The following sample communication UML diagram is a partial look at an online book-ordering system. System participants and their associations are provided:

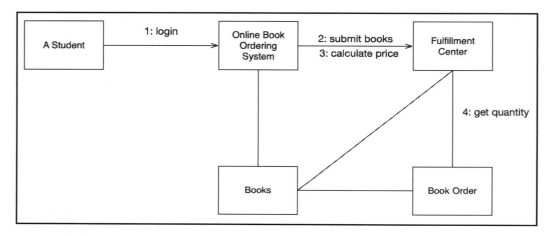

A sample communication diagram

Timing diagrams

Timing UML diagrams provide a visual representation of a system's time constraints.

The following example shows two time constraints in a bank's vault security system. There are two objects:

- **Bio Security System**
- **Vault**

Each starts in the **Off** state. The first time constraint indicates that the vault must be opened within 15 seconds of the **Bio Security System** being activated. The second time constraint is that the vault can only be open for 20 minutes or less:

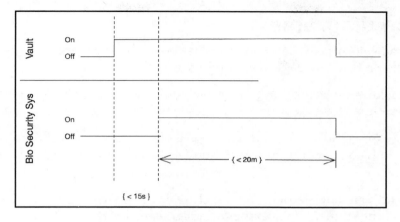

Sample timing diagram

State machine diagrams

State machine diagrams are used to visually describe a system's behavior. The key components of these diagrams include states and transitions. The sample state machine provided in the following diagram is for a bank vault. The solid circle is the initial pseudo state and indicates entry into the system. There are four states—**Wait**, **Unlock**, **Enable**, and **Vault**.

In our bank vault example, the vault is enabled when two bank managers place their thumb on a thumbprint scanner. The vault is unlocked, contingent on a successful thumbprint scan, by entering the correct combination. When these conditions are met, the **Vault** state is reached and the managers can enter it:

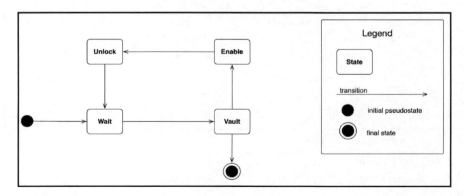

State diagram for bank vault

Use case diagrams

Use case diagrams document the interactions between your users and your system. This is typically done with text, but UML does support use cases.

Let's start by looking at use cases in text, and then review a UML diagram representing the same use cases. We will use an example of a grade book for an online education institution.

The student logs on to the system and selects their class. The student then selects the assignment and uploads their document. Next, the student enters text and selects the submit button.

The instructor logs on to the system and selects their class. The instructor then selects the assignment, and the student. They grade the assignment, enter a grade, and select the submit button.

These use cases are pretty basic and easy to understand in text. There are only a few constructs for the use case diagram in UML:

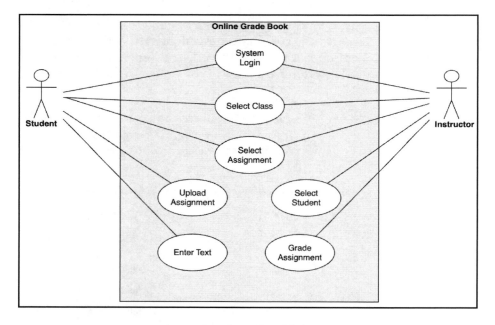

A use case diagram for an online grade book system

There are several visual components to the UML use case diagram:

- **Actor**: The stick figure is referred to as an actor. In our example, student and instructor were both actors. These are the users that use your system. Often, there are multiple user roles in a system.
- **Relationship**: The solid lines indicate which actors interact with which use case items.
- **System**: The overall system is represented by a rectangle. Actors are placed outside of the system and use case items are placed within the system.
- **Use Case Item**: Use case items are represented in ovals, as seen in our preceding *Online Grade Book* example. These are the components of your use case.

These visual components are further illustrated as follows:

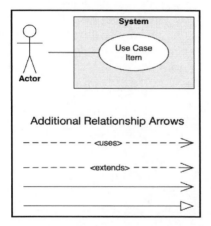

Another use case diagram for an online grade book system

Understanding structural UML diagrams

Structural diagrams illustrate components of a system. The six diagrams listed here are structural, and are briefly described in the subsections that follow:

- Class diagrams
- Component diagrams
- Composite structure diagrams

- Deployment diagrams
- Object diagrams
- Package diagrams

Class diagrams

The class diagram is the most commonly used UML diagram, as it provides a visual description of a system's objects. Consider that, in Java, everything is an object, so you can see the relevance and reason as to why this particular diagram is so widely used. Class diagrams do more than just display objects—they visually depict their construction and relationships with other classes.

As you can see here, the basic component of the class diagram is a rectangle, divided into three sections. Each overall rectangle represents a class, and the class name appears using a bold typeface in the top section. The middle section contains attributes that correlate to variable fields. The third section contains operation data which, in Java, means functions and methods:

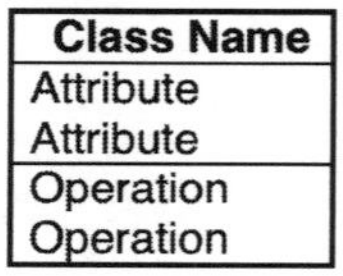

Class Name
Attribute
Attribute
Operation
Operation

The class diagram structure

A simple example of a class diagram for a **Kennel** is displayed in the following diagram. The class name is Kennel, and there are three attributes (**animal**, **breed**, and **name**) and two operations (**intake** and **discharge**):

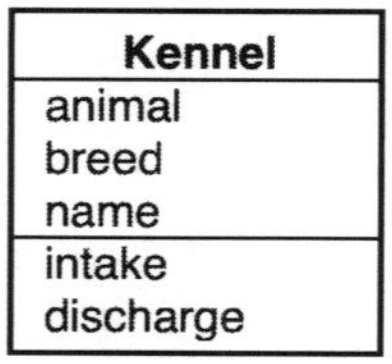

Kennel
animal
breed
name
intake
discharge

A class diagram of our Kennel class

We will further explore class diagrams using our Kennel class example later in this chapter.

Component diagrams

Component diagrams provide a visual representation of a system's physical components. The following example illustrates the three physical components of the system:

- An inventory database
- A customer database
- An order component

The relationships between these components are annotated with dotted lines in the following component diagram:

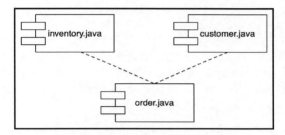

An example component diagram

Composite structure diagrams

The Composite structure UML diagram shows the runtime structure of a system. This diagram can be used to show the internal components of a class. The following example shows a microwave with four structures:

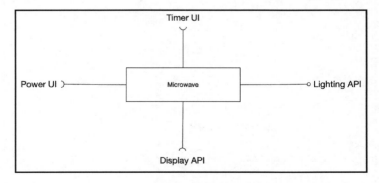

A graphical composite structure diagram

We can also represent a composite structure with a rectangular box, as illustrated in the following diagram:

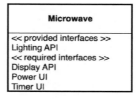

A textual composite structure diagram

Deployment diagrams

Deployment diagrams provide a visual representation of a system's hardware and software. Physical hardware components are illustrated, along with the particular software components that are on them. The hardware components are represented as nodes, and software is represented as an execution environment.

The nodes are drawn as three-dimensional rectangles and represent hardware for a software object, such as a database. As illustrated in the following example, associations are annotated with lines marked with the type of communication protocol used. Our example shows TCP/IP as the communication type:

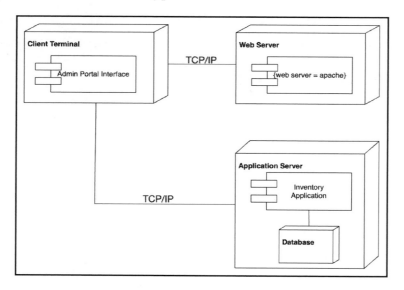

A deployment diagram for a distributed system

Deployment diagrams can be more involved than the example provided here. Our example does, however, provide sufficient insight for you to progress through the proceeding chapters.

Object diagrams

Object diagrams have an unfortunate name, as it does not aptly describe this UML diagram's purpose. The object diagram visually communicates a set of class instances. In fact, the instances have mostly optional components and are often only partially depicted. Therefore, a more apt name for this diagram might be a *loosely defined instance UML diagram*.

The following example depicts four objects and their hierarchy. Because each object is an instance of a class, it is underlined and followed by a colon and the class name:

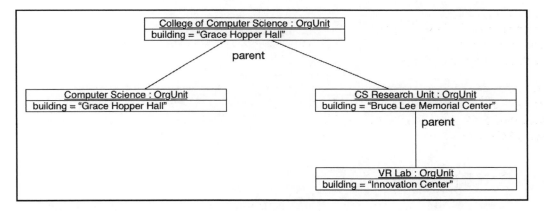

A sample object diagram

Package diagrams

Package diagrams are used to provide a high-level visual depiction of large systems. These diagrams are simplistic and simply show how a system's components are grouped. The following example illustrates nested packages, starting with **Java** and drilling down to the **ArrayList**:

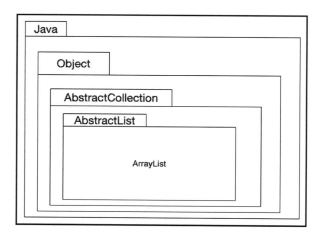

A nested package diagram

Summary

The **Universal Modeling Language** (**UML**) is used to create visual documentation of our systems. This can be used to design a system as well as document a system. UML is widely used by software engineers, software developers, and other professionals.

Two of the 14 UML diagrams are behavioral and structural. Behavioral diagrams illustrate how system components interact to form a system and include activity diagrams, interaction diagrams, state machine diagrams, and use case diagrams. There are several types of interaction UML diagrams, including sequence diagrams, communication diagrams, and timing diagrams.

Structural diagrams illustrate components of a system and include class diagrams, component diagrams, composite structure diagrams, deployment diagrams, object diagrams, and package diagrams.

In the next chapter, *Object-Oriented Design Patterns*, we will explore intermediate and advanced concepts and approaches to object-oriented programming and their applicability to design patterns. A review of the fundamental concepts of object-oriented programming will help to ensure a deep conceptual understanding of object-oriented programming. An overview of object-oriented programming-related design pattern principles will also be provided.

Questions

1. What are the two basic types of UML diagrams?
2. Why was UML initially created?
3. List four behavioral UML diagrams.
4. Which UML diagram provides a system's process flow?
5. Which UML diagram documents the interactions between a system and its users?
6. What is a UML actor?
7. What type of UML diagram illustrates system components?
8. What is the most commonly used UML diagram?
9. Which UML diagram shows the runtime structure of a system?
10. Which UML diagram visually documents a system's hardware and software?

Further reading

- *UML 2.0 in Action: A project-based-tutorial*
  (https://www.packtpub.com/hardware-and-creative/uml-20-action-project-based-tutorial)

2

Object-Oriented Design Patterns

In this chapter, we will explore intermediate and advanced concepts and approaches to **object-oriented programming (OOP)** and their applicability to design patterns. We will review the fundamental concepts of OOP to facilitate a deep conceptual understanding. This chapter also covers the principles of OOP design patterns.

Specifically, we will cover the following topics in this chapter:

- Introduction to object-oriented programming
- Object-oriented programming approaches
- Principles of design patterns
- Complete OOP class

Technical requirements

The code for this chapter can be found at `https://github.com/PacktPublishing/Hands-On-Design-Patterns-with-Java/tree/master/Chapter02`.

Introduction to object-oriented programming

Object-Oriented Programming (OOP) has been around for a couple of decades now, and most software developers are familiar with at least one OOP language, such as C or Java. The introduction of OOP represented a significant computer programming paradigm shift from the prevailing procedural programming technique. With OOP programming, the focus is on objects, and the focus of procedural programming is on procedures. For example, a procedural programming approach to a bicycle management information system would focus on the procedures that the system might perform. The OOP approach would focus on the bicycle and model it as an object. With the physical bicycle represented as an OOP object, we can define characteristics of the object and what behaviors can be taken with respect to the bicycle object.

In this section, we will cover the basics of OOP and use the bicycle object as a common reference. This section is subdivided as follows:

- Primary benefits of OOP
- Sample OOP class
- Instance variables
- The `This` reference

Primary benefits of OOP

There are many benefits of OOP. Chief among them are the following:

- Portability
- Inheritance
- Encapsulation
- Polymorphism

Each of these aspects is detailed in the following sections.

Portability

Portability, also referred to as modularity, is the primary benefit of OOP. With OOP, we program in a series of classes. For example, we would have a bicycle class and other classes for a complete bicycle management system. If there was a problem with a bicycle method, we immediately know to check the bicycle class. That makes source code troubleshooting efficient.

The class structure lends itself well to portability. Our example bicycle class can easily be used in other programs as it is a self-contained object. As mentioned previously, the class contains all the components of a physical bicycle.

Inheritance

Inheritance in programming is the same as in real life. A girl inherits from her mother, who inherits from her mother, and so on. The following diagram shows inheritance in the real world and how it relates to OOP:

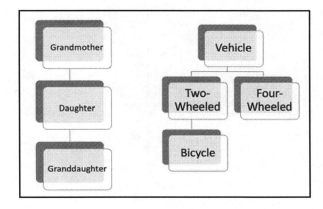

Inheritance examples

On the left-hand side of the preceding diagram, a **Grandmother** passes down traits to the **Daughter**, who passes down traits to the **Granddaughter**. So, the **Granddaughter** inherits from both the **Daughter** and **Grandmother**. The same inheritance concept applies to our **Bicycle** class, which inherits from both the **Two-Wheeled** class and the **Vehicle** class. This is a powerful schema as it avoids class bloating. As an example, if the **Vehicle** class has data elements such as year, make, and model, those elements are automatically part of the **Two-Wheeled** and **Bicycle** classes. We will see an example of this later on in this chapter.

Encapsulation

Encapsulation refers to the hidden nature of an object's data components. We know that the data is there, but cannot access it directly because external entities cannot directly interact with that data:

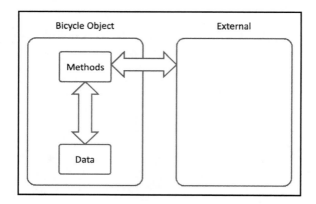

Inheritance examples

The illustration above demonstrates how a `Bicycle` class protects its data from external methods and functions. The object's own methods are the only mechanism that can directly view or alter its data.

Polymorphism

Polymorphism is not a word that non-OOP programmers are likely familiar with. The term *polymorphism* is generally defined as *appearing in multiple forms*. In OOP, polymorphism states that *different types of objects can be accessed via a common interface*. This can be achieved by writing overloaded constructors and methods and is covered later in this chapter. Polymorphism can also be achieved by having subclasses override superclass methods.

Let's take a simple look at this using Java code:

1. First, we create a `Vehicle` class that, by default, extends Java's `Object` class.
2. Next, we create a `TwoWheeled` class that extends the `Vehicle` class.
3. Then, we create a `Bicycle` class that extends the `TwoWheeled` class.

4. Lastly, we create a `Driver` class that creates an instance of the `Bicycle` class and runs four checks using the `instanceof` keyword:

```java
public class Vehicle {
}

public class TwoWheeled extends Vehicle {
}

public class Bicycle extends TwoWheeled {
}

public class Driver {

    public static void main(String[] args) {

        Bicycle myBike = new Bicycle();

        System.out.println("\nmyBike \"Instance of\" Checks");
        if (myBike instanceof Bicycle)
            System.out.println("Instance of Bicycle: True");
        else
            System.out.println("Instance of Bicycle: False");

        if (myBike instanceof TwoWheeled)
            System.out.println("Instance of TwoWheeled: True");
        else
            System.out.println("Instance of TwoWheeled: False");

        if (myBike instanceof Vehicle)
            System.out.println("Instance of Vehicle: True");
        else
            System.out.println("Instance of Vehicle: False");

        if (myBike instanceof Object)
            System.out.println("Instance of Object: True");
        else
            System.out.println("Instance of Object: False");
    }
}
```

The output is as follows:

```
myBike "Instance of" Checks
Instance of Bicycle: True
Instance of TwoWheeled: True
Instance of Vehicle: True
Instance of Object: True
```

Driver class output

As you can see in the preceding screenshot, an instance of the Bicycle class is also an instance of TwoWheeled, Vehicle, and Object. This makes the myBike object polymorphic.

Sample OOP class

Let's develop our Bicycle class further by adding attributes and a behavior. The attributes will be the number of gears, how much the bicycle cost, the weight, and the color. The behavior will be the ability to output the attribute values. Here is the source code:

```
public class Bicycle extends TwoWheeled {

    // instance variable declarations
    private int gears = 0;
    private double cost = 0.0;
    private double weight = 0.0;
    private String color = "";

    // method to output Bicycle's information
    public void outputData() {
        System.out.println("\nBicycle Details:");
        System.out.println("Gears  : " + this.gears);
        System.out.println("Cost   : " + this.cost);
        System.out.println("Weight : " + this.weight + " lbs");
        System.out.println("Color  : " + this.color);
    }
```

Here is the code for Setters:

```
public void setGears(int nbr) {
this.gears = nbr;
}
public void setCost(double amt) {
this.cost = amt;
```

```
  }
public void setWeight(double lbs) {
 this.weight = lbs;
 }
public void setColor(String theColor) {
 this.color = theColor;
 }
}
```

We will take a look at all components of the `Bicycle` class in subsequent sections. For now, focus on the `public void outputData()` method. We will use our `Driver` class to evoke that method. Here is the updated `Driver` class:

```
public class Driver {

    public static void main(String[] args) {

        Bicycle myBike = new Bicycle();

        myBike.setGears(24);
        myBike.setCost(319.99);
        myBike.setWeight(13.5);
        myBike.setColor("Purple");

        myBike.outputData();
    }
}
```

In the preceding `Driver` class, we create an instance of `Bicycle` called `myBike`, assign values to its attributes, and then make a call to the `outputData()` method. Here are the output results:

```
Bicycle Details:
Gears  : 24
Cost   : 319.99
Weight : 13.5 lbs
Color  : Purple
```

Driver class output

Instance variables

In the `Bicycle` class, we had four instance variables. Refer to the following code snippet for reference:

```
// instance variable declarations
private int gears = 0;
private double cost = 0.0;
private double weight = 0.0;
private String color = "";
```

These are instance variables because they exist for every instance of the `Bicycle` class. In our examples thus far, we only had one instance of `Bicycle`, but we can have an unlimited amount, each with their own set of these instance variables.

The this reference

In Java, we can use the `this` keyword as a reference to the current object. For example, the following code snippet sets the color of the current `Bicycle` object:

```
public void setColor(String theColor) {
    this.color = theColor;
}
```

The preceding `setColor` method accepts a `String` parameter and assigns it to the `color` instance variable of the current object.

Object-oriented programming approaches

OOP represents an efficient way to develop portable and secure code. The key to implementing OOP in our applications includes several approaches to include the following:

- Accessors and mutators
- Driver class
- Constructors
- Overloading constructors and methods
- Method call chaining

Each of these approaches is covered in the sections that follow.

Accessors and mutators

Accessor methods are those that allow an object's data to be accessed. These methods can get the data, but not change it. This is a great way to protect the data from being changed. Accessor methods are also referred to as Getters methods.

Mutator methods, also known as setter methods, allow the object's instance variables to be changed.

Here is a complete set of accessors and mutators for our Bicycle class:

```
// Accessors (Getters)
public int getGears() {
    return this.gears;
}

public double getCost() {
    return this.cost;
}

public double getWeight() {
    return this.weight;
}

public String getColor() {
    return this.color;
}

// Mutators (Setters)
public void setGears(int nbr) {
    this.gears = nbr;
}

public void setCost(double amt) {
    this.cost = amt;
}

public void setWeight(double lbs) {
    this.weight = lbs;
}

public void setColor(String theColor) {
    this.color = theColor;
}
```

As you can see in the preceding code, we use the `this` reference for the current object. The accessors do not take any parameters and simply return the value of the instance variable. The mutators take a parameter and use its value in assigning a new value to an instance variable.

Driver class

While driver classes are not specific to OOP languages, they are a best practice approach to implementation. They are used to drive a multi-class program. As you would expect, they contain a `main()` method to signify the starting point for your application's execution.

An example `Driver` class was provided earlier in this chapter.

Constructors

Constructors are a special kind of method that are run when an object is initialized. We use constructors to set up an object with default values. Let's take a look at what our `Bicycle` class constructor would be. The following code should be placed in the `Bicycle` class after the instance variable section:

```
// constructor
Bicycle() {
    this.color = "Navy Blue";
}
```

As you can see from the preceding, the constructor sets the color of the newly instantiated object to `Navy Blue`. When we run the following `Driver` class, an instance of `Bicycle` is instantiated, causing the `Bicycle` class constructor to run, and then a call to the `outputData()` method is made:

```
public class Driver {

    public static void main(String[] args) {

        Bicycle myBike = new Bicycle();

        myBike.outputData();
    }
}
```

The preceding code shows the `Driver` class. The following is the output from the `outputData()` method call.

```
Bicycle Details:
Gears  : 0
Cost   : 0.0
Weight : 0.0 lbs
Color  : Navy Blue
```

outputData() execution results

Overloading constructors and methods

When constructors and methods are declared, we include the expected parameters. For example, our `Bicycle()` constructor does not take any parameters. We can overload that constructor by creating one or more versions of it, each with a different set of parameters. Let's look at our `Bicycle` class with four constructors:

```
// constructor - default
Bicycle() {
}

// constructor - String parameter
Bicycle(String aColor) {
    this.color = aColor;
}

// constructor - int parameter
Bicycle(int nbrOfGears) {
    this.gears = nbrOfGears;
}

// constructor - int, double, double, String parameters
Bicycle(int nbrOfGears, double theCost, double theWeight, String aColor) {
    this.gears = nbrOfGears;
    this.cost = theCost;
    this.weight = theWeight;
    this.color = aColor;
}
```

The default constructor is used when an instance of the object is created without any parameters. We would use the following code link:

```
Bicycle myBike1 = new Bicycle();
```

We can use one of the overloaded methods when creating a Bicycle object, simply by passing the proper arguments, based on what the overloaded method expects as parameters. The following Driver class shows the creation of four Bicycle objects, one using a different constructor:

```java
public class Driver {

    public static void main(String[] args) {

        Bicycle myBike1 = new Bicycle();
        Bicycle myBike2 = new Bicycle("Brown");
        Bicycle myBike3 = new Bicycle(22);
        Bicycle myBike4 = new Bicycle(22, 319.99, 13.5, "White");

        myBike1.outputData();
        myBike2.outputData();
        myBike3.outputData();
        myBike4.outputData();

    }
}
```

As you can see from the following output provided, each Bicycle object was created with a different constructor. Overloading the constructor increases the flexibility in object creation:

```
Bicycle Details:
Gears  : 0
Cost   : 0.0
Weight : 0.0 lbs
Color  :

Bicycle Details:
Gears  : 0
Cost   : 0.0
Weight : 0.0 lbs
Color  : Brown

Bicycle Details:
Gears  : 22
Cost   : 0.0
Weight : 0.0 lbs
Color  :

Bicycle Details:
Gears  : 22
Cost   : 319.99
Weight : 13.5 lbs
Color  : White
```

outputData() execution results

We can also overload methods. For example, we have used the `outputData()` method in our `Bicycle` class several times already. Let's overload that method so that we can pass additional text to be printed in the output. Here are both versions of that method:

```java
// method to output Bicycle's information
public void outputData() {
    System.out.println("\nBicycle Details:");
    System.out.println("Gears  : " + this.gears);
    System.out.println("Cost   : " + this.cost);
    System.out.println("Weight : " + this.weight + " lbs");
    System.out.println("Color  : " + this.color);
}

// method to output Bicycle's information - overloaded
public void outputData(String bikeText) {
    System.out.println("\nBicycle " + bikeText + " Details:");
    System.out.println("Gears  : " + this.gears);
    System.out.println("Cost   : " + this.cost);
    System.out.println("Weight : " + this.weight + " lbs");
    System.out.println("Color  : " + this.color);
}
```

As you can see in the preceding code, our overloaded method accepts a `String` parameter and incorporates that in the first printed line. We can modify our `Driver` class as shown in the following code snippet:

```
myBike1.outputData("Nbr 1");
myBike2.outputData("Nbr 2");
myBike3.outputData("Nbr 3");
myBike4.outputData("Nbr 4");
```

The output is presented here and illustrates how easy it is to create and use overloaded methods:

```
Bicycle Nbr 1 Details:
Gears  : 0
Cost   : 0.0
Weight : 0.0 lbs
Color  :

Bicycle Nbr 2 Details:
Gears  : 0
Cost   : 0.0
Weight : 0.0 lbs
Color  : Brown

Bicycle Nbr 3 Details:
Gears  : 22
Cost   : 0.0
Weight : 0.0 lbs
Color  :

Bicycle Nbr 4 Details:
Gears  : 22
Cost   : 319.99
Weight : 13.5 lbs
Color  : White
```

Overloaded outputData(String) execution results

Method call chaining

OOP affords us the opportunity to use method call chaining. That is the process of making multiple method calls in a single statement. Here is the syntax:

```
object.method1().method2().method3().method4();
```

Using the syntax provided previously, we can walk through the process of method call chaining. The object first calls method1(), which returns the calling object. Next, that returned object calls method2(), which returns the calling object. You can see the process here. It works from left to right.

So, we can implement this in our Driver class, as shown here:

```
// Example using method call chaining
Bicycle myBike5 = new Bicycle(24, 418.50, 17.2, "Green");
myBike5.setColor("Peach").setGears(32).outputData("Number 5");
```

Before this code can work, we will need to make two changes to each method we want to use in our method call chaining:

- Add a return type to the method definition
- Add a return this; statement to each method

Here is an example of the setGears() method that the preceding changes listed made:

```
public Bicycle setGears(int nbr) {
    this.gears = nbr;
    return this;
}
```

Once these changes are made, we can run the Driver class:

```
Bicycle Number 5 Details:
Gears   : 32
Cost    : 418.5
Weight  : 17.2 lbs
Color   : Peach
```

Method call chaining execution results

The preceding screenshot shows the final result.

Principles of design patterns

So far, we have discussed taking a multi-class approach to designing object-oriented programs. We also used examples to demonstrate the use of accessors, mutators, constructors, and driver classes. There are three key principles to bear in mind when studying the design patterns presented in subsequent chapters of this book:

- Creating concise objects
- Encapsulating to protect
- Being purposeful with inheritance

These principles are explored in the subsequent sections.

Creating concise objects

Objects are at the core of OOP. This principle aims to remind software designers and developers to isolate objects to a specific model. Using our `Bicycle` class as an example, we would create `Bicycle` objects that contained the appropriate attributes and behaviors. The bicycle attributes used in this chapter were gears, cost, weight, and color. We created accessors and mutators for each of those attributes. We also created a method that echoed the object's attributes to the output console. No behaviors were added to the `Bicycle` object, but we could have included behaviors such as `upgrade()`.

What we did not include in the `Bicycle` class were attributes and behaviors that were ancillary to the `Bicycle` object. Examples of these include the owner's address, vacation details, and more. While the data might be somewhat related to a specific `Bicycle`, it is not part of a real-world bicycle that we need to model.

Adhering to this principle helps ensure our code is concise, easy to maintain, and portable.

Encapsulating to protect

Earlier in this chapter, we defined encapsulation as the hidden nature of an object's data. Granting access to an object's data via its own accessors and mutators is a great approach to data protection.

We use encapsulation as an approach to data protection in OOP. Encapsulating too much data into a class is an anti-pattern—something that should be avoided. As with the create concise objects approach, we should identify what data all copies of an object have in common and only encapsulate those data elements. Other data might be better suited for an ancillary class.

Being purposeful with inheritance

Inheritance is a powerful OOP construct. We can model objects efficiently, as was illustrated with the bicycle. We know that the following relationships exist:

- Bicycle is a two wheeled
- Bicycle is a vehicle
- Bicycle is a object

When we program inheritance, we should perform the "IS A" Checks using the following pseudo-code logic:

```
if ( <new child object> is a <parent object> ) then relationship = True;
else relationship = False
```

If our "IS A" Checks fails, then inheritance should be avoided. This is an important test that, with dedicated use, can help ensure that inheritance lines between objects are valid.

Let's create the "IS A" Checks for our Bicycle class. We will do this by using Java's instanceof operator. Here is the code in three sections. The first section runs the checks for myBike6 and checks to see whether it is an instance of Bicycle, TwoWheeled, Vehicle, and Object:

```
// "IS A" Checks
System.out.println("\n\"IS A\" CHECKS");

// focus on myBike6
Bicycle myBike6 = new Bicycle();

if (myBike6 instanceof Bicycle)
    System.out.println("myBike6 Instance of Bicycle: True");
else
    System.out.println("myBike6 Instance of Bicycle: False");

if (myBike6 instanceof TwoWheeled)
    System.out.println("myBike6 Instance of TwoWheeled: True");
else
    System.out.println("myBike6 Instance of TwoWheeled: False");
```

```java
if (myBike6 instanceof Vehicle)
    System.out.println("myBike6 Instance of Vehicle: True");
else
    System.out.println("myBike6 Instance of Vehicle: False");

if (myBike6 instanceof Object)
    System.out.println("myBike6 Instance of Object: True");
else
    System.out.println("myBike6 Instance of Object: False");
```

The second section runs the checks for `myTwoWheeled` and checks to see whether it is an instance of `Bicycle`, `TwoWheeled`, `Vehicle`, and `Object`:

```java
// focus on TwoWheeled
TwoWheeled myTwoWheeled = new TwoWheeled();

if (myTwoWheeled instanceof Bicycle)
    System.out.println("\nmyTwoWheeled Instance of Bicycle: True");
else
    System.out.println("\nmyTwoWheeled Instance of Bicycle: False");

if (myTwoWheeled instanceof TwoWheeled)
    System.out.println("myTwoWheeled Instance of TwoWheeled: True");
else
    System.out.println("myTwoWheeled Instance of TwoWheeled: False");

if (myTwoWheeled instanceof Vehicle)
    System.out.println("myTwoWheeled Instance of Vehicle: True");
else
    System.out.println("myTwoWheeled Instance of Vehicle: False");

if (myTwoWheeled instanceof Object)
    System.out.println("myTwoWheeled Instance of Object: True");
else
    System.out.println("myTwoWheeled Instance of Object: False");
```

The third and final section runs the checks for `myVehicle` and checks to see whether it is an instance of `Bicycle`, `TwoWheeled`, `Vehicle`, and `Object`:

```java
// focus on Vehicle
Vehicle myVehicle = new Vehicle();

if (myVehicle instanceof Bicycle)
    System.out.println("\nmyVehicle Instance of Bicycle: True");
else
    System.out.println("\nmyVehicle Instance of Bicycle: False");

if (myVehicle instanceof TwoWheeled)
```

```
        System.out.println("myVehicle Instance of TwoWheeled: True");
    else
        System.out.println("myVehicle Instance of TwoWheeled: False");

    if (myVehicle instanceof Vehicle)
        System.out.println("myVehicle Instance of Vehicle: True");
    else
        System.out.println("myVehicle Instance of Vehicle: False");

    if (myVehicle instanceof Object)
        System.out.println("myVehicle Instance of Object: True");
    else
        System.out.println("myVehicle Instance of Object: False");
```

The output of the three sections of is a code is provided here. As you can see, the myBike6 object is an instance of Bicycle, TwoWheeled, Vehicle, and Object; the myTwoWheeled object is an instance of TwoWheeled, Vehicle, and Object; and the myVehicle object is an instance of Vehicle and Object. We can also see that the myTwoWheeled object is not an instance of Vehicle or Object; and that the myVehicle object is not an instance of Bicycle or TwoWheeled:

```
"IS A" CHECKS
myBike6 Instance of Bicycle: True
myBike6 Instance of TwoWheeled: True
myBike6 Instance of Vehicle: True
myBike6 Instance of Object: True

myTwoWheeled Instance of Bicycle: False
myTwoWheeled Instance of TwoWheeled: True
myTwoWheeled Instance of Vehicle: True
myTwoWheeled Instance of Object: True

myVehicle Instance of Bicycle: False
myVehicle Instance of TwoWheeled: False
myVehicle Instance of Vehicle: True
myVehicle Instance of Object: True
```

Results of "IS A" checks

The preceding screenshot depicts this example.

Learning the complete OOP class

Throughout this chapter, we made use of a `Bicycle` class. As illustrated in the following, we created a hierarchy to demonstrate inheritance as a key feature of OOP. All objects inherit from the `Object` class in Java. Our hierarchy has `Bicycle` inheriting from `TwoWheeled`, which inherits from `Vehicle`, which inherits from `Object`:

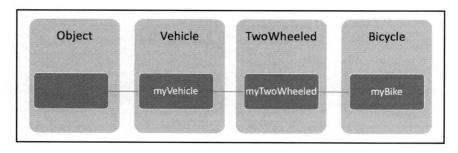

Bicycle class hierarchy

For our `Bicycle` class to work with the intended hierarchy, we created classes for `Vehicle` and `TwoWheeled`. Here are those classes:

```
public class Vehicle {
}

public class TwoWheeled extends Vehicle {
}
```

The `Vehicle` and `TwoWheeled` classes do not offer anything to the `Bicycle` class. Normally, each would have attributes and behaviors associated with them.

The completed `Bicycle` class, as refined throughout this chapter, is provided in the following sections. This first section has the class definition and the four instance variables:

```
public class Bicycle extends TwoWheeled {

    // instance variable declarations
    private int gears = 0;
    private double cost = 0.0;
    private double weight = 0.0;
    private String color = "";
```

The next section of the `Bicycle` class contains the constructors. The first constructor does not take any parameters and is the default constructor. The second constructor accepts a `String` parameter. The third constructor accepts a single `int` parameter. The final constructor accepts four parameters:

```
// constructor - default
Bicycle() {
}

// constructor - String parameter
Bicycle(String aColor) {
    this.color = aColor;
}

// constructor - int parameter
Bicycle(int nbrOfGears) {
    this.gears = nbrOfGears;
}

// constructor - int, double, double, String parameters
Bicycle(int nbrOfGears, double theCost, double theWeight, String
aColor) {
    this.gears = nbrOfGears;
    this.cost = theCost;
    this.weight = theWeight;
    this.color = aColor;
}
```

After the overloaded constructor methods, we have two methods to output data. The `outputData()` method is overloaded so that it can be used without any parameters or with a single `String` parameter:

```
// method to output Bicycle's information
public void outputData() {
    System.out.println("\nBicycle Details:");
    System.out.println("Gears  : " + this.gears);
    System.out.println("Cost   : " + this.cost);
    System.out.println("Weight : " + this.weight + " lbs");
    System.out.println("Color  : " + this.color);
}

// method to output Bicycle's information - overloaded
//  - method call chaining enabled
public Bicycle outputData(String bikeText) {
    System.out.println("\nBicycle " + bikeText + " Details:");
    System.out.println("Gears  : " + this.gears);
    System.out.println("Cost   : " + this.cost);
```

```
        System.out.println("Weight : " + this.weight + " lbs");
        System.out.println("Color   : " + this.color);

        return this;
    }
```

The next section of our `Bicycle` class contains the four `Accessor` methods, one for each of the instance variables:

```
// Accessors (Getters)
public int getGears() {
    return this.gears;
}

public double getCost() {
    return this.cost;
}

public double getWeight() {
    return this.weight;
}

public String getColor() {
    return this.color;
}
```

The final section of our `Bicycle` class contains the four `Mutator` methods, one for each of the instance variables:

```
// Mutators (Setters) - method call chaining enabled
public Bicycle setGears(int nbr) {
    this.gears = nbr;
    return this;
}

public Bicycle setCost(double amt) {
    this.cost = amt;
    return this;
}

public Bicycle setWeight(double lbs) {
    this.weight = lbs;
    return this;
}

public Bicycle setColor(String theColor) {
    this.color = theColor;
    return this;
```

```
    }

}
```

We also made several changes to our `Driver` class. That class is provided here over several successive sections. The code includes in-code comments to organize and identify each code block:

1. This first code block defines the class, includes the `main()` method definition, creates a `myBike` instance of `Bicycle`, and provides example calls to mutators. Then, a sample output statement is provided that makes a call to the `getColor()` accessor method:

```
public class Driver {

    public static void main(String[] args) {

        // Example calls to mutators
        Bicycle myBike = new Bicycle();
        myBike.setGears(24);
        myBike.setCost(319.99);
        myBike.setWeight(13.5);
        myBike.setColor("Purple");
        System.out.println("\nmyBike's color is " +
myBike.getColor());
```

2. The second block of code provides example calls to the overloaded constructor. There are four instances of the `Bicycle` object created, each using a different overloaded constructor:

```
// Example of calls to overloaded constructor
Bicycle myBike1 = new Bicycle();
Bicycle myBike2 = new Bicycle("Brown");
Bicycle myBike3 = new Bicycle(22);
Bicycle myBike4 = new Bicycle(22, 319.99, 13.5, "White");
```

3. Our third code block makes four calls to the overloaded `outputData()` method:

```
myBike1.outputData("Nbr 1");
myBike2.outputData("Nbr 2");
myBike3.outputData("Nbr 3");
myBike4.outputData("Nbr 4");
```

4. The fourth code block provides an example of method call chaining:

```
// Example using method call chaining
Bicycle myBike5 = new Bicycle(24, 418.50, 17.2, "Green");
myBike5.setColor("Peach").setGears(32).outputData("Number 5");
```

5. The fifth code bock provides "IS A" Checks for the Bicycle class. We start by creating an instance of Bicycle and then run our checks against the newly created myBike6 object:

```
// "IS A" Checks
System.out.println("\n\"IS A\" CHECKS");

// focus on myBike6
Bicycle myBike6 = new Bicycle();

if (myBike6 instanceof Bicycle)
    System.out.println("myBike6 Instance of Bicycle: True");
else
    System.out.println("myBike6 Instance of Bicycle: False");

if (myBike6 instanceof TwoWheeled)
    System.out.println("myBike6 Instance of TwoWheeled: True");
else
    System.out.println("myBike6 Instance of TwoWheeled: False");

if (myBike6 instanceof Vehicle)
    System.out.println("myBike6 Instance of Vehicle: True");
else
    System.out.println("myBike6 Instance of Vehicle: False");

if (myBike6 instanceof Object)
    System.out.println("myBike6 Instance of Object: True");
else
    System.out.println("myBike6 Instance of Object: False");
```

6. The sixth code bock provides the "IS A" Checks for the TwoWheeled class. We start by creating an instance of TwoWheeled and then running our checks against the newly created myTwoWheeled object:

```
// focus on TwoWheeled
TwoWheeled myTwoWheeled = new TwoWheeled();

if (myTwoWheeled instanceof Bicycle)
    System.out.println("\nmyTwoWheeled Instance of Bicycle: True");
else
    System.out.println("\nmyTwoWheeled Instance of Bicycle:
```

```
False");

if (myTwoWheeled instanceof TwoWheeled)
    System.out.println("myTwoWheeled Instance of TwoWheeled:
True");
else
    System.out.println("myTwoWheeled Instance of TwoWheeled:
False");

if (myTwoWheeled instanceof Vehicle)
    System.out.println("myTwoWheeled Instance of Vehicle: True");
else
    System.out.println("myTwoWheeled Instance of Vehicle: False");

if (myTwoWheeled instanceof Object)
    System.out.println("myTwoWheeled Instance of Object: True");
else
    System.out.println("myTwoWheeled Instance of Object: False");
```

7. The seventh and final code bock provides the `"IS A"` Checks for the Vehicle class. We start by creating an instance of Vehicle and then running our checks against the newly created myVehicle object:

```
// focus on Vehicle
Vehicle myVehicle = new Vehicle();

if (myVehicle instanceof Bicycle)
    System.out.println("\nmyVehicle Instance of Bicycle:
True");
    else
        System.out.println("\nmyVehicle Instance of Bicycle:
False");

if (myVehicle instanceof TwoWheeled)
    System.out.println("myVehicle Instance of TwoWheeled:
True");
    else
        System.out.println("myVehicle Instance of TwoWheeled:
False");

if (myVehicle instanceof Vehicle)
    System.out.println("myVehicle Instance of Vehicle:
True");
    else
        System.out.println("myVehicle Instance of Vehicle:
False");

    if (myVehicle instanceof Object)
```

```
                    System.out.println("myVehicle Instance of Object:
        True");
              else
                    System.out.println("myVehicle Instance of Object:
        False");
            }
        }
```

The complete output of the `Driver` class is provided as follows:

```
myBike's color is Purple

Bicycle Nbr 1 Details:
Gears  : 0
Cost   : 0.0
Weight : 0.0 lbs
Color  :

Bicycle Nbr 2 Details:
Gears  : 0
Cost   : 0.0
Weight : 0.0 lbs
Color  : Brown

Bicycle Nbr 3 Details:
Gears  : 22
Cost   : 0.0
Weight : 0.0 lbs
Color  :

Bicycle Nbr 4 Details:
Gears  : 22
Cost   : 319.99
Weight : 13.5 lbs
Color  : White

Bicycle Number 5 Details:
Gears  : 32
Cost   : 418.5
Weight : 17.2 lbs
Color  : Peach

"IS A" CHECKS
myBike6 Instance of Bicycle: True
myBike6 Instance of TwoWheeled: True
myBike6 Instance of Vehicle: True
myBike6 Instance of Object: True

myTwoWheeled Instance of Bicycle: False
myTwoWheeled Instance of TwoWheeled: True
myTwoWheeled Instance of Vehicle: True
myTwoWheeled Instance of Object: True

myVehicle Instance of Bicycle: False
myVehicle Instance of TwoWheeled: False
myVehicle Instance of Vehicle: True
myVehicle Instance of Object: True
```

Driver class output

In this section, we demonstrated OOP using a complete OOP `Bicycle` application.

Summary

This chapter started with an introduction to OOP. Portability, inheritance, encapsulation, and polymorphism were deemed to be the primary benefits of OOP and were explored. A sample OOP class was examined in detail. That class, the `Bicycle` class, was used to demonstrate key OOP concepts to include instance variables, the `this` reference, accessors, mutators, driver class, constructors, overloading, and method call chaining. The chapter ended with a look at key OOP principles—create concise objects, encapsulate to protect, and purposeful inheritance.

In the next chapter, *Behavioral Design Patterns*, we will explore the behavioral design pattern category and its individual design patterns of chain of responsibility, mediator, memento, null object, observer, state, strategy, template method, and visitor. We will examine the programming challenges and design patterns that resolve them.

Questions

1. What are the primary benefits of OOP languages?
2. Which OOP construct lends itself well to portability?
3. What refers to the hidden nature of an object's data components?
4. What is the definition of polymorphism in relation to OOP?
5. What is the `this` reference used for?
6. What is an `accessor` method?
7. What is a `mutator` method?
8. What is a constructor?
9. How are overloaded constructors or methods unique?
10. In what direction are chained method calls executed?

Further reading

- *Hands-On Object-Oriented Programming with Java 11 [Video]* (https://www.packtpub.com/application-development/hands-object-oriented-programming-java-11-video)
- *Learning Object-Oriented Programming* (https://www.packtpub.com/application-development/learning-object-oriented-programming)

Section 2: Original Design Patterns

2

In this section, the categories behavioral, creational, and structural will be explored. For each of these categories, their design patterns will be explained along with step-by-step instructions on how to solve the underlying design challenge. The behavioral category contains 12 design patterns; the creational category contains 6 design patterns, and the structural category contains 7 design patterns.

The following chapters will be covered:

- Chapter 3, *Behavioral Design Patterns*
- Chapter 4, *Creational Design Patterns*
- Chapter 5, *Structural Design Patterns*

Behavioral Design Patterns 3

In the previous chapter, we explored **Object-Oriented Programming (OOP)** and accepted it as the preferred programming approach for this and the remaining chapters in the book. We learned the key OOP principles—concise objects, encapsulation to protect, and purposeful inheritance—and we will see evidence of those principles in the design patterns and source code presented throughout this book.

In this chapter, we will explore the behavioral design pattern category and its individual design patterns listed as follows. We will examine programming challenges and the behavioral design patterns that solve them:

- Introducing behavioral design patterns
- Chain of responsibility pattern
- Command pattern
- Interpreter pattern
- Iterator pattern
- Mediator pattern
- Memento pattern
- Null object pattern
- Observer pattern
- State pattern
- Strategy pattern
- Template method pattern
- Visitor pattern

Technical requirements

The code for this chapter can be found here: `https://github.com/PacktPublishing/Hands-On-Design-Patterns-with-Java/tree/master/Chapter03`.

Introducing behavioral design patterns

In `Chapter 1`, *Unified Modeling Language Primer*, we learned that behavioral diagrams illustrate how system components interact to form a system. We examined the following behavioral diagrams—activity diagram, interaction diagram, state Machine diagram, and use case diagram. It follows that behavioral design patterns are focused on the interaction of objects and classes in a system. The key component here is the interaction, also referred to as the communication between objects and classes.

The twelve behavioral design patterns presented in this chapter can be grouped into two subcategories—those that focus on classes and those that focus on objects. The following table details the subcategories:

Object Scope	Class Scope
Chain of responsibility pattern	Interpreter pattern
Command pattern	Template method pattern
Iterator pattern	
Mediator pattern	
Memento pattern	
Null object pattern	
Observer pattern	
State pattern	
Strategy pattern	
Visitor pattern	

Behavioral design pattern subcategories

The behavioral design patterns listed in the preceding table are detailed in the remaining sections of this chapter. They are presented in alphabetical order to illustrate that one is not more important than the others. Here is a brief description of each design pattern's applicability to the behavioral design category. These are further detailed in subsequent sections of this chapter:

- **Chain of responsibility pattern**: An object submits a request to multiple objects without knowing which object will handle the request

- **Command pattern**: Permits the sending of requests without knowing details about the receiver or even about what is being requested
- **Interpreter pattern**: Used to establish a grammatical representation and an interpreter that interprets language
- **Iterator pattern**: Grants access to an object's members without sharing the encapsulated data structures
- **Mediator pattern**: Used to permit object interactions without using explicit object references
- **Memento pattern**: Saves an object's current internal state as a memento so that it can be referred to and restored to
- **Null object pattern**: Negates the need to search for the null condition
- **Observer pattern**: Updates subscriber objects when a change is made to the publisher object's state
- **State pattern**: Allows an object to change its behavior based on internal state changes
- **Strategy pattern**: Allows us to individually encapsulate a set of interchangeable algorithms
- **Template method pattern**: Involves creating an algorithm template with processing steps relegated to child classes
- **Visitor pattern**: Performs operations on an object without altering its structure

Understanding the chain of responsibility pattern

The purpose of the chain of responsibility design pattern involves senders and receivers. Specifically, the chain of responsibility design pattern calls for the decoupling of the sender and receiver. Objects can be sent to a series of receivers without the sender being concerned about which receiver handles the request. The request is sent along a chain of receivers and only one of them will process the request. Let's look at some examples of this.

Consider a large customer service agency that handles thousands of incoming emails each day. Instead of having a person or persons manually review each one to determine which department should process the email, we can write a Java program using the chain of responsibility design pattern to send the emails along the chain so that they are processed by the appropriate department.

Another example is a call center. Many call centers now ask the caller to briefly describe what they are calling about and then the caller is placed in a queue. The caller's brief descriptions are recorded and then analyzed for key words. The calls are routed along the chain and then processed by the appropriate agent. In cases when an agent receives a call that is not appropriate for them, say it is regarding billing and the agent handles shipping, then the call can be sent further down the chain.

We will further explore a third example that involves incoming emails to a university. The university has several functional areas and wants to ensure the emails are routed to the appropriate team. We will look at the use case, UML class diagram, and the source code necessary to implement the chain of responsibility design pattern for this scenario.

Use case

To demonstrate the chain of responsibility design pattern, we will use the university email scenario briefly mentioned in the previous section. For our example, we design a system that takes incoming emails and searches for specific keywords to help determine which university team the email should be routed to. Specifically, we will account for the following:

Keywords	University Team	Java Handler
academic	Academic Team	AcademicEmailHandler()
alumni, transcript	Alumni Affairs	AlumniEmailHandler()
advising, schedule, course	Advising Staff	AdvisingEmailHandler()
financial, student aid, tuition	Finance Staff	FinanceEmailHandler()
career, job, faculty	Human Resources	HREmailHandler()
other	Admin Team	AdminEmailHandler()

As you can see from the table, we identified handler classes to be implemented in Java. Having individual handlers for each type of email request will improve our application's efficiency.

UML class diagram

Before we look at the UML class diagram, let's determine the chain of responsibility flow. As emails are received, they will be sent down the chain until they are processed by a team. We do have to provide the path, and that path, for our example, is illustrated here:

Chain of responsibility path

The following UML class diagram shows how we will implement the university email system. First, we will create a `UniversityEmailHandler` interface, a `MainEmailHandler` class, and six email handler classes, one for each of the university teams that will receive emails for processing:

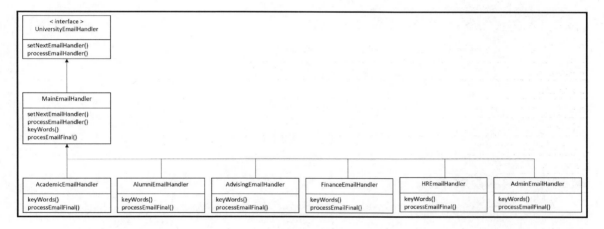

Chain of responsibility—UML diagram

The chain of responsibility's directional flow is implied by the UML class diagram's layout.

Programming the design pattern

The source code for the university email system is provided here:

- `UnversityEmailHandler()`
- `MainEmailHandler()`

- AcademicEmailHandler()
- AlumniEmailHandler()
- AdvisingEmailHandler()
- FinanceEmailHandler()
- HREmailHandler()
- AdminEmailHandler()

The interface and classes are detailed next, along with the full source code.

University email handler interface

The `UniversityEmailHandler` interface has two methods. The first method, `setNextEmailHandler()`, accepts a `UniversityEmailHandler` argument, which will be the next handler in the chain of authority. The second method, `processEmailHandler()`, is used if the email is processed by the current handler:

```
public interface UniversityEmailHandler {

 public void setNextEmailHandler(UniversityEmailHandler emailHandler);

    public void processEmailHandler(String emailText);

}
```

The preceding code explains the handler interface.

Main email handler

`MainEmailHandler()` is the primary handler and implements the `UniversityEmailHandler` interface. The first part of this class contains the `processEmailHandler()` method, which performs the search of the email text for the keywords assigned to each email handler. The following code shows this:

```
public abstract class MainEmailHandler implements UniversityEmailHandler {

    private UniversityEmailHandler theNextHandlerInTheChain;

    public void setNextEmailHandler(UniversityEmailHandler emailHandler) {
        theNextHandlerInTheChain = emailHandler;
    }

    public void processEmailHandler(String emailText) {
```

```
        // starting value
        boolean keyWordFound = false;

        // check for a matching keyword in emailText
        if (keyWords().length == 0) {
            keyWordFound = true;
        } else {
            for (String oneKeyWord : keyWords()) {
                if (emailText.indexOf(oneKeyWord) >= 0) {
                    keyWordFound = true;  // change value if match is found
                    break; // leave loop if match is found
                }
            }
        }
```

Next, we check to determine whether the email can be processed by the current email handler based on the keyword match:

```
if (keyWordFound) {
    processEmailHandler(emailText);
} else {
    // pass along the chain if the email is not processed
    // by the current email handler
    theNextHandlerInTheChain.processEmailHandler(emailText);
    }
}
```

The third part of the MainEmailHandler() class contains the handleEmail() method, which takes the email text as a parameter. It then creates instances of each handler:

```
public static void handleEmail(String emailText) {
    UniversityEmailHandler academic = new AcademicEmailHandler();
    UniversityEmailHandler alumni = new AlumniEmailHandler();
    UniversityEmailHandler advising = new AdvisingEmailHandler();
    UniversityEmailHandler finance = new FinanceEmailHandler();
    UniversityEmailHandler hr = new HREmailHandler();
    UniversityEmailHandler admin = new AdminEmailHandler();
```

The final part of the MainEmailHandler() class sets up the direction for the chain by making calls to the setNextEmailHandler() method for each of the email handlers except for the last one, AdminEmailHandler(), since that is our catchall email handler:

```
        // setup chain direction
        academic.setNextEmailHandler(alumni);
        alumni.setNextEmailHandler(advising);
        advising.setNextEmailHandler(finance);
        finance.setNextEmailHandler(hr);
        hr.setNextEmailHandler(admin);
```

```
            // we do not need to set the next email handler after admin
            // because it is the end of the chain of responsibility

            // this line will start the chain
            academic.processEmailHandler(emailText);
    }
    protected abstract String[] keyWords();
    protected abstract void processEmailFinal(String emailText);
}
```

The `MainEmailHandler()` code provided is the primary handler and contains the `processEmailHandler()` method, which performs the search of the email text for the keywords assigned to each email handler.

Academic email handler

The `AcademicEmailHandler` class extends the `MainEmailHandler` class. It assigns the keywords specific to the academic email handler and contains the `processEmailFinal()` method:

```
    public class AcademicEmailHandler extends MainEmailHandler {

        protected String[] keyWords() {
            // setup keywords for the receiver team
            return new String[] {"academic"};
        }

        protected void processEmailFinal(String emailText) {
            System.out.println("The Academic Team processed the email.");
        }

        @Override
        public void setNextEmailHandler(UniversityEmailHandler emailHandler) {

        }
    }
```

The `processEmailFinal()` method of the `AcademicEmailHandler` class shown informs the user that the academic email handler took care of the received email.

Alumni email handler

The `AlumnicEmailHandler` class extends the `MainEmailHandler` class. It assigns the keywords specific to the alumni email handler and contains the `processEmailFinal()` method:

```
public class AlumniEmailHandler extends MainEmailHandler {

    protected String[] keyWords() {
        // setup keywords for the receiver team
        return new String[] {"alumni", "transcript"};
    }

    protected void processEmailFinal(String emailText) {
        System.out.println("The Alumni Team processed the email.");
    }

    @Override
    public void setNextEmailHandler(UniversityEmailHandler emailHandler) {

    }
}
```

The `processEmailFinal()` method just shown informs the user that the alumni email handler took care of the received email.

Advising email handler

The `AdvisingEmailHandler` class extends the `MainEmailHandler` class. It assigns the keywords specific to the advising email handler and contains the `processEmailFinal()` method:

```
public class AdvisingEmailHandler extends MainEmailHandler {

  protected String[] keyWords() {
  // setup keywords for the receiver team
  return new String[] {"advising", "schedule", "course"};
  }

  protected void processEmailFinal(String emailText) {
  System.out.println("The Advising Team processed the email.");
  }

  @Override
  public void setNextEmailHandler(UniversityEmailHandler emailHandler) {
```

```
        }
    }
```

The `processEmailFinal()` method just shown informs the user that the advising email handler took care of the received email.

Finance email handler

The `FinanceEmailHandler` class extends the `MainEmailHandler` class. It assigns the keywords specific to the finance email handler and contains the `processEmailFinal()` method:

```
public class FinanceEmailHandler extends MainEmailHandler {

    protected String[] keyWords() {
        // setup keywords for the receiver team
        return new String[] {"financial", "student aid", "tuition"};
    }

    protected void processEmailFinal(String emailText) {
        System.out.println("The Finance Team processed the email.");
    }

    @Override
    public void setNextEmailHandler(UniversityEmailHandler emailHandler) {

    }
}
```

The `processEmailFinal()` method just shown informs the user that the finance email handler took care of the received email.

HR email handler

The `HREmailHandler` class extends the `MainEmailHandler` class. It assigns the keywords specific to the HR email handler and contains the `processEmailFinal()` method:

```
public class HREmailHandler extends MainEmailHandler {

    protected String[] assignedKeyWords() {
        // setup keywords for the receiver team
        return new String[]{"career", "job", "faculty"};
    }

    @Override
```

```
    protected String[] keyWords() {
        return new String[0];
    }

    protected void processEmailFinal(String emailText) {
        System.out.println("The Human Resources Team processed the
email.");
    }

    @Override
    public void setNextEmailHandler(UniversityEmailHandler emailHandler) {

    }
}
```

The `processEmailFinal()` method just shown informs the user that the HR email handler took care of the received email.

Admin email handler

The `AdminEmailHandler` class extends the `MainEmailHandler` class. Unlike the other classes, it does not assign any keywords specific to the admin email handler. If an email is sent to this handler, the last one in the chain of responsibility, it will process the email and inform the user via the `processEmailFinal()` method:

```
public class AdminEmailHandler extends MainEmailHandler {

    protected String[] keyWords() {
        // Here it does not matter what the keywords are
        return new String[0];
    }

    protected void processEmailFinal(String emailText) {
        System.out.println("The Admin Team processed the email.");
    }

    @Override
    public void setNextEmailHandler(UniversityEmailHandler emailHandler) {

    }
}
```

The `processEmailFinal()` method just shown informs the user that the admin email handler took care of the received email.

This section featured the university email system's source code, demonstrating the chain of responsibility design pattern.

Exploring the command pattern

The purpose of the command design pattern is to send requests as objects. This pattern, also referred to as the transaction or action design pattern, permits the sending of requests without knowing any details about the receiver or even about what is being requested. This might sound counter-intuitive, and requires that it be looked at from a systems perspective and not a human-managed operation. With the command pattern, we encapsulate requests as objects and transmit them to a receiver.

We will look at an example use case, the UML class diagram, and the source code necessary to implement the command design pattern for this scenario.

Use case

A common use of the command pattern is with user interfaces and related frameworks. This can be extended to both hardware and software interfaces. To demonstrate the command pattern, we will model a hardware control box that contains an on/off toggle, a slider that has a range between 0 and 100, and a digital display for the slider value. Key to our example is that the hardware control box is manufactured without knowing what specifically it will be used for. The following diagram depicts this:

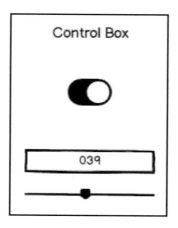

Command design pattern—ControlBox example

In the next section, we will review a UML class diagram associated with our control box example.

UML class diagram

Core to the control box example is a `ControlBox` Java class. The UML class diagram illustrated next shows four attributes—SLIDER_MIN, SLIDER_MAX, poweredOn, and sliderValue; the first two are capitalized to denote their final status:

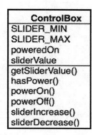

UML class diagram—ControlBox example

The UML class diagram also shows six behaviors that are the `ControlBox` class methods. Those are shown in Java code in the next section.

Programming the design pattern

In order to implement our control box example, we need to create a `ControlBox` class based on the UML diagram in the previous section. The class is presented in the following sections:

- Class variables
- Constructor
- Accessor methods
- Power-related methods
- Slider-related methods

Class variables

There are four class variables in the ControlBox class. The first two set the minimum and maximum values for the slider and are final int variables. The second two class variables are poweredOn and sliderValue. The poweredOn variable is of the Boolean type and will be used to store the state of the power. The sliderValue is an int variable and simply holds the current value of the slider:

```
public class ControlBox {

// Class Variables - Public / Final
public static final int SLIDER_MIN = 0;
public static final int SLIDER_MAX = 100;

// Class Variables - Private
private boolean poweredOn;
    private int sliderValue;
```

The initial part of the ControlBox class is provided.

Constructor

The ControlBox class constructor sets the initial values when an instance of the class is instantiated. The power will be set to off based on the Boolean value of false, and the initial slidervalue will be set to 0:

```
// Constructor
public ControlBox () {
    poweredOn = false; // default value
    sliderValue = 0;   // default value
}
```

The ControlBox class constructor does not take any arguments and sets default values.

Accessor methods

There are only two variables that require accessor methods—sliderValue and poweredOn. Accessor methods for those variables are provided here:

```
// Accessor Methods
public int getSliderValue() {
    return sliderValue;
}
```

```
public boolean hasPower () {
    return poweredOn;
}
```

The accessor methods just shown can also be referred to as `getter` methods.

Power-related methods

Two methods are required to manage power—`powerOn()` and `powerOff()`:

```
// Method to turn power on
public void powerOn() {
    poweredOn = true;
}

// Method to turn power off
public void powerOff() {
    poweredOn = false;
}
```

The preceding methods serves a toggles for the `poweredOn` variable.

Slider-related methods

The final section of the `ControlBox` class provides methods to increase or decrease the slider value. It is important to check two things when adjusting the slider value. First, we need to ensure the power is on. We can check that by making a call to our `hasPower()` method. The second check is to ensure we do not go outside the minimum-maximum range, as follows:

```
    // Method to increase slider value
    public void sliderIncrease () {
        if (hasPower()) {
            if (getSliderValue() < SLIDER_MAX) {
                sliderValue++;
                System.out.println(sliderValue); // simulate sending value
to digital display
            }
        }
    }

    // Method to decrease slider value
    public void sliderDecrease () {
        if (hasPower()) {
            if (getSliderValue() > SLIDER_MIN) {
```

```
                    sliderValue--;
                    System.out.println(sliderValue); // simulate sending value
    to digital display
                }
            }
        }

    }
```

The slider value can be used to manage temperature, volume, quantity, or other values based on what system the control box is integrated with. This demonstrates the command pattern.

This section featured the source code that demonstrates the command design pattern.

Using the interpreter pattern

The interpreter design pattern is used to establish a grammatical representation and an interpreter that interprets language. That might sound a bit complex and, although the concept is simple, their implementation often is not. This design pattern can be used for the interpretation of interpreted programming languages or languages that are compiled in byte code or other intermediate languages such as the **Microsoft Intermediate Language (MSIL)**.

We will look at an example use case, the UML class diagram, and the source code necessary to implement the interpreter design pattern for this scenario.

Use case

We will demonstrate the interpreter design pattern by using a simple number-to-character scenario. Our Code Interpreter program will accept numeric input and translate it to a series of characters. For example, an input string of 319 might return a value of YES. We will use an expression interface and three classes to demonstrate this relatively simple use case.

The following screenshot shows the example program's output, given the user's input:

```
CODE INTERPRETER

Enter your code: 319
Your code: 319
Decrypted Message: YES
```

Code Interpreter output

The preceding screenshot shows the user input as 319.

UML class diagram

As illustrated in the following UML class diagram, our Code Interpreter example consists of an interface and three classes. All of these four components will be described in the next section along with their implementation in Java:

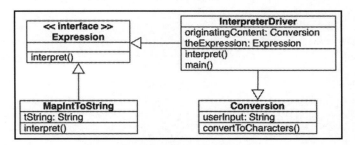

UML class diagram—Code Interpreter example

As illustrated, the MapIntToCharacters class implements the Expression interface.

Programming the design pattern

The Code Interpreter application is an example implementation of the interpreter design pattern. Our application consists of the following components:

- Expression interface
- MapIntToCharacters class
- Conversion class
- InterpreterDriver class

The Expression interface

The **Expression interface** declares the `interpret()` method, which receives a `Conversion` object as an argument:

```
interface Expression {

    void interpret(Conversion orignalContent);

}
```

As shown, the `Expression` interface consists of a single `interpret()` method.

The MapIntToCharacters class

The `MapIntToCharacters` class includes a single `String` class variable and a constructor method. The constructor expects a `String` argument:

```
public class MapIntToCharacters implements Expression {

    // class variable
    private String tString;

    // constructor
    public MapIntToCharacters(String tString) {
        this.tString = tString;
    }

    @Override
    public void interpret(Conversion orignalContent) {
        orignalContent.convertToCharacters(tString);
    }
}
```

The `MapIntToCharacters` class overrides the `interpret()` method.

The Conversion class

The Conversion class applies when there is conversion from numbers to letters (int to char). The class has a single String class variable and a constructor method that is passed to the user's input. The class has one additional method, the convertToCharacters() method. That method converts the user's input into a character array and then processes that array, one character at a time. The processing is implemented with a simple switch statement. Each numerical value, from 0 through 9, has a corresponding character. The characters are printed one at a time until the entire character array has been processed.

The first section of our Conversion class follows:

```java
public class Conversion {

    // class variable
    public String userInput;

    // constructor
    public Conversion(String userInput) {
        this.userInput = userInput;
    }

    public void convertToCharacters(String userInput) {

        this.userInput = userInput;

        System.out.print("Decrypted Message: ");
        char answer[] = userInput.toCharArray();
```

The remaining code from the Conversion class is provided here:

```java
        for (int i=0; i < answer.length; i++) {
            switch (answer[i]) {
                case '0':
                    System.out.print("A");
                    break;
                case '1':
                    System.out.print("E");
                    break;
                case '2':
                    System.out.print("I");
                    break;
                case '3':
                    System.out.print("Y");
                    break;
                case '4':
                    System.out.print("O");
```

```
                break;
        case '5':
            System.out.print("L");
            break;
        case '6':
            System.out.print("R");
            break;
        case '7':
            System.out.print("T");
            break;
        case '8':
            System.out.print("C");
            break;
        case '9':
            System.out.print("S");
            break;
        }
    }
  }
}
```

The preceding code implements a 10-character mapping of integers. A complete implementation would account for the entire alphabet or, depending on the language, alphabets.

InterpreterDriver class

The InterpreterDriver class is the class that drives the application and therefore contains the main() method. There are two class variables, originatingContent and theExpression; both are initially set to null.

In addition to the constructor method, there is also an interpret() method that does the following:

1. Uses the Scanner class
2. Instantiates a new Expression instance
3. Calls the interpret() method on the new Expression instance

The `InterpreterDriver` class is provided next:

```java
import java.util.Scanner;

public class InterpreterDriver {

    // class variables
    public Conversion originatingContent = null;
    public Expression theExpression = null;

    public InterpreterDriver(Conversion content) {
        originatingContent = content;
    }

    public void interpret(String tString) {

        Scanner in = new Scanner(System.in);
        theExpression = new MapIntToCharacters(tString);
        theExpression.interpret(originatingContent);
    }
```

Execution of the `InterpreterDriver` `main()` method starts by printing the output header, CODE INTERPRETER, and prompts users for their input. Next, the `Scanner` class is used to obtain user input via their keyboard. That input is used to create a new `Conversion` instance. That instance is used to instantiate a new `InterpreterDriver` object. Finally, the `interpret()` method is called on that `InterpreterDriver` object:

```java
    public static void main(String[] args) {
        System.out.println("\n\nCODE INTERPRETER\n");
        System.out.print("Enter your code: ");
        Scanner in = new Scanner(System.in);
        String userInput = in.nextLine();
        System.out.println("Your code: " + userInput);
        Conversion conversion = new Conversion(userInput);
        InterpreterDriver userCode = new InterpreterDriver(conversion);
        userCode.interpret(userInput);
        System.out.println("\n\n");
    }
}
```

The program's output is provided here:

```
CODE INTERPRETER

Enter your code: 319
Your code: 319
Decrypted Message: YES
```

Code Interpreter program—console output

This section featured the source code, demonstrating the interpreter design pattern.

Using the iterator pattern

The purpose of the iterator design pattern is to grant access to an object's members without sharing the encapsulated data structures. There are two main motivations for using the iterator design pattern. First, not all object data is stored in the same manner. For example, an online store that aggregates content from other vendors might have a vendor that uses an array, another that uses a list, and a third that uses an `ArrayList`. A second reason is to avoid exposing data structures. Both the variability of storage approaches and data security can be addressed with the iterator design pattern.

The iterator design pattern is implemented by using the `Iterator` interface, part of the `java.util` package.

We will look at a simple use case, the UML class diagram, and the source code necessary to implement the iterator design pattern for this scenario.

Use case

Implementing the iterator design pattern essentially makes use of Java's `Iterator` interface. We will use a single class example that creates an `ArrayList` of strings and uses an iterator to iterate through the list, printing each element.

UML class diagram

Java's Iterator interface is part of the `java.util` package and is a member of the Java collections framework. As you can see from the UML class diagram, the interface includes four methods:

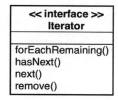

UML class diagram—interface Iterator

The `forEachRemaining()` method iterates through an object's elements. The `hasNext()` method returns a Boolean value depending on whether there are more iterations to go through. The `next()` method simply returns the next sequential iteration element. The final method, `remove()`, removes that last iterated element from the object.

Programming the design pattern

The first part of our source code includes `import` statements for `ArrayList` and `Iterator`. In the `main()` method, we create a `colonies ArrayList` of strings. We then populate `12` elements to the `ArrayList`:

```
import java.util.ArrayList;
import java.util.Iterator;

public class IteratorExample {

    public static void main(String[] args) {

        ArrayList<String> colonies = new ArrayList<>();

        colonies.add("Aerlion");
        colonies.add("Aquaria");
        colonies.add("Canceron");
        colonies.add("Caprica");
        colonies.add("Gemenon");
        colonies.add("Leonis");
        colonies.add("Libran");
        colonies.add("Picon");
        colonies.add("Sagittaron");
```

```
            colonies.add("Scorpia");
            colonies.add("Tauron");
            colonies.add("Virgon");
```

The second half of the source code does three things. First, it instantiates an iterator named `myIterator`. Next, a simple text header is printed to the console. Lastly, the code iterates through the `ArrayList`, printing each element:

```
        // instantiate iterator
        Iterator myIterator = colonies.iterator();

        // console output
        System.out.println("\n\nOriginal Colonies of Kobol:");

        // iterate through the list
        while (myIterator.hasNext())
        System.out.println("\t\t" + myIterator.next());

    }
}
```

The iteration was able to take place without knowing that the `colonies` object stored its data in an `ArrayList`.

The output of our sample application is illustrated here:

```
Original Colonies of Kobol:
        Aerlion
        Aquaria
        Canceron
        Caprica
        Gemenon
        Leonis
        Libran
        Picon
        Sagittaron
        Scorpia
        Tauron
        Virgon
```

Iterator application output

This section featured the source code and output, demonstrating the iterator design pattern.

Understanding the mediator pattern

The mediator design pattern is used to permit object interactions without using explicit object references. This is an advanced use of the object-oriented programming encapsulation concept. Mediators manage the interactions between two or more objects. A real-world example is a legal mediator where both sides of a lawsuit communicate to the mediator, but not directly to each other.

We will look at an example use case, the UML class diagram, and the source code necessary to implement the mediator design pattern for this scenario.

Use case

To demonstrate the mediator design pattern, we will emulate a widget production system that includes a hopper for parts, a starter to start the system, an assembly system to combine hopper components, an accelerator, and an emergency break to manage the speed of the system.

There are inter-relations between the various components for our mediator to manage. These inter-relationships are detailed here:

Components in the left column have the listed impact on the components listed in columns two through six.					
	Starter	**Assembly System**	**Hopper**	**Accelerator**	**Decelerator**
Starter	N/A	Powers this component	Powers this component	Powers this component	Powers this component
Assembly System	Starter must be on for the assembly system to function	N/A	Engages Hopper	N/A	N/A
Hopper	Starter must be on for the hopper to function	Hopper must be on for the assembly system to function	N/A	N/A	N/A
Accelerator	Starter must be on for the accelerator to function	Increases speed of this component	Increases speed of this component	N/A	When accelerator is engaged, this component is not available

				When emergency break is engaged, this component is not available	
Emergency Break	Starter must be on for the emergency break to function	Sets speed to zero for this component	Sets speed to zero for this component		N/A

Widget production system inter-relationships

As you can see from the table, there are 16 inter-relationships among the 5 system components for the mediator to manage.

UML class diagram

The UML diagram illustrated next documents the six classes required for our WidgetProductionSystem. The WidgetProductionSystem class serves as the mediator between the other five classes, which do not interact directly:

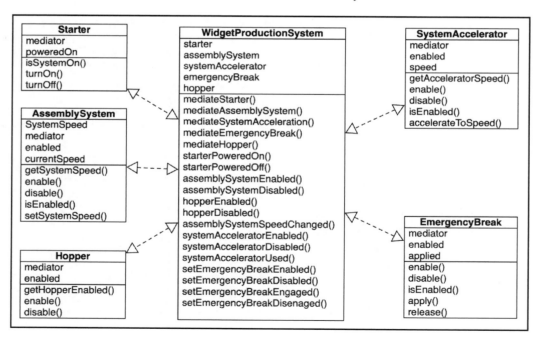

UML class diagram—mediator design pattern implementation

The preceding UML diagram shows six classes required for the implementation of the WidgetProductionSystem.

Programming the design pattern

The following classes are required to implement the WidgetProductionSystem system:

- Starter
- AssemblySystem
- Hopper
- SystemAccelerator
- EmergencyBreak
- WidgetProductionSystem

All of these classes are detailed in subsequent sections.

Starter

The Starter class includes two class variables, a constructor method, an accessor method, and two methods that toggle the starter on and off. The constructor is used to instantiate copies of the class. The accessor method simply returns the value of the poweredOn variable:

```
public class Starter {

    private WidgetProductionSystem mediator;
    private boolean poweredOn;

    // Constructor
    public Starter(WidgetProductionSystem mediator) {
        this.mediator = mediator;
        poweredOn = false;

        mediator.mediateStarter(this);
    }

    // accessor
    public boolean isSystemOn() {
        return poweredOn;
    }

    public void turnOn() {
```

```
        poweredOn = true;
        mediator.starterPoweredOn();
        System.out.println("Mediated Event: Started Powered On");
    }

    public void turnOff() {
        poweredOn = false;
        mediator.starterPoweredOff();
        System.out.println("Mediated Event: Starter Powered Off");
    }
}
```

Also provided are the `turnOn()` and `turnOff()` methods, which simply toggle the value of the `powerOn` variable.

AssemblySystem

The `AssemblySystem` class is presented here in two chunks, shown as follows:

1. The first chunk starts with `SystemSpeed` enum creation, class variables, and the constructor method. Accessor and mutator methods are also included for the `currentSpeed` variable:

```
public class AssemblySystem {

    public enum SystemSpeed {ZERO, ONE, TWO, THREE, FOUR, FIVE,
        SIX, SEVEN, EIGHT, NINE, TEN};

    private WidgetProductionSystem mediator;
    private boolean enabled;
    private SystemSpeed currentSpeed;

    // constructor
    public AssemblySystem(WidgetProductionSystem mediator) {
        this.mediator = mediator;
        enabled = false;
        currentSpeed = SystemSpeed.ZERO;
        mediator.mediateAssemblySystem(this);
    }

    // accessor
    public SystemSpeed getSystemSpeed() {
        return currentSpeed;
    }

    // mutator
```

```
public void setSystemSpeed(SystemSpeed speed) {
    if ((isEnabled()) && (getSystemSpeed() != speed)) {
        currentSpeed = speed;
        mediator.assemblySystemSpeedChanged();
        System.out.println("Mediated Event: System Speed
Changed to "
            + currentSpeed + ".");
    }
}
```

2. The second chunk of the `AssemblySystem` class has methods that enable and disable the system as well as one to check whether it is currently enabled:

```
// additional methods
public void enable() {
    enabled = true;
    mediator.assemblySystemEnabled();
    System.out.println("Mediated Event: System Initialized.");
}

public void disable() {
    enabled = false;
    mediator.assemblySystemDisabled();
    System.out.println("Mediated Event: System
Deinitialized.");
}

public boolean isEnabled() {
    return enabled;
}
}
```

The final method shown returns the Boolean value of `Enabled`.

Hopper

The `Hopper` class contains two class variables, a constructor method and an accessor method, to determine whether the hopper is currently enabled. The class code is as follows:

```
public class Hopper {

    private WidgetProductionSystem mediator;
    private boolean enabled;

    // constructor
    public Hopper(WidgetProductionSystem mediator) {
```

```
        this.mediator = mediator;
        enabled = false;
        mediator.mediateHopper(this);
    }

    // accessor
    public boolean getHopperEnabled() {
        return enabled;
    }

    public void enable() {
        enabled = true;
        mediator.hopperEnabled();
        System.out.println("Mediated Event: Hopper Initialized.");
    }

    public void disable() {
        enabled = false;
        mediator.hopperDisabled();
        System.out.println("Mediated Event: Hopper Deinitialized.");
    }
}
```

The final two methods shown, enable() and disable(), toggle the Boolean value of the enabled variable.

The SystemAccelerator class

The SystemAccelerator class is presented here in two parts. The first part establishes the class variables, the constructor method, an accessor method that returns the speed, and an isEnabled() method that returns the value of the enabled variable:

```
public class SystemAccelerator {

    // class variables
    private WidgetProductionSystem mediator;
    private boolean enabled;
    private int speed;

    // constructor
    public SystemAccelerator(WidgetProductionSystem mediator) {
        this.mediator = mediator;
        enabled = false;
        speed = 0;
        mediator.mediateSystemAcceleration(this);
    }
```

```
    // accessor
    public int getAcceleratorSpeed() {
        return speed;
    }

    public boolean isEnabled() {
        return enabled;
    }
```

The second part of the `SystemAccelerator` class contains three methods. The `enable()` and `disable()` methods toggle the value of the enabled variable:

```
public void enable() {
    enabled = true;
    mediator.systemAcceleratorEnabled();
    System.out.println("Mediated Event: System Accelerator Enabled.");
}

public void disable() {
    enabled = false;
    mediator.systemAcceleratorDisabled();
    System.out.println("Mediated Event: System Accelerator Disabled.");
}

public void accelerateToSpeed(int speed) {
    if (isEnabled()) {
        this.speed = speed;
        mediator.systemAcceleratorUsed();
        System.out.println("Mediated Event: System Accelerator Set to "
            + speed + ".");
    }
}
}
```

The third method in the `SystemAccelerator` class is the `accelerateToSpeed()` method, which handles the `speed` change.

EmergencyBreak

The `EmergencyBreak` class is presented in two parts. The first part defines the class variables: the `constructor` method, and the `enable()` and `disable()` methods:

```
public class EmergencyBreak {

    // class variables
    private WidgetProductionSystem mediator;
```

```
    private boolean enabled;
    private boolean applied;

    // constructor
    public EmergencyBreak(WidgetProductionSystem mediator) {
        this.mediator = mediator;
        enabled = false;
        applied = false;
        mediator.mediateEmergencyBreak(this);
    }

    public void enable() {
        enabled = true;
        mediator.setEmergencyBreakEnabled();
        System.out.println("Mediated Event: System Decelerator Enabled.");
    }

    public void disable() {
        enabled = false;
        mediator.setEmergencyBreakDisabled();
        System.out.println("Mediated Event: System Decelerator Disabled.");
    }
```

The remaining part of the EmergencyBreak class has the isEnabled(), apply(), and release() methods:

```
    public boolean isEnabled() {
        return enabled;
    }

    public void apply() {
        if (isEnabled()) {
            applied = true;
            mediator.setEmergencyBreakEngaged();
            System.out.println("Mediated Event: Emergency Break Engaged.");
        }
    }
    public void release() {
        if (isEnabled()) {
            applied = false;
            mediator.setEmergencyBreakDisengaged();
            System.out.println("Mediated Event: Emergency Break
Disengaged.");
        }
    }
}
```

As shown, the `isEnabled()` method simply returns the Boolean value of the `enabled` variable. The `apply()` and `release()` methods simulate the emergency break being applied and released.

WidgetProductionSystem

Our example `WidgetProductionSystem` class manages mediation between the other classes. The source code is presented in six sequential parts. The first part of the class defines the class variables and contains the `constructor` method:

```java
public class WidgetProductionSystem {

    // class variables
    private Starter starter;
    private AssemblySystem assemblySystem;
    private SystemAccelerator systemAccelerator;
    private EmergencyBreak emergencyBreak;
    private Hopper hopper;
    private int currentSpeed;

    // constructor
    public WidgetProductionSystem() {
        currentSpeed = 0;
    }
```

The second part of the `WidgetProductionSystem` class contains five `mediation` methods:

```java
    // mediation methods
    public void mediateStarter(Starter starter) {
        this.starter = starter;
    }

    public void mediateAssemblySystem(AssemblySystem assemblySystem) {
        this.assemblySystem = assemblySystem;
    }

    public void mediateSystemAcceleration(SystemAccelerator systemAccelerator)
    {
        this.systemAccelerator = systemAccelerator;
    }

    public void mediateEmergencyBreak(EmergencyBreak emergencyBreak) {
        this.emergencyBreak = emergencyBreak;
    }

    public void mediateHopper(Hopper hopper) {
```

```
        this.hopper = hopper;
    }
```

The third part of the `WidgetProductionSystem` class contains the first two object interaction methods. The two featured here are `starterPoweredOn()` and `starterPoweredOff()`. Based on the power status, several other component settings are changed:

```
// object interaction methods
public void starterPoweredOn() {
    assemblySystem.enable();
    hopper.enable();
    systemAccelerator.enable();
    emergencyBreak.enable();
}

public void starterPoweredOff() {
    assemblySystem.disable();
    hopper.disable();
    systemAccelerator.disable();
    emergencyBreak.disable();
}
```

Part four of the `WidgetProductionSystem` class contains seven additional object interaction methods:

```
public void assemblySystemEnabled() {
    System.out.println("Mediation Decision: Hopper Enabled.");
}

public void assemblySystemDisabled() {
    System.out.println("Mediation Decision: Hopper Disabled.");
}

public void hopperEnabled() {
    System.out.println("Mediation Decision: Assembly System Enabled.");
}

public void hopperDisabled() {
    System.out.println("Mediation Decision: Assembly System Disabled.");
}

public void assemblySystemSpeedChanged() {
    System.out.println("Mediation Decision: Permissible Speed Change.");
}

public void systemAcceleratorEnabled() {
```

```
        System.out.println("Mediation Decision: Emergency Break Enabled");
    }

    public void systemAcceleratorDisabled() {
        System.out.println("Mediation Decision: Emergency Break Disabled");
    }
```

The fifth part of the `WidgetProductionSystem` class contains the `systemAcceleratorUsed()` method. This method converts the `int` speed set to the appropriate `enum` system speed:

```
public void systemAcceleratorUsed() {
    emergencyBreak.disable();
    while (currentSpeed < systemAccelerator.getAcceleratorSpeed()) {
        currentSpeed ++;
        System.out.println("Mediation Event: Speed Changed to " +
currentSpeed + ".");

        if (currentSpeed <= 10) {
            assemblySystem.setSystemSpeed(AssemblySystem.SystemSpeed.ONE);
        } else if (currentSpeed <= 20) {
            assemblySystem.setSystemSpeed(AssemblySystem.SystemSpeed.TWO);
        } else if (currentSpeed <= 30) {
assemblySystem.setSystemSpeed(AssemblySystem.SystemSpeed.THREE);
        } else if (currentSpeed <= 40) {
            assemblySystem.setSystemSpeed(AssemblySystem.SystemSpeed.FOUR);
        } else if (currentSpeed <= 50) {
            assemblySystem.setSystemSpeed(AssemblySystem.SystemSpeed.FIVE);
        } else if (currentSpeed <= 60) {
            assemblySystem.setSystemSpeed(AssemblySystem.SystemSpeed.SIX);
        } else if (currentSpeed <= 70) {
assemblySystem.setSystemSpeed(AssemblySystem.SystemSpeed.SEVEN);
        } else if (currentSpeed <= 80) {
assemblySystem.setSystemSpeed(AssemblySystem.SystemSpeed.EIGHT);
        } else if (currentSpeed <= 90) {
            assemblySystem.setSystemSpeed(AssemblySystem.SystemSpeed.NINE);
        } else {
assemblySystem.setSystemSpeed(AssemblySystem.SystemSpeed.TEN); }
    }
    emergencyBreak.enable();
}
```

Next, the `WidgetProductionSystem` class contains the last four object `interaction` methods:

```
    public void setEmergencyBreakEnabled() {
        System.out.println("Mediation Decision: System Accelerator
Disabled.");
    }

    public void setEmergencyBreakDisabled() {
        System.out.println("Mediation Decision: System Accelerator
Enabled.");
    }

    public void setEmergencyBreakEngaged() {
        systemAccelerator.disable();
        currentSpeed = 0;
    }

    public void setEmergencyBreakDisengaged() {
        assemblySystem.setSystemSpeed(AssemblySystem.SystemSpeed.ZERO);
        currentSpeed = 0;
    }
}
```

This section featured the source code, demonstrating the mediator design pattern.

Examining the memento pattern

The memento design pattern saves an object's current internal state as a memento so that it can be referred to and restored to. If you have ever used *Ctrl + Z* (Windows) or *Cmd + Z* (Mac) to undo a change, you were restoring to a previous state using the memento design pattern. A benefit of using this design pattern is that we honor encapsulation, providing data protection.

We will look at an example use case, the UML class diagram, and the source code necessary to implement the memento design pattern for this scenario.

Use case

An example case for using the memento design pattern is with video game progress. When a player fails a mission and the game is over, the scores and other values are often reset to an earlier save point. We will use a simple game mission example to demonstrate the memento design pattern.

UML class diagram

Our implementation of the memento design pattern involves two classes—GameMission and GameMissionMemento. All of these classes is detailed along with their source code in the next section of this chapter:

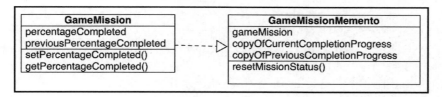

UML class diagram—memento design pattern implementation

As illustrated in the UML class diagram, the two classes do not share an inheritance relationship.

Programming the design pattern

The first class in our example is the GameMission class. As you can see, we have two class variables. The percentageCompleted int is private and the getPercentageCompleted() accessor method is used to obtain the variable's value. The second class variable is previousPercentageCompleted. This is assumed private to the current Java package; there is no associated accessor method for this variable:

```
public class GameMission {

    // class variables
    private int percentageCompleted;
    int previousPercentageCompleted;

    // constructor
    public GameMission() {
        percentageCompleted = 0;
        previousPercentageCompleted = 0;
    }

    // mutator
    public void setPercentageCompeted(int percentage) {
        previousPercentageCompleted = percentageCompleted;
        percentageCompleted = percentage;
    }
```

```
    // accessor
    public int getPercentageCompleted() {
        return percentageCompleted;
    }
}
```

The GameMissionMemento class contains three class variables, a constructor method, and the resetMissionStatus() method. A review of the constructor method reveals different approaches to gaining access to the GameMission data. The gameMission.getPercentageCompleted() method call uses the accessor method in the GameMission class. The gameMission.previousPercentageCompleted statement accesses the data directly. The following code shows this:

```
public class GameMissionMemento {

    // class variables
    private GameMission gameMission;
    private int copyOfCurrentCompletionProgress;
    private int copyOfPreviousCompletionProgress;

    // constructor
    public GameMissionMemento(GameMission gameMission) {
        this.gameMission = gameMission;
        copyOfCurrentCompletionProgress =
gameMission.getPercentageCompleted();
        copyOfPreviousCompletionProgress =
gameMission.previousPercentageCompleted;
    }

    public void resetMissionStatus() {
        gameMission.setPercentageCompeted(copyOfCurrentCompletionProgress);
        gameMission.previousPercentageCompleted =
copyOfPreviousCompletionProgress;
    }
}
```

This section featured the source code, demonstrating the memento design pattern.

Using the null object pattern

The null object design pattern is relatively straightforward. It is a common task to check for null values during routine programming. We check for null so that we do not receive a null pointer exception from the **Java Virtual Machine (JVM)** at runtime.

The null object design pattern negates the need to search for the null condition. This is accomplished by creating a null object class. The null object class is designed to implement the same interface as other classes in the package. No functionality is included in the null object class.

We will look at an example use case, the UML class diagram, and the source code necessary to implement the null object design pattern for this scenario.

Use case

We will demonstrate the null object design pattern with a simple TrainStatus interface that has three methods to activate, deactivate, and check whether the object is currently activated. Five classes will be used, each implementing the TrainStatus interface. The NorthernTrain, EasternTrain, SouthernTrain, and WesternTrain classes will be identical. The NullObjectTrain class will be similar to the other classes in that it will implement the TrainStatus interface, but it will have no functionality. This is illustrated with the UML class diagram in the next section and then again with the source code in an additional section.

UML class diagram

The following UML class diagram shows the `TrainStatus` interface, which is implemented by five additional classes. Each of those classes is identical with the exception of the `NullObjectTrain` class, which will have no functionality:

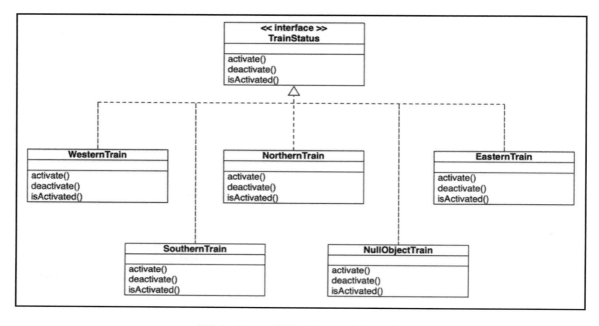

UML class diagram—null object design pattern implementation

As indicated in the UML class diagram, the `WesterTrain`, `NorthernTrain`, `EasterTrain`, `SouthernTrain`, and `NullObjectTrain` classes each implement the `TrainStatus` interface.

Programming the design pattern

The source code for the `TrainStatus` interface follows:

```
public interface TrainStatus {
    public void activate();
    public void deactivate();
    public boolean isActivated();
}
```

The source code for the NorthernTrain, EasternTrain, SouthernTrain, and WesternTrain classes is identical, so only the WesternTrain class is shown here:

```
public class WesternTrain implements TrainStatus {

    private boolean activated;

    public void activate() {
        activated = true;
        System.out.println("Train Status Update: Western Train
Activated.");
    }

    public void deactivate() {
        activated = false;
        System.out.println("Train Status Update: Western Train
Deactivated.");
    }

    public boolean isActivated() {
        return activated;
    }
}
```

The NullObjectTrain class is slightly different from the other classes in that it does not contain any functionality. Also, the isActivated() method returns false, as this is not an actual train and will never be activated:

```
public class NullObjectTrain implements TrainStatus {

    public void activate() {
        // no functionality
    }

    public void deactivate() {
        // no functionality
    }

    public boolean isActivated() {
        return false;
    }
}
```

Use of the null object design pattern negates the need to test for a null condition.

This section featured the source code, demonstrating the null object design pattern.

Observing the observer pattern

The observer design pattern requires a one-to-many object dependency. The purpose of the dependency is to update subscriber objects when a change is made to the publisher object's state. An example is an online university course discussion forum. There is one forum and many subscribers. When an update to the forum is made, the subscribers are notified. Subscribers have the option of unsubscribing when they no longer want to be notified of changes to the discussion forum.

We will look at an example use case, the UML class diagram, and the source code necessary to implement the observer design pattern for this scenario.

Use case

We will utilize the discussion forum example to demonstrate the observer design pattern. Our example will consist of one discussion forum and multiple subscribers. We can also refer to these subscribers as **observers**.

UML class diagram

The UML class diagram illustrates a basic implementation of the observer design pattern:

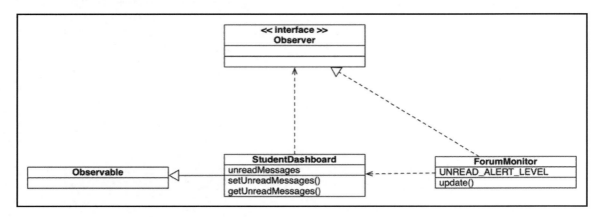

UML class diagram—observer design pattern implementation

As shown in the UML class diagram, the `StudentDashboard` class extends the `Observable` class, and the `ForumMonitor` implements the `Observer` interface.

Programming the design pattern

The StudentDashboard class extends the Observable class and has a single class variable, the unreadMessages int. There are three methods in this class: the constructor class and the setter (mutator) and getter (accessor) methods:

```
public class StudentDashboard extends Observable {

    private int unreadMessages;

    // constructor
    public StudentDashboard() {
        unreadMessages = 0;
    }

    public void setUnreadMessages(int messages) {
        unreadMessages = messages;

        /*
            Add methods here to notify observers of a change
         */

    }

    public int getUnreadMessages() {
        return unreadMessages;
    }
}
```

The ForumMonitor class implements the Observer interface. It includes a final UNREAD_ALERT_LEVEL variable that is used as an alert threshold. In our example, an observer will be alerted if there are more than zero unread messages:

```
public class ForumMonitor implements Observer {

    public static final int UNREAD_ALERT_LEVEL = 0;

    public void update(Observable observable, Object object) {
        StudentDashboard messages = (StudentDashboard) observable;
        if (messages.getUnreadMessages() > UNREAD_ALERT_LEVEL) {
            System.out.println("You have " + messages.getUnreadMessages()
                + " unread messages.");
        } else {
            System.out.println("No unread messages found.");
        }
    }
}
```

In order to complete this example application, the `Observer` interface and the `Observable` class need to be written.

This section featured the source code, demonstrating the observer design pattern.

Understanding the state pattern

The state design pattern allows an object to change its behavior based on internal state changes. The effect is that the object may seem to change its class. We will use the use case of a print job queue to demonstrate the state design pattern.

We will look at an example use case, the UML class diagram, and the source code necessary to implement the state design pattern for this scenario.

Use case

Our state design pattern implementation example is a print-job application. The application receives a print request and either processes it or puts the job on hold. In our example, the print-job application can only print one job at a time.

UML class diagram

The solution to the state design pattern implementation requires an abstract `PrinterController` class that is extended by both the `PrinterOnLine` and `PrinterOffLine` classes:

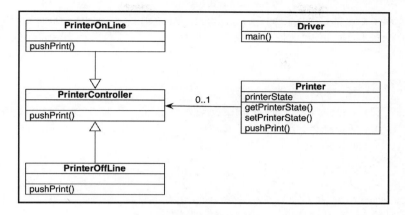

UML class diagram—state design pattern implementation

Also indicated in the UML class diagram are the `Printer` and `Driver` classes.

Programming the design pattern

The implementation example for the state design pattern consists of the following classes:

- `PrinterOnLine`
- `PrinterOffLine`
- `Printer`
- `PrinterController`
- `Driver`

PrinterOnLine

The `PrinterOnLine` class extends the `PrinterController` class and overrides the `pushPrint()` method. When called, this method clears the printer buffer and shuts down. Here is the code:

```
public class PrinterOnLine extends PrinterController {

    @Override
    public void pushPrint(Printer printJob) {
        System.out.println("\nClearing buffer and shutting down. . .");
        printJob.setPrinterState(new PrinterOffLine());
    }
}
```

As you can see in the code, the pushPrint() method in the PrinterOnLine class results in the printer going from online to offline.

PrinterOffLine

The PrinterOffLine class extends the PrinterController class and overrides the pushPrint() method. When called, this method powers the printer on. The printer goes from being offline to online:

```
public class PrinterOffLine extends PrinterController {

    @Override
    public void pushPrint(Printer printJob) {
        System.out.println("\nPowering printer on please wait. . .");
        printJob.setPrinterState(new PrinterOnLine());
    }
}
```

As you can see in the preceding code, the pushPrint() method in the PrinterOffLine class results in the printer going from offline to online.

Printer

The Printer class has a single class variable, printerState. It contains constructor, accessor, and mutator methods. Here is the Printer class source code:

```
public class Printer {

    // class variable
    private PrinterController printerState;

    // constructor
    public Printer(PrinterController pState) {
        this.printerState = pState;
    }

    // accessor / getter
    public PrinterController getPrinterState() {
        return printerState;
    }

    // mutator / setter
    public void setPrinterState(PrinterController pState) {
        this.printerState = pState;
```

```
    }

    public void pushPrint() {
        printerState.pushPrint(this);
    }
}
```

The `Printer` class also contains the `pushPrint()` method, which simulates pushing a printer's power button.

PrinterController

The `PrinterController` class contains a single abstract `pushPrint()` method:

```
abstract class PrinterController {

    public abstract void pushPrint(Printer printJob);
}
```

The `pushPrint()` abstract method shown receives a `Printer` object as an argument.

Driver

The `Driver` class is created to test the functionality of the state design pattern implementation:

```
public class Driver {

    public static void main(String[] args) {

        PrinterOffLine initialPrinterState = new PrinterOffLine();
        Printer printer = new Printer(initialPrinterState);

        System.out.println("\n");

        printer.pushPrint();
        printer.pushPrint();
        printer.pushPrint();

        System.out.println("\n\n");
    }
}
```

The `Driver` class contains a `main()` method that drives the application's execution.

Application output

The completed application generates the following lines of console output. The `Driver` class contains three calls to the `pushPrint()` method. As shown, each line of the console output is created as a result of a call to the `printer.pushPrint()` method:

```
Powering printer on please wait. . .

Clearing buffer and shutting down. . .

Powering printer on please wait. . .
```

State design pattern implementation—application output

This section featured the source code, demonstrating the state design pattern.

Strategizing with the strategy pattern

The strategy design pattern allows you to individually encapsulate a set of interchangeable algorithms. This results in algorithm variability depending on the calling client. This is similar to method overloading, which allows a class to have more than one method with the same name. The difference between the same-named methods is their argument list.

The strategy design pattern differs from the method overloading example when each algorithm is individually encapsulated.

A sample UML class diagram is provided in the next section.

UML class diagram

As you can see from the UML class diagram, there are multiple options for a single algorithm, represented here with the `sampleAlgorithm()` method:

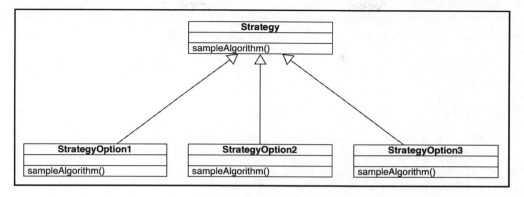

UML class diagram—strategy design pattern

As illustrated by the UML class diagram, the strategy design pattern allows you to individually encapsulate a set of interchangeable algorithms.

Understanding the template method pattern

The template method design pattern involves creating an algorithm template with processing steps relegated to child classes. The purpose is to give the child classes the ability to specify their own steps while still remaining true to the algorithm structure.

As the design pattern's name suggests, we create a template that can be followed by subordinate classes. An example is a recipe template that has bakers following the steps to create the shell and then adding their own pie filling based on their preference. At the end of the process, all the pies will look similar but will have different fillings.

Another example is creating a syllabus or resume template. Each use of the template can be used for unique content and would still not alter the template.

Understanding the visitor pattern

The visitor design pattern allows us to perform operations on an object without altering its structure. Essentially, we can add functionalities to an object with it changing the original object structure. An example is when a person goes to a hair salon and asks for a haircut. Once in the chair, the parameters of what is desired are changed. This does not change the structure of the operation; it just adds new functionality such as having hair colored as well as cut and styled.

Using object-oriented programming, we can extend the visitor design pattern so it affects the way inheritance works. We can extend a class and then add functionality to it in a child class.

Summary

In this chapter, we learned that behavioral diagrams illustrate how system components interact to form a system. We also learned that behavioral design patterns focus on the interaction of objects and classes in a system. We explored the behavioral design pattern category and 12 individual design patterns, which were then listed. We also looked at programming challenges and the behavioral design patterns that solve them.

In the next chapter, *Creational Design Patterns*, we will explore the creational design pattern category and its individual design patterns—abstract factory, builder, factory method, prototype, simple factory, and singleton. We will examine the programming challenges and creational design patterns that solve them.

Questions

1. Which design pattern would likely be used to restore a system based on previous settings?
2. What design pattern category does the null object pattern belong to?
3. What is the purpose of the object dependency in the observer design pattern?
4. Which design pattern allows an object to change its behavior based on internal state changes?
5. Which design pattern allows you to individually encapsulate a set of interchangeable algorithms?
6. Which design pattern involves creating an algorithm template with processing steps relegated to child classes?
7. Which design pattern permits objects to be sent to a series of receivers without the sender being concerned about which receiver handles the request?
8. What other name is the command design pattern referenced?
9. What is the Interpreter design pattern used for?
10. Under which Java interface does the iterator design pattern rely on?

Further reading

- *Java EE 8 Design Patterns and Best Practices* (`https://www.packtpub.com/application-development/java-ee-8-design-patterns-and-best-practices`)
- *Learn Design Patterns with Java [Video]* (`https://www.packtpub.com/application-development/learn-design-patterns-java-video`)
- *Design Patterns and Best Practices in Java* (`https://www.packtpub.com/application-development/design-patterns-and-best-practices-java`)

Creational Design Patterns

4

In the last chapter, *Behavioral Design Patterns*, we learned that behavioral diagrams illustrate how system components interact to form a system. We also learned that behavioral design patterns focus on the interaction of objects and classes in a system. We explored the behavioral design pattern category and 12 individual design patterns (chain of responsibility, command, interpreter, iterator, mediator, memento, null object, observer, state, strategy, template method, and visitor). Our coverage included an examination of programming challenges and the behavioral design patterns that solve them.

In this chapter, *Creational Design Patterns*, we will explore the creational design pattern category and its individual design patterns. We will examine the programming challenges and creational design patterns that solve them:

- Introducing creational design patterns
- Abstract factory
- Builder
- Factory method
- Prototype
- Simple factory
- Singleton

Technical requirements

The code for this chapter can be found in this book's GitHub repository: `https://github.com/PacktPublishing/Hands-On-Design-Patterns-with-Java/tree/master/Chapter04`.

Introducing creational design patterns

Creational design patterns are used to manage the objects as they are instantiated (created). In Java, there are two basic creation patterns. When we create classes, we use inheritance. When creating objects, we can assign the creation task to other objects.

The purposes of creational design patterns are as follows:

- Separate object creation from the system
- Support reliance on object creation vice inheritance
- Encapsulate information regarding which classes are used by a system
- Protect object creation details

The six creational design patterns presented in this chapter can be grouped into two subcategories—those that focus on classes and those that focus on objects. The following table details these subcategories:

Object Scope	Class Scope
Abstract factory pattern	Factory pattern
Builder pattern	Simple factory pattern
Prototype pattern	Singleton pattern

The creational design patterns listed in the preceding table are detailed in the remaining sections of this chapter. They are presented in alphabetical order to illustrate that one is not more important than the others.

Understanding the abstract factory design pattern

Before we look at the abstract factory design pattern, let's first review the term *abstract* and how it applies to Java classes and the programs we develop.

The term *abstract* refers to something not having a definitive existence. In Java, abstract classes cannot be instantiated, but they can be inherited. Let's consider an example of an abstract Grandmother class that is extended by a Mother class. A third class, Daughter, is used to house the main() method. Here is the code for the Grandmother class:

```
abstract class Grandmother {

    // Constructor
```

```
Grandmother() {
    System.out.println("Grandmother constructor executed.");
}
}
```

Next, we have the `Mother` class, which extends `Grandmother` and has its own constructor method:

```
public class Mother extends Grandmother {

    // Constructor
    Mother() {
        System.out.println("Mother constructor executed.");
    }
}
```

The final class in this example is the `Daughter` class. Here is the code:

```
public class Daughter {

    public static void main(String[] args) {
        Mother mom = new Mother();
    }
}
```

When the application is run, the following results are provided in the console window:

```
Grandmother constructor executed.
Mother constructor executed.
```

Abstract class sample program output

As you can see in the following screenshot, if we try to instantiate the `Grandmother` class, we are presented with the error that the class is abstract and cannot be instantiated:

```
public class Daughter {

    public static void main(String[] args) {
        Mother mom = new Grandmother();
    }                    'Grandmother' is abstract; cannot be instantiated
}
```

Error in abstract class instantiation

The abstract factory design pattern creates an interface that is used to create multiple objects without knowledge of the concrete class. A concrete class in Java is a non-abstract class that implements all of the methods in its hierarchy. This is a high-powered demonstration of encapsulation. This design pattern allows us to change implementations without changing source code.

We will look at an example use case, the UML class diagram, and the source code necessary to implement the abstract factory design pattern for this scenario.

Use case

We will use a motor-home manufacturing example to demonstrate the abstract factory design pattern. When motor homes are manufactured, there are many details that must be determined. At a high level, the manufacturer must decide on the type (type A, type B, or type C), the style (for example, camper van, bus, truck), the frame, engine, and kitchen. Our example will support type A, type B, and type C motorhomes, all of which require a style, frame, engine, and kitchen.

The abstract factory design pattern will be used to create object sets, one for each motor-home type.

UML class diagram

The following UML class diagram shows the relationships between the interfaces and classes that are used in the abstract factory design pattern implementation:

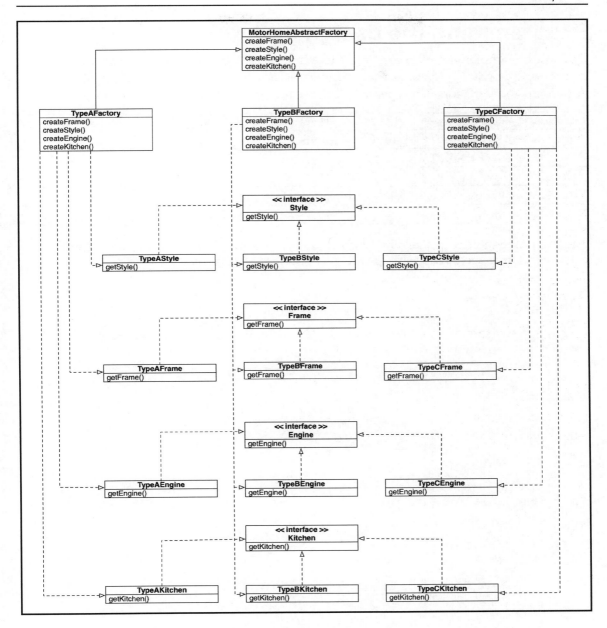

UML class diagram—abstract factory implementation

As indicated in the UML class diagram, our implementation solution will require 5 interfaces and 17 classes.

Programming the design pattern

Our solution implementation consists of five interfaces (Type, Style, Frame, Engine, and Kitchen), a MotorHomeAbstractFactory class, a MotorHomeDriver class, and 15 additional classes, 5 for each type. Here is the complete list of interfaces and classes:

Interfaces	General Classes	TypeA Classes	TypeB Classes	TypeC Classes
Type	MotorHomeAbstractFactory	TypeAFactory	TypeBFactory	TypeCFactory
Style	MotorHomeDriver	TypeAStyle	TypeBStyle	TypeCStyle
Frame		TypeAFrame	TypeBFrame	TypleCFrame
Engine		TypeAEngine	TypeBEngine	TypleCEngine
Kitchen		TypeAKitchen	TypeBKitchen	TypeCKitchen

The preceding table organizes the types of Java classes that were used in the solution. The classes that are specific to each type are very similar to one another.

Interfaces

Each of the five interfaces in our abstract factory design pattern implementation consist of a single accessor method. Their source code is listed here:

```
public interface Type {
    public String getType();
}

public interface Style {
    public String getStyle();
}

public interface Frame {
    public String getFrame();
}

public interface Engine {
    public String getEngine();
}

public interface Kitchen {
    public String getKitchen();
}
```

As you can see, the interfaces each return a String value.

Abstract Factory class

The `MotorHomeAbstractFactory` class defines four `abstract` methods. Here is the code:

```
public abstract class MotorHomeAbstractFactory {
  public abstract Frame createFrame();
  public abstract Style createStyle();
  public abstract Engine createEngine();
  public abstract Kitchen createKitchen();
}
```

The abstract methods defined in the preceding code correspond to the `Factory` classes that are defined in subsequent sections.

TypeA classes

Our solution includes a `Factory` class for each of the three types of motor homes (type A, type B, and type C). The `TypeAFactory` class shown in the following code extends the `MotorHomeAbstractFactory` class:

```
public class TypeAFactory extends MotorHomeAbstractFactory {

    public Frame createFrame() {
        return new TypeAFrame();
    }

    public Style createStyle() {
        return new TypeAStyle();
    }

    public Engine createEngine() {
        return new TypeAEngine();
    }

    public Kitchen createKitchen() {
        return new TypeAKitchen();
    }
}
```

In addition to a `Factory` class, we need a class to implement the class hierarchy. Here, you see can each of the interfaces that were implemented:

```
public class TypeAStyle implements Style {

    public String getStyle() {
```

```
            return "[Type A] Style:\t\tOff the Grid";
        }
    }

    public class TypeAEngine implements Engine {

        public String getEngine() {

            return "[Type A] Engine:\tFord V10";
        }
    }

    public class TypeAFrame implements Frame {

        public String getFrame() {

            return "[Type A] Frame:\t\tBus";
        }
    }

    public class TypeAKitchen implements Kitchen {

        public String getKitchen() {

            return "[Type A] Kitchen:\tFull";
        }
    }
```

The four classes defined implement the appropriate `accessor` method and return a contextual `String`.

TypeB classes

Our solution includes a `Factory` class for each of the three types of motor homes (type A, type B, and type C). The `TypeBFactory` class shown here extends the `MotorHomeAbstractFactory` class:

```
    public class TypeBFactory extends MotorHomeAbstractFactory {

        public Frame createFrame() {
            return new TypeBFrame();
        }

        public Style createStyle() {
            return new TypeBStyle();
```

```
    }

    public Engine createEngine() {
        return new TypeBEngine();
    }

    public Kitchen createKitchen() {
        return new TypeBKitchen();
    }
}
```

In addition to a `Factory` class, we need a class to implement the class hierarchy. Here, you can see each of the interfaces implemented:

```
public class TypeBStyle implements Style {

    public String getStyle() {

        return "[Type B] Style:\t\tWeekender";
    }
}

public class TypeBEngine implements Engine {

    public String getEngine() {

        return "[Type B] Engine:\tFord Transit 350 HD";
    }
}

public class TypeBFrame implements Frame {

    public String getFrame() {

        return "[Type B] Frame:\t\tCamper Van";
    }
}

public class TypeBKitchen implements Kitchen {

    public String getKitchen() {

        return "[Type B] Kitchen:\tCompact";
    }
}
```

The four classes that were defined implement the appropriate `accessor` method and return a contextual `String`.

Type-C classes

Our solution includes a Factory class for each of the three types of motor homes (type A, type B, and type C). The TypeCFactory class shown in the following code extends the MotorHomeAbstractFactory class:

```java
public class TypeCFactory extends MotorHomeAbstractFactory {


    public Frame createFrame() {
        return new TypeCFrame();
    }

    public Style createStyle() {
        return new TypeCStyle();
    }

    public Engine createEngine() {
        return new TypeCEngine();
    }

    public Kitchen createKitchen() {
        return new TypeCKitchen();
    }

}
```

In addition to a Factory class, we need a class to implement the class hierarchy. Here, you can see each of the interfaces that were implemented:

```java
public class TypeCStyle implements Style {

    public String getStyle() {

        return "[Type C] Style:\t\tExtended Trip";
    }
}

public class TypeCEngine implements Engine {

    public String getEngine() {

        return "[Type C] Engine:\tFord E-450";
    }
}

public class TypeCFrame implements Frame {
```

```
    public String getFrame() {

        return "[Type C] Frame:\t\tTruck";
    }
}

public class TypeCKitchen implements Kitchen {

    public String getKitchen() {

        return "[Type C] Kitchen:\tFull";
    }
}
```

The four classes that were defined implement the appropriate `accessor` method and return a contextual `String`.

Driver class

The `Driver` class for our abstract factory design pattern implementation is the `MotorHomeDriver` class. It is presented here in four sequential sections:

1. The first section defines the `main()` method and creates an instance of `MotorHomeAbstractFactory` named `mhFactory`:

   ```
   public class MotorHomeDriver {

       public static void main(String[] args) {

           // Step 1
           // create abstract factory
           MotorHomeAbstractFactory mhFactory = null;
   ```

2. The second section of code shows the second step in our process, creating a factory instance. We start by simulating user input where the user would select which motor home type (type A, type B, or type C) to manufacture. Based on the user input, descriptive text is printed and a new factory instance is created. When the program was started, the type of factory was not identified:

   ```
   // Step 2
   // Create a factory instance
   String nextMotorHome = "TypeA"; // simulated user input

   if (nextMotorHome.equals("TypeA")) {
       System.out.println("\nType A motor home selected");
   ```

```
        mhFactory = new TypeAFactory();
    } else if (nextMotorHome.equals("TypeB")) {
        System.out.println("\nType B motor home selected");
        mhFactory = new TypeBFactory();
    } else if (nextMotorHome.equals("TypeC")) {
        System.out.println("\nType C motor home selected");
        mhFactory = new TypeCFactory();
    } else {
        System.out.println("Invalid motor home type entered.");
    }
```

3. The third section of code creates the motor-home components based on the factory instance that was created in the previous step:

```
// Step 3
// Create motor home components
Style mhStyle = mhFactory.createStyle();
Frame mhFrame = mhFactory.createFrame();
Engine mhEngine = mhFactory.createEngine();
Kitchen mhKitchen = mhFactory.createKitchen();
```

4. The final step is to provide output to the user:

```
    // Step 4
    // Provide Output
    System.out.println("\nComponent list for " + nextMotorHome
+ " motor home");
        System.out.println(mhStyle.getStyle());
        System.out.println(mhFrame.getFrame());
        System.out.println(mhEngine.getEngine());
        System.out.println(mhKitchen.getKitchen());
    }
}
```

The output results show the output for each possible type (type A, type B, type C) that the user could select:

```
Type A motor home selected            Type B motor home selected              Type C motor home selected

Component list for TypeA motor home   Component list for TypeB motor home     Component list for TypeC motor home
[Type A] Style:    Off the Grid       [Type B] Style:    Weekender            [Type C] Style:    Extended Trip
[Type A] Frame:    Bus                [Type B] Frame:    Camper Van           [Type C] Frame:    Truck
[Type A] Engine:   Ford V10           [Type B] Engine:   Ford Transit 350 HD  [Type C] Engine:   Ford E-450
[Type A] Kitchen:  Full               [Type B] Kitchen:  Compact              [Type C] Kitchen:  Full
```

Abstract factory implementation—application output

This section provided the source code implementation and console output for our abstract factory application.

Building with the builder design pattern

The builder design pattern is used to create a separation between object instantiation and representation. The purpose is to permit different representations with the same instantiation process.

 In this context, *representation* refers to the description of an object.

This design pattern is typically only used for complex objects. Using the builder design pattern, complex objects are created in separate steps. This allows us to build different objects based on the building steps taken.

We will look at an example use case, the UML class diagram, and the source code that's necessary to implement the builder design pattern for this scenario.

Use case

To demonstrate the builder design pattern, we will implement a coffee roaster manufacturing application. This app will facilitate the creation of two different coffee roaster models: personal and commercial. There are a total of eight components; some components are used for both roaster models, and the components indicated as model-specific indicate that they are different for each roaster model. Additionally, the platform component is only required for the commercial roaster model. The following table provides an overview of these components:

Component	Personal Roaster	Commercial Roaster
Cooling tray	Model-Specific	Model-Specific
Exhaust system	Model-Specific	Model-Specific
Gas burner	Model-Specific	Model-Specific
Inner drum	Model-Specific	Model-Specific
Main body	Model-Specific	Model-Specific
Motor	Standard	Standard
Platform	Not required	Standard
Thermocouples	Standard	Standard

As you can see from the preceding table, five of the components are unique to the roaster model and three are standard. One of the components, the platform, is not required for a personal roaster build.

UML class diagram

The UML class diagram for our `Coffee Roaster Manufacturing` implementation is provided here:

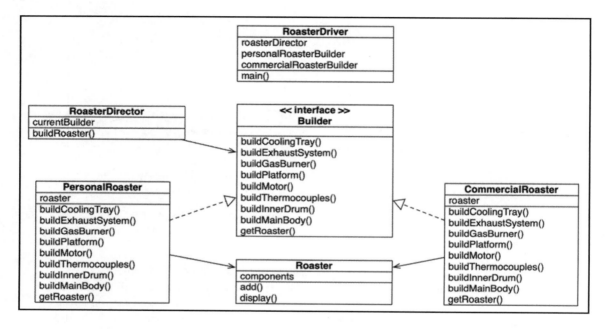

UML class diagram—builder design pattern implementation

As indicated in the UML class diagram, our solution includes a `Builder` interface and five classes.

Programming the design pattern

The programming solution to our `Coffee Roaster Manufacturing` implementation of the builder design pattern consists of a `Roaster` class, an interface, a `Driver` class, and four additional classes. Each is detailed in this section.

Roaster class

The first class in our solution is the `Roaster` class. This class allows for the instantiation of multiple `Roaster` objects. The class contains a constructor method and an `add()` method for adding components to a roaster, and a `display()` method for displaying a roaster's components list:

```
import java.util.LinkedList;

public class Roaster {

    private LinkedList<String> components;

    public Roaster() {
        components = new LinkedList<>();
    }

    public void add(String component) {
        components.addLast(component);
    }

    public void display() {
        System.out.println("\n\nROASTER BUILD:");
        for (int i=0; i<components.size(); i++) {
            System.out.println(components.get(i));
        }
    }
}
```

As shown in the preceding code, the `java.util.LinkedList` package was imported because the `Roaster` class made use of a `LinkedList` object.

Interface

The `Builder` interface is provided in the following code and consists of eight methods, one for each roaster component:

```
public interface Builder {

    void buildCoolingTray();
    void buildExhaustSystem();
    void buildGasBurner();
    void buildPlatform();
    void buildMotor();
    void buildThermocouples();
    void buildInnerDrum();
```

```
    void buildMainBody();

    Roaster getRoaster();
}
```

The `Builder` interface also includes a `getRoaster()` method that returns a `Roaster` object.

Builder classes

Our solution involves two builder classes—`PersonalRoaster` and `CommercialRoaster`. The following code is the first half of the `PersonalRoaster` class. It implements the `Builder` interface and instantiates a `Roaster` object.

In this code section, there are four methods for building specific components, each utilizing the `add()` method:

```
public class PersonalRoaster implements Builder {

    private Roaster roaster = new Roaster();

    @Override
    public void buildCoolingTray() {
        roaster.add("Personal Roaster Cooling Tray added");
    }

    @Override
    public void buildExhaustSystem() {
        roaster.add("Personal Roaster Exhaust System added");
    }

    @Override
    public void buildGasBurner() {
        roaster.add("Personal Roaster Gas Burner added");
    }

    @Override
    public void buildPlatform() {
        // do nothing - not applicable for personal roasters
    }
```

It is important to note that the `buildPlatform()` method does not perform any functionality in the `PersonalRoaster` class.

The following code is the second half of the `PersonalRoaster` class. There are four methods for building specific components, each utilizing the `add()` method:

```
@Override
public void buildMotor() {
    roaster.add("Standard Motor added");
}

@Override
public void buildThermocouples() {
    roaster.add("Standard Thermocouples added");
}

@Override
public void buildInnerDrum() {
    roaster.add("Personal Roaster Inner Drum added");
}

@Override
public void buildMainBody() {
    roaster.add("Personal Roaster Main body added");
}

@Override
public Roaster getRoaster() {
    return roaster;
}
}
```

The `PesonalRoaster` class also includes a `getRoaster()` method, which returns a `Roaster` object.

The following code is the first half of the `CommercialRoaster` class. It implements the `Builder` interface and instantiates a `Roaster` object. In this code section, there are four methods for building specific components, each utilizing the `add()` method:

```
public class CommercialRoaster implements Builder {

    private Roaster roaster = new Roaster();

    @Override
    public void buildCoolingTray() {
        roaster.add("Commercial Roaster Cooling Tray added");

    }

    @Override
```

```
public void buildExhaustSystem() {
    roaster.add("Commercial Roaster Exhaust System added");

}

@Override
public void buildGasBurner() {
    roaster.add("Commercial Roaster Gas Burner added");

}

@Override
public void buildPlatform() {
    roaster.add("Standard Platform added");

}
```

It is important to note that the `buildPlatform()` method makes a call to the `add()` method, unlike the same method in the `PersonalRoaster` class.

The following code is the second half of the `CommercialRoaster` class. There are four methods for building specific components, each utilizing the `add()` method:

```
@Override
public void buildMotor() {
    roaster.add("Standard Motor added");

}

@Override
public void buildThermocouples() {
    roaster.add("Standard Thermocouples added");

}

@Override
public void buildInnerDrum() {
    roaster.add("Commercial Roaster Inner Drum added");
}

@Override
public void buildMainBody() {
    roaster.add("Commercial Roaster Main body added");

}

@Override
public Roaster getRoaster() {
```

```
            return roaster;
    }
}
```

The `CommercialRoaster` class also includes a `getRoaster()` method, which returns a `Roaster` object.

Director class

The `RoasterDirector` class creates a `Builder` instance and then uses a sequence of steps to build the roaster. The `RoasterDirector` class is unaware of whether the roaster being created is for personal or commercial use:

```
public class RoasterDirector {
    Builder currentBuilder;

    // roaster building steps
    public void buildRoaster(Builder builder) {

        currentBuilder = builder;
        currentBuilder.buildCoolingTray();
        currentBuilder.buildExhaustSystem();
        currentBuilder.buildGasBurner();
        currentBuilder.buildInnerDrum();
        currentBuilder.buildMainBody();
        currentBuilder.buildMotor();
        currentBuilder.buildPlatform();
        currentBuilder.buildThermocouples();
    }
}
```

The order of the steps in the build process is not important.

Driver class

The `RoasterDriver` class contains our program's `main()` method and drives the application. The functionality starts by creating a `RoasterDirector` instance and two `Builder` instances. Next, the build sequence is called once each for a personal roaster and a commercial roaster:

```
public class RoasterDriver {

    public static void main(String[] args) {
```

```
RoasterDirector roasterDirector = new RoasterDirector();

Builder personalRoasterBuilder = new PersonalRoaster();
Builder commercialRoasterBuilder = new CommercialRoaster();

// Build a Personal Roaster
roasterDirector.buildRoaster(personalRoasterBuilder);
Roaster unit1 = personalRoasterBuilder.getRoaster();
unit1.display();

// Build a Commercial Roaster
roasterDirector.buildRoaster(commercialRoasterBuilder);
Roaster unit2 = commercialRoasterBuilder.getRoaster();
unit2.display();
        }
    }
```

The `display()` method is called after each build sequence completes. As illustrated in the following screenshot, the components are different for both roaster models:

```
ROASTER BUILD:
Personal Roaster Cooling Tray added
Personal Roaster Exhaust System added
Personal Roaster Gas Burner added
Personal Roaster Inner Drum added
Personal Roaster Main body added
Standard Motor added
Standard Thermocouples added


ROASTER BUILD:
Commercial Roaster Cooling Tray added
Commercial Roaster Exhaust System added
Commercial Roaster Gas Burner added
Commercial Roaster Inner Drum added
Commercial Roaster Main body added
Standard Motor added
Standard Platform added
Standard Thermocouples added
```

Builder design pattern implementation—console output

This section provided the source code and the console output for our `Coffee Roaster Manufacturing` implementation of the builder design pattern.

Exploring the factory method design pattern

The factory method design pattern allows subclasses to determine which class to create. This is achieved by removing details about which class to create away from the framework. Instead, the subclasses are given the responsibility for object creation. This design pattern is useful when the framework is unaware of what is to be instantiated.

We will look at an example use case, the UML class diagram, and the source code that's necessary to implement the factory method design pattern for this scenario.

Use case

To demonstrate the factory method design pattern, we will create a `Mower Selection Helper` implementation. The system will provide helpful information to aid users in their selection of a lawnmower type. The types that are supported are *riding* and *push*. We will create an abstract `Factory` class with a method to retrieve the mower type. We will also create a factory method for the concrete classes for the instantiation of specific mower objects.

UML class diagram

The UML class diagram for the `Mower Selection Helper` implementation of the factory method design pattern consists of an interface that is implemented by two classes.

The `ConcreteMowerFactory` class is where the object instantiation occurs:

UML class diagram—factory method design pattern implementation

As indicated in the UML class diagram, the `RidingMower` and `PushMower` classes implement the `Mower` interface, and the `MowerFactory` class is removed from the object creation process.

Programming the design pattern

Our implementation starts with a `Mower` interface. It has a single `mow()` method:

```
public interface Mower {
    void mow();
}
```

The following segment of code is the `MowerFactor` abstract class. There, we will have the `ConcreteMowerFactory` subclass:

```
abstract class MowerFactory {

    public abstract Mower getMowerType(String mowerType);
}
```

The `Riding` class represents the class object for this type of mower. It implements the `Mower` interface. It overrides the `mow()` method and outputs text that's specific to this type of `Mower`:

```
public class Riding implements Mower {

    @Override
    public void mow() {
        System.out.println("Riding mowers provide safety and comfort.");
    }
}
```

The `Push` class represents the class object for the push mower type. It implements the `Mower` interface. The `Push` class overrides the `mow()` method and outputs text that's specific to this type of `Mower`:

```
public class Push implements Mower {

    @Override
    public void mow() {
        System.out.println("Push mowers are good for small yards.");
    }
}
```

The `ConcreteMowerFactory` class that's shown in the following code extends the `MowerFactory` class. This class is used to determine which mower type is instantiated based on the `String` argument:

```
public class ConcreteMowerFactory extends MowerFactory {

    @Override
    public Mower getMowerType(String mowerType) {
        if (mowerType.equals("Riding")) {
            return  new Riding();
        } else if (mowerType.equals("Push")) {
            return new Push();
        } else {
            System.out.println("Invalid mower type selected.");
            return null;
        }
    }
}
```

The final class in our implementation is the `MowerDriver` class. This class contains the `main()` method and drives the application. The `main()` method starts by printing a simple output header. Then, two mower instances are created, one for each mower type:

```
public class MowerDriver {

    public static void main(String[] args) {

        // output header
        System.out.println("\n\nMOWER SELECTION HELPER");

        // create first mower
        MowerFactory mowerFactory = new ConcreteMowerFactory();
        Mower rideIt = mowerFactory.getMowerType("Riding");
        rideIt.mow();

        // create second mower
        Mower pushIt = mowerFactory.getMowerType("Push");
        pushIt.mow();
    }
}
```

As shown in the following screenshot, our `Mower Selection Helper` implementation prints the output header from the `MowerDriver` class `main()` method and then a line from the `mow()` method from each of the instantiated objects:

```
MOWER SELECTION HELPER
Riding mowers provide safety and comfort.
Push mowers are good for small yards.
```

Factory method design pattern implementation—console output

This section provided the source code and the console output for our `Mower Selection Helper` implementation of the factory method design pattern.

Using the prototype design pattern

The prototype design pattern allows us to specify a category of objects using a prototype instance. This instance is then copied in order to create new objects. The prototype design pattern is ideal for situations when you want object creation to be independent of the system. For example, we might be developing a game with multiple levels. Each level is based on a core level and modified thereafter. We can clone the prototype level in order to create subsequent levels and avoid having to start level creation from scratch.

Object creation requires processing time, and reducing the time it takes to create objects is a goal of the prototype design pattern.

We will look at an example use case, the UML class diagram, and the source code that's necessary to implement the prototype design pattern for this scenario.

Use case

We will use a game-level creation system as an example application that implements the prototype design pattern. We will have a `BaseLevel` prototype class and three concrete prototype classes, each for a different type of game level. These concrete prototype classes will implement the `BaseLevel clone()` method. Different game-level attributes will be applied individually to the three different game levels.

UML class diagram

The UML class diagram, as shown in the following diagram, shows the implementation of our game-level creation system. Our implementation has a `BaseLevel` class, which includes the `clone()` method. This method is overridden by each of the three subclasses—`Dungeon`, `Forest`, and `City`:

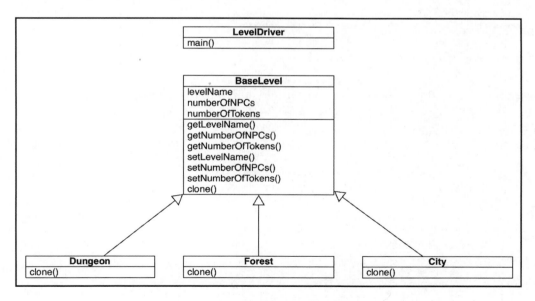

UML class diagram—prototype design pattern implementation

As indicated in the UML class diagram, the `LevelDriver` class contains our application's `main()` method and is used to drive the program's functionality.

Programming the design pattern

Our game-level creation system starts with the abstract `BaseLevel` class. This class implements Java's `Cloneable` interface. There are three class variables that will be part of each game level that's created—`levelName`, `numberOfNPCs`, and `numberOfTokens`. Following the class variables are the three `accessor` methods, one for each of the variables:

```
public abstract class BaseLevel implements Cloneable {

    public String levelName;
    public int numberOfNPCs;
    public int numberOfTokens;

    // accessor methods
    public String getLevelName() {
        return levelName;
    }

    public int getNumberOfNPCs() {
        return numberOfNPCs;
    }

    public int getNumberOfTokens() {
        return numberOfTokens;
    }
```

The second half of the `BaseLevel` class contains the mutator methods for the class variables. At the bottom of the class is the `clone()` method, which is used to create a clone of the `BaseLevel` class:

```
    // mutator methods
    public void setLevelName(String levelName) {
        this.levelName = levelName;
    }

    public void setNumberOfNPCs(int npc) {
        this.numberOfNPCs = npc;
    }

    public void setNumberOfTokens(int tokens) {
        this.numberOfTokens = tokens;
```

```
    }

    // level clone method
    public BaseLevel clone() throws CloneNotSupportedException {
        return (BaseLevel)super.clone();
    }
}
```

Our implementation includes three classes that extend the BaseLevel class. The following code is for the Dungeon class. This class contains a constructor and overrides the clone() method from the BaseLevel class:

```
public class Dungeon extends BaseLevel {

    public Dungeon(String name) {
        levelName = name;
    }

    @Override
    public BaseLevel clone() throws CloneNotSupportedException {
        return (Dungeon)super.clone();
    }
}
```

The Forest class, as shown in the following code, extends the BaseLevel class. This class contains a constructor and overrides the clone() method from the BaseLevel class:

```
public class Forest extends BaseLevel {

    public Forest(String name) {
        levelName = name;
    }

    @Override
    public BaseLevel clone() throws CloneNotSupportedException {
        return (Forest)super.clone();
    }
}
```

Like the Dungeon and Forest classes, the City class, which is shown in the following code, extends the BaseLevel class. This class contains a constructor and overrides the clone() method from the BaseLevel class:

```
public class City extends BaseLevel {

    public City(String name) {
        levelName = name;
```

```
    }

    @Override
    public BaseLevel clone() throws CloneNotSupportedException {
        return (City)super.clone();
    }
}
```

The last class that's required to implement our game-level creation system is the
`LevelDriver` class. This class only contains a `main()` method. This method is displayed in
two sections, as we will see in the following code snippets. The first section starts with an
output header and then creates a `Dungeon` object, a `Forest` object, and a `City` object. As
each object is created, the game-level name, number of `NPCs`, and number of `Tokens` is
provided:

```
public class LevelDriver {

    public static void main(String[] args) throws
CloneNotSupportedException {

        System.out.println("\n\nGAME LEVEL CREATION\n");

        // Create Dungeon Game Level
        BaseLevel dungeon = new Dungeon("Slasher\'s Dungeon Level 1");
        dungeon.numberOfNPCs = 500;
        dungeon.numberOfTokens = 80;

        // Create Forest Game Level
        BaseLevel forest = new Forest("Acid Rain Forest Level");
        forest.numberOfNPCs = 250;
        forest.numberOfTokens = 120;

        // Create City Game Level
        BaseLevel city = new City("Industrial City Level");
        city.numberOfNPCs = 319;
        city.numberOfTokens = 600;
```

The second portion of the `LevelDriver` `main()` method does two things. First, it creates a
clone of the already created `Dungeon` object, naming it `levelClone1`. New values are
provided for the level name, number of `NPCs`, and `Tokens`. The second set of tasks this
code performs is to display output to verify the application's functionality:

```
// Clone Dungeon Object
        BaseLevel levelClone1;
        levelClone1 = dungeon.clone();
        levelClone1.setLevelName("Slasher\'s Dungeon Level 2");
        levelClone1.setNumberOfNPCs(1000);
```

```
        levelClone1.setNumberOfTokens(40);

        // Display output for functionality verification
        System.out.println("Dungeon Level information");
        System.out.println("Level Name      : " + dungeon.getLevelName());
        System.out.println("Number of NPCS  : " +
dungeon.getNumberOfNPCs());
        System.out.println("Number of Tokens: " +
dungeon.getNumberOfTokens());

        System.out.println("\nCloned Level information");
        System.out.println("Level Name : " + levelClone1.getLevelName());
        System.out.println("Number of NPCS : " +
levelClone1.getNumberOfNPCs());
        System.out.println("Number of Tokens: " +
levelClone1.getNumberOfTokens());
    }
}
```

The application's console output is then provided:

```
GAME LEVEL CREATION

Dungeon Level information
Level Name      : Slasher's Dungeon Level 1
Number of NPCS  : 500
Number of Tokens: 80

Cloned Level information
Level Name      : Slasher's Dungeon Level 2
Number of NPCS  : 1000
Number of Tokens: 40
```

Prototype design pattern implementation—console output

This section provided the source code and the console output for our game-level creation system implementation of the prototype design pattern.

Examining the simple factory design pattern

Earlier in this chapter, we identified the abstract factory design pattern as creating an interface to create multiple objects without knowledge of the concrete class. We also stated that the factory method design pattern allows subclasses to determine which class to create. The simple factory design pattern is used to delegate object creation to a specific class.

We will look at an example use case, the UML class diagram, and the source code that's necessary to implement the simple factory design pattern for this scenario.

Use case

We will implement a lawnmower seat creation system to demonstrate the simple factory design pattern. Our example will include an abstract LawnMowerSeat class, two subclasses that extend the LawnMowerSeat class, a factory class, and a Driver class. The following section contains our system's UML class diagram, which depicts class relationships.

UML class diagram

The UML class diagram for our lawnmower seat creation system illustrates key relationships among the system's classes. The abstract LawnMowerSeat class is extended by both the ResidentialLawnMowerSeat class and the CommercialLawnMowerSeat class:

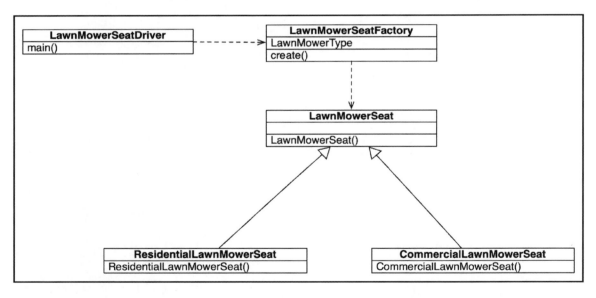

UML class diagram—simple factory deign pattern implementation

As indicated in the UML class diagram, the LawnMowerSeatDriver class contains the main() method and drives the system's execution.

Programming the design pattern

Our lawnmower seat creation system starts with the `LawnMowerSeat` abstract class. This class only contains a constructor and, by its abstract nature, cannot be instantiated:

```
public abstract class LawnMowerSeat {

    public LawnMowerSeat() {

    }
}
```

The next class is `ResidentialLawnMowerSeat`. This class extends the `LawnMowerSeat` class and contains a constructor that prints class-specific output:

```
public class ResidentialLawnMowerSeat extends LawnMowerSeat {

    public ResidentialLawnMowerSeat() {

        System.out.println("Residential lawnmower seat with seat belt
created.");

    }
}
```

The class that's shown in the following code is `CommercialLawnMowerSeat`. This class extends the `LawnMowerSeat` class and contains a constructor that prints class-specific output:

```
public class CommercialLawnMowerSeat extends LawnMowerSeat {

    public CommercialLawnMowerSeat() {

        System.out.println("Commercial lawnmower seat with roll bar
created.");
    }
}
```

Next is our `Factory` class—the `LawnMowerSeatFactory` class. This is the class with the ability to create the residential and commercial iterations of the `LawnMowerSeat`:

```
public class LawnMowerSeatFactory {

    public enum LawnMowerType {RESIDENTIAL, COMMERCIAL};

    public static LawnMowerSeat create(LawnMowerType mowerType) {
        if (mowerType == LawnMowerType.RESIDENTIAL) {
```

```
        return new ResidentialLawnMowerSeat();
    } else if (mowerType == LawnMowerType.COMMERCIAL) {
        return new CommercialLawnMowerSeat();
    } else {
        return null;
    }
}
}
```

The last class in our solution is the `LawnMowerSeatDriver` class. This class contains the main method and makes calls to the `Factory` class for object creation:

```
public class LawnMowerSeatDriver {

    public static void main(String[] args) {

        System.out.println("\n\n");

        // Create a Residential Lawnmower Seat
        LawnMowerSeat residential =
LawnMowerSeatFactory.create(LawnMowerSeatFactory.LawnMowerType.RESIDENTIAL)
;

        // Create a Commercial Lawnmower Seat
        LawnMowerSeat commercial =
LawnMowerSeatFactory.create(LawnMowerSeatFactory.LawnMowerType.COMMERCIAL);

    }
}
```

After each object is created, contextual text is printed on the console. That output is displayed here:

```
Residential lawnmower seat with seat belt created.
Commercial lawnmower seat with roll bar created.
```

Simple factory design pattern implementation—console output

This section provided the source code and the console output for our lawnmower seat creation system implementation of the simple factory design pattern.

Implementing the singleton design pattern

The singleton design pattern is perhaps the easiest of the creational design patterns to understand and to implement. The purpose of this design pattern is to ensure there is only one instance of the class, and it must be externally accessible. It is common for security-based systems to implement the singleton design pattern. An example would be a banking system that creates new account numbers. It is important that these account numbers are only generated by a single system.

We will implement the singleton design pattern simply by making the singleton class constructor private.

We will look at an example use case, the UML class diagram, and the source code that's necessary to implement the singleton design pattern for this scenario.

Use case

To demonstrate the singleton design pattern, we will create a bank account number generation system. This system will consist of a singleton class that can only be instantiated once. Our system will attempt to create more than one instance of the singleton class to verify our application's functionality.

UML class diagram

As indicated by the UML class diagram, only two classes are required to demonstrate our singleton design pattern implementation:

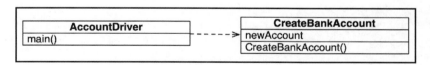

UML class diagram—singleton design pattern implementation

The UML class diagram aptly indicates that the `AccountDriver` class contains the `main()` method and will be used to drive the program's execution.

Programming the design pattern

The CreateBankAccount class includes a private constructor, which will prevent attempts to instantiate more than one instance of the CreateBankAccount object. The getNewAccount() method checks whether the newAccount already exists and provides contextual feedback to the user:

```java
public class CreateBankAccount {

    private static CreateBankAccount newAccount;

    // constructor
    private CreateBankAccount() {

    }

    public static CreateBankAccount getNewAccount() {
        if (newAccount == null) {
            newAccount = new CreateBankAccount();
            System.out.println("New Account created.");
        } else {
            System.out.println("Account already opened.");
        }
        return newAccount;
    }
}
```

The Driver class, AccountDriver, prints a header label and then attempts to create two instances of the CreateBankAccount object, which is shown as follows:

```java
public class AccountDriver {

    public static void main(String[] args) {

        System.out.println("\n\nBank Account Number Generation System");

        // create new account
        CreateBankAccount account1 = CreateBankAccount.getNewAccount();

        // create second account
        CreateBankAccount account2 = CreateBankAccount.getNewAccount();
    }
}
```

As shown by the following console output, the first attempt at object creation was successful and the subsequent attempt failed. This shows that the singleton design pattern was properly implemented:

```
Bank Account Number Generation System
New Account created.
Account already opened.
```

Builder design pattern implementation—console output

This section provided the source code and the console output for our bank account number generation system implementation of the singleton design pattern.

Summary

In this chapter, *Creational Design Patterns*, we explored the creational design pattern category and its individual design patterns: abstract factory, builder, factory method, prototype, simple factory, and singleton. We learned that creational design patterns are used to mange object instantiation. The purposes of creational design patterns are to separate object creation from the system, support reliance on object creation via inheritance, encapsulate information regarding which classes are used by a system, and to protect object creation details.

In the next chapter, *Structural Design Patterns*, we will explore the structural design pattern category and its individual design patterns of adapter, bridge, composite, facade, flyweight, and proxy.

Questions

1. What are the four purposes of creational design patterns?
2. What are the six creational design patterns?
3. What are the two categories of creational design patterns?
4. What is unique about abstract classes in Java?
5. Which design pattern creates an interface that is used to create multiple objects without prior knowledge of the concrete class?
6. Which design pattern is used to create separation between object instantiation and representation?

7. Which design pattern allows subclasses to determine which class to create?
8. Which design pattern allows us to specify a category of objects using a prototype instance?
9. Which design pattern is used to delegate object creation to a specific class?
10. Which design pattern ensures there is only one instance of the class?

Further reading

- *Java EE 8 Design Patterns and Best Practices* (https://www.packtpub.com/application-development/java-ee-8-design-patterns-and-best-practices)
- *Learn Design Patterns with Java* (https://www.packtpub.com/application-development/learn-design-patterns-java-video)
- *Design Patterns and Best Practices in Java* (https://www.packtpub.com/application-development/design-patterns-and-best-practices-java)

5
Structural Design Patterns

In the last chapter, *Creational Design Patterns*, we explored the creational design pattern category and its individual design patterns, namely, abstract factory, builder, the `factory` method, prototype, simple factory, and singleton. We learned that creational design patterns are used to manage object instantiation. The purposes of creational design patterns are to separate object creation from the system, support reliance on object creation vice inheritance, encapsulate information regarding which classes are used by a system, and to protect object creation details.

In this chapter, *Structural Design Patterns*, we will explore the structural design pattern category. Structural design patterns are used to identify how system components are related. Seven specific structural design patterns, listed here, will be covered in this chapter. We will examine the programming challenges and creational design patterns that solve them:

- Introduction to creational design patterns
- Adapter
- Bridge
- Composite
- Decorator
- Facade
- Flyweight
- Proxy

Technical requirements

The code for this chapter can be found at https://github.com/PacktPublishing/Hands-On-Design-Patterns-with-Java/tree/master/Chapter05.

Introduction to structural design patterns

Structural design patterns focus on how objects and classes are combined to form a system. There are two categories of structural design patterns:

- **Object design patterns**: Structural object design patterns are used to describe how to create objects with new functionality
- **Class design patterns**: Structural class design patterns utilize inheritance to create interfaces and combine multiple classes to form a larger structure

Examples of both the approaches are provided in this chapter.

The seven structural design patterns presented in this chapter all have an object scope, with the exception of the adapter design pattern. The adapter design pattern has both object and class scope, as illustrated in the following table:

Object scope	Class scope
Adapter object pattern	Adapter class pattern
Bridge pattern	
Composite pattern	
Decorator pattern	
Facade pattern	
Flyweight pattern	
Proxy pattern	

The structural design patterns listed in the preceding table are detailed in the remaining sections of this chapter. They are presented in alphabetical order to illustrate that one is not more important than the others.

Understanding the adapter design pattern

The adapter design pattern is used to convert an interface of one class into another interface expected by the system. This design pattern empowers classes to work in concert with one another regardless of the compatibility of their interfaces.

Consider the real-world case of a motorhome. In order to connect to shore power, an electric cord is plugged into the motorhome. The other end of that cord is plugged into a power source receptacle. If the power receptacle does not fit the plug, an adapter is required. We can translate this real-world scenario into a computer model. The motorhome and power source receptacles are both classes with their own interfaces. These interfaces restrict the two classes from communicating with each other without the use of an adapter.

Use case

We will use a real estate land area calculation program to demonstrate how to implement the adapter design pattern. We will have two similar classes that do not inherit from the same class and cannot communicate directly with each other without an adapter. The Lot class will simply contain a length and width so acreage can be computed as square feet. This assumes small lot sizes. The Estate class acreage will be computed as acreage as those lots sizes are much larger.

UML class diagram

As indicated by the following UML class diagram, the AcreageDeterminatorAdapter class is the adapter that facilitates communication between the Lot and Estate classes:

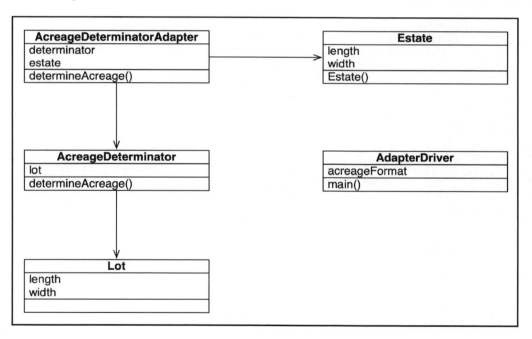

UML class diagram—adapter design pattern implementation

As illustrated, the AdapterDriver class is used to drive the application and contains the main() method.

Programming the design pattern

The Lot class shown here only contains two variables that can be used to calculate the square footage land area of instances of the Lot class:

```
public class Lot {

    // class variables
    public double length;
    public double width;
}
```

The Estate class contains the same two variables as the Lot class and also contains a constructor method:

```
public class Estate {

    // class variables
    public double length;
    public double width;

    // constructor
    public Estate(int length, int width) {
        this.length = length;
        this.width = width;
    }
}
```

The AcreageDeterminator class is used to compute the square footage of a Lot instance:

```
public class AcreageDeterminator {
    Lot lot;

    public double determineAcreage(Lot tLot) {
        lot = tLot;
        return lot.length * lot.width;
    }
}
```

The `AcreageDeterminatorAdapter` class is the adapter class that permits the communication between the `Lot` and `Estate` classes. The class uses instances of `AcreageDeterminator` and `Estate` to determine acreage. The `determineAcreage()` method creates instances of both the `Lot` and `Estate` classes. The `Estate` instance values are assigned to the `Lot` instance variables. Then, the method performs the calculation specific to the `Estate` instance and returns that value, which is shown in the following code:

```
public class AcreageDeterminatorAdapter {

    AcreageDeterminator determinator;
    Estate estate;

    public double determineAcreage(Estate tEstate) {
        determinator = new AcreageDeterminator();
        estate = tEstate;
        Lot tLot = new Lot();

        tLot.length = estate.length;
        tLot.width = estate.width;

        return (determinator.determineAcreage(tLot) / 43560);
    }
}
```

The `AdapterDriver` class is the application's class that contains the `main()` method. This method contains some housekeeping functionality to include an output header and to allow formatting the output for two decimal places. The core functionality in the `main()` method is to create `AcreageDeterminatorAdapter` and `Estate` instances. The `Estate` instance is created with sample values of `2300` and `6325` for length and width respectively. A call is made to the `determineAcreage()` method of the `AcreageDeterminatorAdapter` instance, with the `Estate` instance used as a parameter to the method call. The following code shows this:

```
import java.text.DecimalFormat;

public class AdapterDriver {

 private static DecimalFormat acreageFormat = new DecimalFormat(".##");

 public static void main(String[] args) {

 System.out.println("\n\nReal Estate Land Area Calculation");
        AcreageDeterminatorAdapter adAdapter = new
AcreageDeterminatorAdapter();
```

```
        Estate estate = new Estate(2300, 6325);

        System.out.print("Estate Acreage: ");
   System.out.print(acreageFormat.format(adAdapter.determineAcreage(estate)));
      }
   }
```

The application's console output is displayed here:

```
Real Estate Land Area Calculation
Estate Acreage: 333.96
```

Adapter design pattern implementation—console output

This section provided the source code and the console output for our real estate land area calculation program implementation of the adapter design pattern.

Crossing the bridge design pattern

The bridge design pattern simply separates abstraction from implementation. This design pattern involves creating a bridge between abstraction and implementation. Before exploring this design pattern further, it is important to thoroughly understand how abstraction works in Java.

Learning about abstraction

Abstraction is one of the core principles of **Object-Oriented Programming (OOP)** and is used to hide object implementation details. It is important to understand abstraction to support correct implementation.

An example of abstraction is when we have an abstract User class and multiple subclasses that inherit from it. For example, we might have a **Learning Management System (LMS)** User class and three subclasses—Student, Teacher, and Administrator. We can implement a method overriding the inherited methods that would otherwise expose the implementation details. More specifically, the superclass defines the methods and the subclasses implement them.

As you can see in the following UML diagram, the Student, Teacher, and Administrator classes all inherit from the User class and override the computeCredits() method:

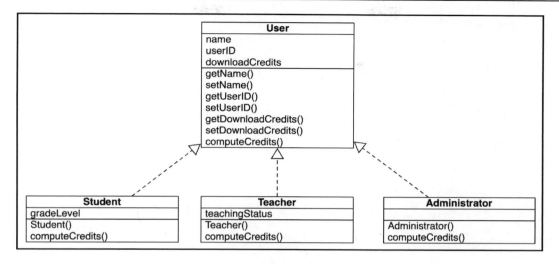

UML class diagram—abstraction example

The preceding abstraction example illustrates how the Student, Teacher, and Administrators subclasses have different class variables and all implement the same computeCredits() method from the superclass.

Implementing the abstraction example

The User class, shown here, is abstract and has three class variables. A default constructor has been added. In addition, the computeCredits() method has been made abstract and therefore cannot have a method body:

```
public abstract class User {

    // class variables
    private String name;
    private String userID;
    private int downloadCredits;

    // constructor
    public User(String name, String userID, int downloadCredits) {
        this.name = name;
        this.userID = userID;
        this.downloadCredits = downloadCredits;
    }

    // abstract method
    public abstract int computeCredits();
```

The second half of the `User` class is provided in the following code block. It contains the accessor and `mutator` methods for each of the three class variables:

```
// accessor methods
public String getName() {
    return name;
}

public String getUserID() {
    return userID;
}

public int getDownloadCredits() {
    return downloadCredits;
}

// mutator methods
public void setName(String name) {
    this.name = name;
}

public void setUserID(String userID) {
    this.userID = userID;
}

public void setDownloadCredits(int downloadCredits) {
    this.downloadCredits = downloadCredits;
}
}
```

The `Student` class extends the `User` class. It contains a private variable named `gradeLevel` and a constructor method. The constructor uses both the `super` constructor's and its own. The class has its own implementation of the `User` class `computeCredits()` method. The calculation is unique to the `Student` class:

```
public class Student extends User {

    private int gradeLevel;

    public Student(String name, String userID, int downloadCredits, int
gradeLevel) {
        super(name, userID, downloadCredits);
        this.gradeLevel = gradeLevel;
    }

    @Override
    public int computeCredits() {
```

```
        return getDownloadCredits() * gradeLevel;
    }
}
```

The `Teacher` class extends the `User` class. It contains a private variable named
`teachingStatus` and a constructor method. The constructor uses both the `super`
constructor's and its own. The class has its own implementation of the `User` class
`computeCredits()` method. The calculation is unique to the `Teacher` class:

```java
public class Teacher extends User {

    private int teachingStatus;

    public Teacher(String name, String userID, int downloadCredits, int
teachingStatus) {
        super(name, userID, downloadCredits);
        this.teachingStatus = teachingStatus;
    }

    @Override
    public int computeCredits() {
        return getDownloadCredits() * teachingStatus;
    }
}
```

The `Administrator` class extends the `User` class. It implements the `User` class constructor
method without modification. The class has its own implementation of the `User` class
`computeCredits()` method. Since administrative users are not permitted download
credits, 0 is returned:

```java
public class Administrator extends User {

    public Administrator(String name, String userID, int downloadCredits) {
        super(name, userID, downloadCredits);
    }

    @Override
    public int computeCredits() {
        return 0;
    }
}
```

The four preceding classes demonstrate how to implement abstraction in Java. Armed with
this knowledge, we can explore the bridge design pattern.

Use case

To demonstrate the bridge design pattern and how abstraction and implementation can be efficiently decoupled, we will use `Medication Administering System`. This system will support the administering of specific mediations to both adult and children patients. The dosage will be variable. Using the bridge design pattern, we will create a bridge between the `Medicine` interface and the `Patient` superclass.

UML class diagram

The UML class diagram provided here shows the seven classes involved in `Medication Administering System`. The `Antibiotic` and `PainRelief` classes implement the `Medicine` interface. The `Adult` and `Child` classes extend the `Patient` class. Our system's bridge is between the `Medicine` interface and `Patient` class:

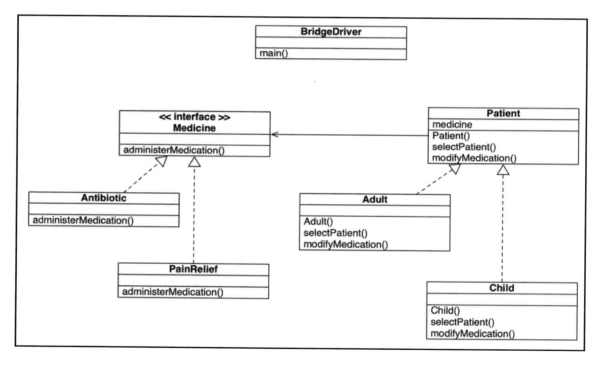

UML class diagram—bridge design pattern implementation

As illustrated in the preceding image, the `BridgeDriver` class is used to drive the application and contains the `main()` method.

Programming the design pattern

Medication Administering System starts with a Medicine interface. Let's see how that works:

1. As shown here, the interface contains an administerMedication() method:

```
public interface Medicine {

    void administerMedication(int amount);
}
```

2. The Antibiotic class is one of the two classes that implement the Medicine interface. The class overrides the administerMedication() method:

```
public class Antibiotic implements Medicine {
    @Override
    public void administerMedication(int amount) {
        System.out.print(amount + " antibiotic pills
administered.");
    }
}
```

3. The PainRelief class is the second of the two classes that implement the Medicine interface. The class overrides the administerMedication() method with tailored output text:

```
public class PainRelief implements Medicine {

    @Override
    public void administerMedication(int amount) {
        System.out.print(amount + " pain relief pills
administered.");
    }
}
```

4. The Patient class is the superclass to the Adult and Child classes. It includes two abstract methods: selectPatient() and modifyMedication(). These abstract methods will have to be implemented by the Adult and Child classes:

```
abstract class Patient {

    protected Medicine medicine;
    protected Patient(Medicine med) {
        this.medicine = med;
    }
```

```
        abstract void selectPatient(int dose);
        abstract void modifyMedication(int dose, int increment);
}
```

5. The `Adult` class extends the `Patient` superclass and overrides the abstract methods of `selectPatient()` and `modifyMedication()`. The `selectPatient()` method is used for issuing new doctor dosage orders. The `modifyMedication()` method is used to modify the dosage for an already prescribed medication:

```java
public class Adult extends Patient {

    protected Adult(Medicine med) {
        super(med);
    }

    @Override
    void selectPatient(int dose) {
        System.out.print("\tDoctor\'s Order: ");
        medicine.administerMedication(dose);

    }

    @Override
    void modifyMedication(int dose, int increment) {

        String message = "";

        if (increment < 0) {
            dose = dose - Math.abs(increment);
            message = "minus ";
        } else {
            dose = dose + increment;
            message = "plus ";
        }

        System.out.println("\n\tDoctor-ordered dosage change: " +
                message + Math.abs(increment) + " pills.");
        selectPatient(dose);
    }
}
```

6. The `Child` class extends the `Patient` superclass and overrides the abstract methods of `selectPatient()` and `modifyMedication()`. As with the `Adult` class, the `selectPatient()` method is used for issuing new doctor dosage orders. The `modifyMedication()` method is used to modify the dosage for an already prescribed medication:

```java
public class Child extends Patient {

    public Child(Medicine med) {
        super(med);
    }

    @Override
    void selectPatient(int dose) {
        System.out.print("\tDoctor\'s Order: ");
        medicine.administerMedication(dose);
    }

    @Override
    void modifyMedication(int dose, int increment) {

        String message = "";

        if (increment < 0) {
            dose = dose - Math.abs(increment);
            message = "minus ";
        } else {
            dose = dose + increment;
            message = "plus ";
        }

        System.out.println("\n\tDoctor-ordered dosage change: " +
                message + Math.abs(increment) + " pills.");
        selectPatient(dose);
    }
}
```

7. The final class in our system is the `BridgeDriver` class that contains the `main()` method. There are two code blocks in the `main()` method: one for administering antibiotic pills to an adult patient, and the other to administer pain relief pills to a child patient:

```java
public class BridgeDriver {

    public static void main(String[] args) {

        System.out.println("\n\nMedication Administering
```

```
System\n");

            // administer antibiotic pills to adult
            System.out.println("Adult Patient:");
            Medicine antibiotic = new Antibiotic();
            Patient adultPatient = new Adult(antibiotic);
            adultPatient.selectPatient(2);
            adultPatient.modifyMedication(2, 2);

            // administer pain relief pills to child
            System.out.println("\n\nChild Patient:");
            Medicine painRelief = new PainRelief();
            Patient childPatient = new Child(painRelief);
            childPatient.selectPatient(4);
            childPatient.modifyMedication(4, -2);

            System.out.println("\n\n");
        }
    }
```

The application's console output is displayed here:

```
Medication Administering System

Adult Patient:
    Doctor's Order: 2 antibiotic pills administered.
    Doctor-ordered dosage change: plus 2 pills.
    Doctor's Order: 4 antibiotic pills administered.

Child Patient:
    Doctor's Order: 4 pain relief pills administered.
    Doctor-ordered dosage change: minus 2 pills.
    Doctor's Order: 2 pain relief pills administered.
```

Bridge design pattern implementation—console output

This section provided the source code and the console output for our Medication Administering System implementation of the bridge design pattern.

Combining objects with the composite design pattern

The composite design pattern allows us to create an object tree structure. We can then treat both objects and the tree structures in the same manner, as individual objects. Without this design pattern, we can run into problems when we create structures from multiple objects. The problems stem from the need to treat primitive objects and the composite differently. The composite design pattern was created to overcome the aforementioned problem.

In order to implement the composite design pattern, we first create an abstract class to represent the primitive and tree structures.

Use case

To implement the composite design pattern, we will create a kitchen staff management system that includes a KitchenStaff interface and a Chef class. We will use the following chef hierarchy in our implementation—Executive Chef, Head Chef, Sous Chef, Line Chef, and Commis Chef. Using the composite design pattern, we will be able to treat the chef tree structure as if it were a single object.

UML class diagram

The following UML class diagram illustrates the relationships between the three classes in our implementation of the composite design pattern. The KitchenStaff interface is implemented by the Chef class.

The staffList class also has a direct relationship with the interface:

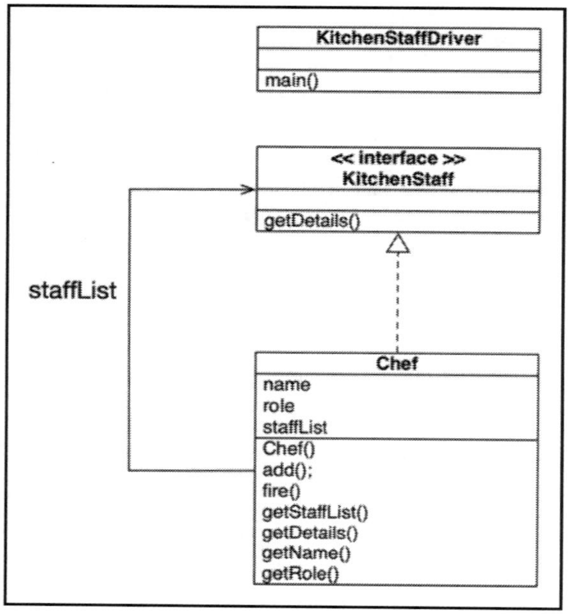

UML class diagram—composite design pattern implementation

As illustrated here, the KitchenStaffDriver class is used to drive the application and contains the main() method.

Programming the design pattern

Our program begins with a KitchenStaff interface that contains an empty getDetails() method:

```
public interface KitchenStaff {

    public String getDetails();
}
```

The Chef class, shown here, implements the KitchenStaff class. It contains three class variables and a constructor:

```
import java.util.ArrayList;
import java.util.List;
```

```
public class Chef implements KitchenStaff {

    private String name;
    private String role;
    private List<KitchenStaff> staffList;

    Chef(String name, String role) {
        this.name = name;
        this.role = role;
        staffList = new ArrayList<KitchenStaff>();
    }
```

The next section of the Chef class contains three methods—add(), fire(), and getStaffList():

```
public void add(Chef chef) {
    staffList.add(chef);
}

public void fire(Chef chef) {
    staffList.remove(chef);
}

public List<KitchenStaff> getStaffList() {
    return staffList;
}
```

The last section of the Chef class contains three accessor methods—getDetails(), which is overridden from the KitchenStaff interface, getName(), and getRole():

```
    @Override
    public String getDetails() {
        return (name + " is assigned the role of " + role);
    }

    public String getName() {
        return name;
    }

    public String getRole() {
        return role;
    }
}
```

Our program's `Driver` class is the `KitchenStaffDriver` class. The first part of this class, shown here, instantiates several `Chef` objects. The purpose of these objects is for illustration purposes:

```
import java.util.List;

public class KitchenStaffDriver {

    public static void main(String[] args) {

        // create sample data
        Chef execChef = new Chef("Gemma Patron", "Executive Chef");
        Chef headChef = new Chef("Tiksha Century", "Head Chef");
        Chef sousChef1 = new Chef ("Tilly Hope", "Sous Chef");
        Chef sousChef2 = new Chef ("Pat Stringe", "Sous Chef");
        Chef lineChef1 = new Chef ("Seth Arpage", "Line Chef");
        Chef lineChef2 = new Chef ("Diego Salazar", "Line Chef");
        Chef lineChef3 = new Chef ("Cersei Butrix", "Line Chef");
        Chef lineChef4 = new Chef ("Marissa Parth", "Line Chef");
        Chef commisChef1 = new Chef ("Johnny Ferd", "Commis Chef");
        Chef commisChef2 = new Chef ("Kay Fleping", "Commis Chef");
```

The second part of the `KitchenStaffDriver` class subordinates `Head Chef` to `Executive Chef`, `Sous Chef` to `Head Chef`, `Line Chef` to `Sous Chefs`, and `Commis Chef` to `Line Chef`:

```
        // establish Executive Chef at top of tree structure
        // make Head Chef subordinate to Executive Chef
        execChef.add(headChef);

        // subordinate Sous Chefs to Head Chef
        headChef.add(sousChef1);
        headChef.add(sousChef2);

        // subordinate Line Chefs to Sous Chefs
        sousChef1.add(lineChef1);
        sousChef1.add(lineChef2);
        sousChef1.add(lineChef3);
        sousChef1.add(lineChef4);

        // subordinate Commmis Chefs under Line Chef 1
        lineChef1.add(commisChef1);
        lineChef1.add(commisChef2);
```

In the next section of code, we use null to indicate no subordinates. This establishes the end of the tree structure:

```
// no subordinates to other Line Chefs
lineChef2.add(null);
lineChef3.add(null);
lineChef4.add(null);

// no subordinates to Commis Chefs
commisChef1.add(null);
commisChef2.add(null);
```

The `Driver` class also provides console output based on the sample data. The `getDetails()` method is used to retrieve details from `Executive Chef`. Next, details are provided using the `getStaffList()` and `getDetails()` methods for `Sous Chef`, `Line Chef`, and `Commis Chef`. Output is provided in tabbed form to indicate the tree structure:

```
// provide console output
System.out.println("\n\nKitchen Staff Management System\n");
System.out.println(execChef.getDetails());

List<KitchenStaff> head = execChef.getStaffList();
for (int i=0; i < head.size(); i++) {
 System.out.println("\t" + head.get(i).getDetails());
}

List<KitchenStaff> sous = headChef.getStaffList();
for (int i=0; i < sous.size(); i++) {
    System.out.println("\t\t" + sous.get(i).getDetails());
}

List<KitchenStaff> line = sousChef1.getStaffList();
for (int i=0; i < line.size(); i++) {
    System.out.println("\t\t\t" + line.get(i).getDetails());
}

List<KitchenStaff> commis = lineChef1.getStaffList();
for (int i=0; i < commis.size(); i++) {
    System.out.println("\t\t\t\t" + commis.get(i).getDetails());
}
```

The final section of the `KitcheStaffDriver` class processes a firing event for a line chef. The `fire()` method is used to remove the chef from the staff list. Finally, an updated list of line chefs is provided for visual verification of the code:

```
// firing a line chef
System.out.println("\n\nKITCHEN STAFF UPDATE");
```

```
        System.out.println("\t" + lineChef1.getName() +
                ", " + lineChef1.getRole() + ", has been terminated.");
        sousChef1.fire(lineChef1);
        System.out.println("\nHere is the updated list of Line Chefs:");
        List<KitchenStaff> newLine = sousChef1.getStaffList();
        for (int i=0; i < newLine.size(); i++) {
            System.out.println("\t" + newLine.get(i).getDetails());
        }
    }
}
```

The application's console output is displayed here:

```
Kitchen Staff Management System

Gemma Patron is assigned the role of Executive Chef
     Tiksha Century is assigned the role of Head Chef
        Tilly Hope is assigned the role of Sous Chef
        Pat Stringe is assigned the role of Sous Chef
            Seth Arpage is assigned the role of Line Chef
            Diego Salazar is assigned the role of Line Chef
            Cersei Butrix is assigned the role of Line Chef
            Marissa Parth is assigned the role of Line Chef
                Johnny Ferd is assigned the role of Commis Chef
                Kay Fleping is assigned the role of Commis Chef


KITCHEN STAFF UPDATE
     Seth Arpage, Line Chef, has been terminated.

Here is the updated list of Line Chefs:
     Diego Salazar is assigned the role of Line Chef
     Cersei Butrix is assigned the role of Line Chef
     Marissa Parth is assigned the role of Line Chef
```

Composite design pattern implementation—console output

This section provided the source code and the console output for our kitchen staff management system implementation of the composite design pattern.

Understanding the decorator design pattern

The decorator design pattern allows us to assign responsibilities to an object without impacting the class. Without the decorator design pattern, we can assign responsibilities to objects through inheritance. A more streamlined approach is to use the decorator design pattern to assign additional responsibilities to specific objects. The key goal is to add the additional responsibility to objects dynamically and without impacting other objects.

This design pattern is commonly used with graphical software that includes layering objects over one another. For example, building a **Graphical User Interface (GUI)** or creating a **Heads Up Display (HUD)** for a game.

The decorator design pattern is occasionally referred to as a wrapper design pattern because the decorator essential wraps around the object and its dynamically created responsibilities.

Use case

We will create a `Printer Buffer Flusher Demo` application to demonstrate how to implement the decorator design pattern. We have a `flushBuffer()` method that will not be modified. Functionality will be added using decorators. As you will see, the new functionality works without impacting the original `flushBuffer()` functions.

UML class diagram

The following UML class diagram shows that our `Printer Buffer Flusher Demo` application includes a `Printer` class and a `ConcretePrinter` class that extends the `Printer` class. There are also two concrete decorator classes (`ConcreteDecorator1` and `ConcreteDecorator2`) that extend the `AbstractDecorator` class:

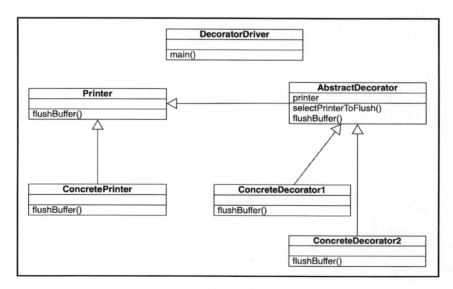

UML class diagram—decorator design pattern implementation

As illustrated here, the `DecoratorDriver` class is used to drive the application and contains the `main()` method.

Programming the design pattern

Our `Printer Buffer Flusher Demo` application starts with an abstract `Printer` class that has an empty `flushBuffer()` method. Since it is an abstract method, it cannot have a method body. The following code shows this:

```
abstract class Printer {
    public abstract void flushBuffer();
}
```

Next, we have a `ConcretePrinter` class that extends the `Printer` class. The `flushBuffer()` method is overridden and includes a contextual message that is printed to the console:

```
public class ConcretePrinter extends Printer {

    @Override
    public void flushBuffer() {
        System.out.println("Message from Concrete Printer: Printer Buffer
Flushed");
    }
}
```

The `AbstractDecorator` class is abstract and extends the `Printer` class. The class instantiates a `Printer` object, has a `selectPrinterToFlush()` method and the `flushBuffer()` method:

```
abstract class AbstractDecorator extends Printer {

    protected Printer printer;

    public void selectPrinterToFlush(Printer ptr) {
        printer = ptr;
    }

    public void flushBuffer() {
        if (printer != null) {
            printer.flushBuffer();
        }
    }
}
```

The first concrete decorator class, `ConcreteDecorator1`, extends the abstract `AbstractDecorator` class. The `flushBuffer()` method is implemented and includes contextual text for console output:

```
public class ConcreteDecorator1 extends AbstractDecorator {

    public void flushBuffer() {
        super.flushBuffer();
        System.out.println("Message from Concrete Decorator 1: " +
                "Printer Buffer Flushed");
    }
}
```

The second concrete decorator class, `ConcreteDecorator2`, extends the abstract `AbstractDecorator` class. The `flushBuffer()` method is implemented and includes contextual text for console output. This output varies from the first concrete decorator class for illustration purposes:

```
public class ConcreteDecorator2 extends AbstractDecorator {

    public void flushBuffer() {

        System.out.println("\n[ START ] Concrete Decorator 2 Wrapper [
START ]");
        super.flushBuffer();
        System.out.println("Message from Concrete Decorator 2: " +
                    "Printer Buffer Flushed");
        System.out.println("[ END ] Concrete Decorator 2 Wrapper [ END ]");
    }
}
```

The last class in our `Printer Buffer Flusher Demo` implementation of the decorator design pattern is the `DecoratorDriver` class. This is the `Driver` class for the application and includes the `main()` method. After printing a decorative header, a `ConcretePrinter` instance is created and then two concrete decorators are created:

```
public class DecoratorDriver {

    public static void main(String[] args) {

System.out.println("\n\n=======================================================
===");
        System.out.println("\t\t\tPrinter Buffer Flusher Demo");
System.out.println("======================================================="
);
        ConcretePrinter concreteFlush = new ConcretePrinter();
```

```
            // create concrete decorator
            ConcreteDecorator1 cd1 = new ConcreteDecorator1();
            // decorate cd1
            cd1.selectPrinterToFlush(concreteFlush);
            cd1.flushBuffer();

            // create concrete decorator
            ConcreteDecorator2 cd2 = new ConcreteDecorator2();
            // decorate cd2
            cd2.selectPrinterToFlush(cd1);
            cd2.flushBuffer();
        }
    }
```

The application's console output is displayed here:

```
===============================================
                Printer Buffer Flusher Demo
===============================================
Message from Concrete Printer: Printer Buffer Flushed
Message from Concrete Decorator 1: Printer Buffer Flushed

[ START ] Concrete Decorator 2 Wrapper [ START ]
Message from Concrete Printer: Printer Buffer Flushed
Message from Concrete Decorator 1: Printer Buffer Flushed
Message from Concrete Decorator 2: Printer Buffer Flushed
[ END ] Concrete Decorator 2 Wrapper [ END ]
```

Decorator design pattern implementation—console output

This section provided the source code and the console output for our `Printer Buffer Flusher Demo` implementation of the decorator design pattern.

Implementing the facade design pattern

The facade design pattern creates an interface that is served as an interface to other interfaces within a system or subsystem. The benefits of using this design pattern are that subsystems are less complex, the reliance components is reduced, and communication between system components is minimized.

Consider the following illustrations. The image on the left shows the organization of a system and subsystems without a facade interface. The right-hand image shows the facade interface layered between the main classes and the subsystem:

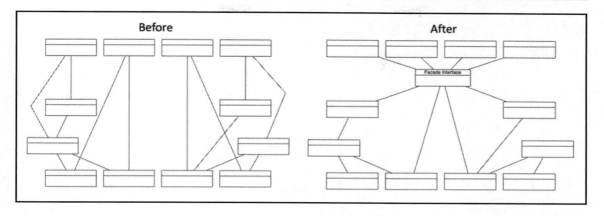

System representation with and without a facade interface

As indicated in the diagram, the facade interface serves as an interface between the system and subsystem. It can also be correction inferred that the facade interface will prevent the unnecessary exposure of details to the system.

Use case

To demonstrate the facade design pattern, we will create a meal assembly service application. The app will assemble meals with protein, vegetable, and starch components. Our classes will be organized into multiple Java projects to help protect information details. Here is an overview of the package organization:

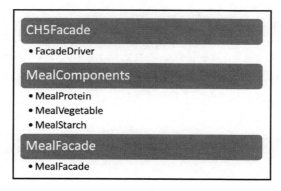

Package structure of meal assembly service app

As illustrated in the previous image, there are three Java packages and five classes in the meal assembly service application.

UML class diagram

The UML class diagram shows that the MealFacade class serves as a facade for the MealProtein, MealVegetable, and MealStarch classes:

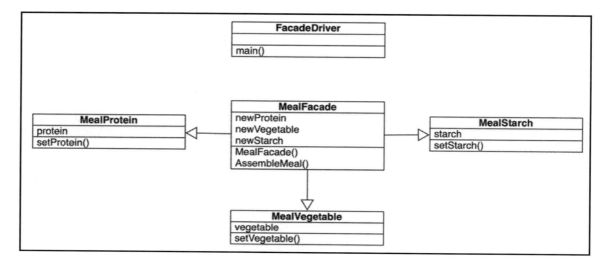

UML class diagram—facade design pattern implementation

As illustrated, the FacadeDriver class is used to drive the application and contains the main() method.

Programming the design pattern

The MealProtein class is one of the three component classes of a meal. Let's see how that goes:

1. It contains a protein class variable and the mutator method to assign the provided input to the class variable:

```
package CH5Facade.MealComponents;

public class MealProtein {

    private String protein;

    public void setProtein(String protein) {
        this.protein = protein;
```

```
        System.out.println("\t\tProtein (" + this.protein + ")
added to meal.");
    }
}
```

2. The `MealVegetable` class is similar to the `MealProtein` class as it is one of the three component classes of a meal. It contains a `vegetable` class variable and the `mutator` method to assign the provided input to the class variable:

```
package CH5Facade.MealComponents;

public class MealVegetable {

    private String vegetable;

    public void setVegetable(String vegetable) {
        this.vegetable = vegetable;
        System.out.println("\t\tVegetable (" + this.vegetable + ")
added to meal.");
    }
}
```

3. The `MealStarch` class is the third component class of a meal. It contains a `starch` class variable and the `mutator` method to assign the provided input to the class variable:

```
package CH5Facade.MealComponents;

public class MealStarch {

    private String starch;

    public void setStarch(String starch) {
        this.starch = starch;
        System.out.println("\t\tStarch (" + this.starch + ") added
to meal.");
    }
}
```

4. The `MealFacade` class is in its own package and imports the `MealProtein`, `MealVegetable`, and `MealStarch` classes. The first part of the `MealFacade` class is provided here. This segment of code defines three class variables and contains the `constructor` method:

```
package CH5Facade.MealFacade;

import CH5Facade.MealComponents.MealProtein;
```

```
import CH5Facade.MealComponents.MealVegetable;
import CH5Facade.MealComponents.MealStarch;

public class MealFacade {

    MealProtein newProtein;
    MealVegetable newVegetable;
    MealStarch newStarch;

    public MealFacade() {
        newProtein = new MealProtein();
        newVegetable = new MealVegetable();
        newStarch = new MealStarch();
    }
```

5. The final part of the MealFacade class, provided in the following code block, contains the assembleMeal() method. This method provides console output for the beginning and ending of the meal assembly process. It makes calls to the setProtein(), setVegetable(), and setStarch() methods:

```
    public void assembleMeal(String protein, String vegetable,
String starch) {

        System.out.println("\n\tMeal assembly process initiated. .
. ");
        newProtein.setProtein(protein);
        newVegetable.setVegetable(vegetable);
        newStarch.setStarch(starch);
        System.out.println("\tMeal assembly process completed. . .
\n");
    }
}
```

6. Our application's driver class, FacadeDriver, contains the main() method. That method starts by printing a decorative header to the console. Next, a series of three meals are created by first instantiating a MealFacade object and then calling that object's assembleMeal() method:

```
package CH5Facade;

import CH5Facade.MealFacade.MealFacade;

public class FacadeDriver {

    public static void main(String[] args) {

System.out.println("\n\n==============================================
```

```
===========");
        System.out.println("\t\t\tMeal Assembly Service Demo");
System.out.println("=================================================
=======");

        // assemble three meals
        MealFacade meal1 = new MealFacade();
        meal1.assembleMeal("Steak", "Asparagus", "Wild Rice");

        MealFacade meal2 = new MealFacade();
        meal2.assembleMeal("Chicken", "Green Beans", "Potato
Wedges");

        MealFacade meal3 = new MealFacade();
        meal3.assembleMeal("Meatloaf", "Brussel Sprouts", "Mashed
Potatoes");
    }
}
```

The application's console output is displayed here:

```
=====================================================
                Meal Assembly Service Demo
=====================================================

    Meal assembly process initiated. . .
        Protein (Steak) added to meal.
        Vegetable (Asparagus) added to meal.
        Starch (Wild Rice) added to meal.
    Meal assembly process completed. . .


    Meal assembly process initiated. . .
        Protein (Chicken) added to meal.
        Vegetable (Green Beans) added to meal.
        Starch (Potato Wedges) added to meal.
    Meal assembly process completed. . .


    Meal assembly process initiated. . .
        Protein (Meatloaf) added to meal.
        Vegetable (Brussel Sprouts) added to meal.
        Starch (Mashed Potatoes) added to meal.
    Meal assembly process completed. . .
```

Facade design pattern implementation—console output

This section provided the source code and the console output for our meal assembly service implementation of the facade design pattern.

Soaring with the flyweight design pattern

The flyweight design patterns offer great efficiency and improved processing when dealing with a large number of similar objects. The pattern uses sharing of identical object components. Consider programming a video game that has thousands of tile objects that are used to build architectural structures. The tile objects will likely only have a color attribute. So repeating the `Tiles tile = new Tiles("beige")` line of code 1,000 times is not efficient, especially since all of the objects will contain the same attribute value. The flyweight design pattern addresses this issue by permitting the reference of numerous same-type objects that have the same state.

Use case

We will create a `Mattress Manufacturing Factory Demo` application to implement the flyweight design pattern. We will create an interface, a `Mattress` class, a `MattressFactory` class, and a `Driver` class. Our application will facilitate the ability to create mattresses of size crib, twin, and full. If a mattress already exists, then new objects will not be created; instead, `MattressFactory` will provide the size and then the mattress firmness can be determined.

UML class diagram

The following UML class diagram visually details the class relationship for the mattress manufacturing factory application implementation of the flyweight design pattern:

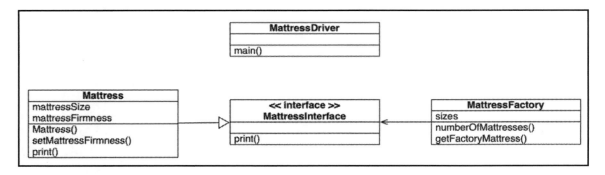

UML class diagram—flyweight design pattern implementation

As illustrated, the `MattressDriver` class is used to drive the application and contains the `main()` method.

Programming the design pattern

We will consider the following case to understand the programming design pattern:

1. Our `Mattress Manufacturing Factory Demo` project starts with a `MattressInterface` interface. That interface contains a `print()` method with no body:

```
public interface MattressInterface {

    void print();
}
```

2. The `Mattress` class implements `MattressInterface`. It contains two class variables (`mattressSize` and `mattressFirmness`). The class also contains the `setMattressFirmness()` mutator method and overrides the interface's `print()` method:

```
public class Mattress implements MattressInterface {
    // class variables
    String matrressSize;
    public String mattressFirmness;

    // constructor
    public Mattress(String matrressSize) {
        this.matrressSize = matrressSize;
    }

    // mutator
    public void setMattressFirmness(String mattressFirmness) {
        this.mattressFirmness = mattressFirmness;
    }

    @Override
    public void print() {
        System.out.println("\t\tThis is a " + mattressFirmness +
                " " + matrressSize + " mattress.");
    }
}
```

3. The `MattressFactory` class, presented here in two sections, relies on Java's `HashMap` and `Map` packages:

```
import java.util.HashMap;
import java.util.Map;
```

```
public class MattressFactory {

    Map<String, MattressInterface> sizes = new HashMap<String,
MattressInterface>();

    public int numberOfMattresses() {
        return sizes.size();
    }
```

4. The second section of the `MattressFactory` class contains the `getFactoryMattress()` method. This method includes exception handling and a `switch` construct based on the mattress size. Here is the first section of that method:

```
public MattressInterface getFactoryMattress(String mSize) throws
Exception {
        MattressInterface mattressSize = null;
        if (sizes.containsKey(mSize)) {
            mattressSize = sizes.get(mSize);
        } else {
            switch (mSize) {
                // switch statements go here
            }
        }
        return mattressSize;
    }
}
```

5. The `switch()` code block for the `getFactoryMattress()` method is provided here:

```
switch (mSize) {
    case "Crib":
        System.out.println("\tA Crib Mattress did not exist, but
does now");
        mattressSize = new Mattress("Crib");
        sizes.put("Crib", mattressSize);
        break;

    case "Twin":
        System.out.println("\tA Twin Mattress did not exist, but
does now");
        mattressSize = new Mattress("Twin");
        sizes.put("Twin", mattressSize);
        break;

    case "Full":
```

```
            System.out.println("\tA Full Mattress did not exist, but
does now");
            mattressSize = new Mattress("Full");
            sizes.put("Full", mattressSize);
            break;

        default:
            throw new Exception("\tMattress Creation Request Error: " +
                invalid mattress size defined.");
```

6. The final class is the `MattressDriver` class that contains the `main()` method. After printing a decorative header to the console, there are three `for` loops, each for a different size of mattress. Each of these loops attempts to create five mattress objects. As designed, our implementation only supports creating one of each size:

```
public class MattressDriver {

    public static void main(String[] args) throws Exception {

        MattressFactory theFactory = new MattressFactory();

System.out.println("\n\n==========================================
===========");
        System.out.println("\t\t\tMattress Manufacturing Factory
Demo");
System.out.println("==============================================
=======");

        Mattress newMattress;

        for (int i = 0; i < 5; i++) {
            newMattress =
(Mattress)theFactory.getFactoryMattress("Crib");
            newMattress.setMattressFirmness("Firm");
            newMattress.print();
        }

        for (int i = 0; i < 5; i++) {
            newMattress =
(Mattress)theFactory.getFactoryMattress("Twin");
            newMattress.setMattressFirmness("Soft");
            newMattress.print();
        }

        for (int i = 0; i < 5; i++) {
            newMattress =
```

```
                      (Mattress)theFactory.getFactoryMattress("Full");
                            newMattress.setMattressFirmness("Extra Firm");
                            newMattress.print();
                  }
            }
      }
```

The application's console output is displayed here:

```
==============================================
            Mattress Manufacturing Factory Demo
==============================================
A Crib Mattress did not exist, but does now
      This is a Firm Crib mattress.
      This is a Firm Crib mattress.
      This is a Firm Crib mattress.
      This is a Firm Crib mattress.
      This is a Firm Crib mattress.
A Twin Mattress did not exist, but does now
      This is a Soft Twin mattress.
      This is a Soft Twin mattress.
      This is a Soft Twin mattress.
      This is a Soft Twin mattress.
      This is a Soft Twin mattress.
A Full Mattress did not exist, but does now
      This is a Extra Firm Full mattress.
      This is a Extra Firm Full mattress.
      This is a Extra Firm Full mattress.
      This is a Extra Firm Full mattress.
      This is a Extra Firm Full mattress.
```

Flyweight design pattern implementation—console output

This section provided the source code and the console output for our mattress manufacturing factory implementation of the flyweight design pattern.

Implementing the proxy design pattern

Proxy, in the Java context, is defined as having the authority to represent another object. The proxy design pattern is true to its name in that it establishes a placeholder so that an object other than itself can control access. Pointer object references lack sophistication. Proxy references can accomplish the following with regards to an object reference:

- Utilize smart pointers that can count the number of references to a given object. This supports garbage collection.
- Object locking so it cannot be modified by other objects.
- Memory loading enhancements.

The primary justification for using the proxy design pattern is to save the tremendous memory and processing time that is required to create complex objects.

Use case

We will create a proxy weather forecast application to demonstrate the proxy design pattern implementation. We will create an abstract class and extend it with a concrete class. Next, we will create a Proxy class for the Driver class to reference. We will organize our classes into two packages, one for the master classes and the other for proxy classes.

UML class diagram

Our weather forecast application consists of four classes—Weather, ConcreteWeather, Proxy, and ProxyDriver:

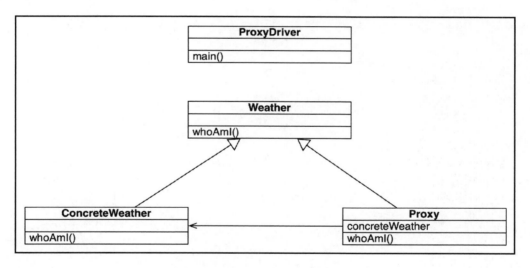

UML class diagram—proxy design pattern implementation

As illustrated, the ProxyDriver class is used to drive the application and contains the main() method.

Programming the design pattern

The first class in our solution is the abstract `Weather` class. It contains the empty `whoAmI()` method:

```
package Proxy.MasterClasses;

public abstract class Weather {

    public abstract void whoAmI();
}
```

The `ConcreteWeather` class extends the `Weather` class. It is a concrete class because it implements all of the hierarchical methods. Specifically, the `ConcreteWeather` class overrides the `whoAmI()` method. This method simply outputs to the console, informing the user where the method call came from and provides a weather forecast:

```
package Proxy.MasterClasses;

public class ConcreteWeather extends Weather {

    @Override
    public void whoAmI() {
        System.out.println("\tMethod Call from " +
                this.getClass().getSimpleName() + " class");
        System.out.println("\t\tWeather forcast is sunny\n");
    }
}
```

The `Proxy` class also extends the abstract `Weather` class. The class overrides the `whoAmI()` method. This method simply outputs to the console, informing the user where the method call came from and provides a weather forecast:

```
package Proxy.ProxyClasses;

import Proxy.MasterClasses.ConcreteWeather;
import Proxy.MasterClasses.Weather;

public class Proxy extends Weather {

    ConcreteWeather concreteWeather;

    @Override
    public void whoAmI() {
        System.out.println("\tMethod Call from " +
                this.getClass().getSimpleName() + " class");
        System.out.println("\t\tWeather forcast is overcast and rain\n");
```

```
        if (concreteWeather == null) {
            concreteWeather = new ConcreteWeather();
        }
        concreteWeather.whoAmI();
    }
}
```

The final class in our solution is the `ProxyDriver` class, which contains the `main()` method. This method produces decorative console output, creates a new `Proxy` instance, and then calls the `whoAmI()` method on the new object:

```
package Proxy.ProxyClasses;

public class ProxyDriver {

    public static void main(String[] args)  {

System.out.println("\n\n=============================================
===");
        System.out.println("\t\t\tProxy Weather Forecast Demo");
System.out.println("====================================================="
);

        Proxy proxyCall = new Proxy();
        proxyCall.whoAmI();
    }
}
```

The application's console output is displayed here:

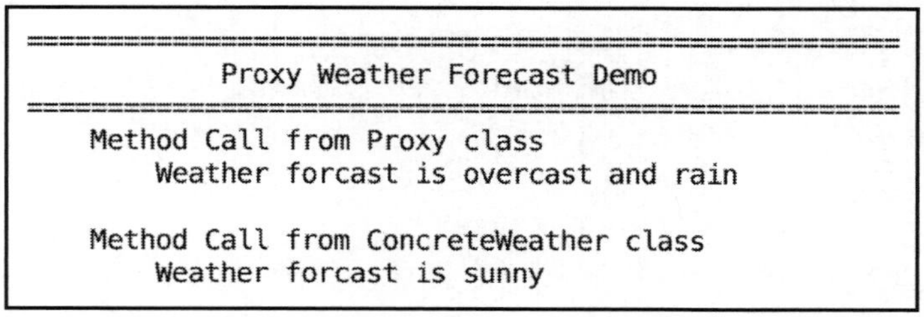

```
=========================================================
               Proxy Weather Forecast Demo
=========================================================
    Method Call from Proxy class
        Weather forcast is overcast and rain

    Method Call from ConcreteWeather class
        Weather forcast is sunny
```

Proxy design pattern implementation—console output

This section provided the source code and the console output for our proxy weather forecast implementation of the proxy design pattern.

Summary

In this chapter, we reviewed seven structural design patterns that focus on how objects and classes are combined to form a system. The two structural design pattern categories were identified as object design patterns and class design patterns. The structural object design patterns are used to describe how to create objects with new functionality. Structural class design patterns utilize inheritance to create interfaces and combine multiple classes to form a larger structure. Examples of both approaches are provided in this chapter using multiple design pattern implementations.

In the next chapter, we will shift our focus to architectural design patterns. The chapter starts with an overview of architectural design patterns and covers the application, layered, and microservice design patterns.

Questions

1. What is the focus of structural design patterns?
2. What are the seven structural design patterns?
3. Which structural design pattern has both a class and object scope?
4. Which structural design pattern category is used to describe how to create objects with new functionality?
5. Which design pattern is used to convert an interface of one class into another interface expected by the system?
6. Which design pattern allows us to create an object tree structure and treat both objects and the tree structures in the same manner?
7. Which design pattern is commonly used with graphical software that includes layering objects over one another?
8. Which design pattern creates an interface that serves as an interface to other interfaces within a system or subsystem?
9. Which design pattern uses sharing of identical object components in its implementation?
10. Which design pattern's purpose is to save memory and processing required to create complex objects?

Further reading

- *Java EE 8 Design Patterns and Best Practices* (`https://www.packtpub.com/application-development/java-ee-8-design-patterns-and-best-practices`)
- *Learn Design Patterns with Java* (`https://www.packtpub.com/application-development/learn-design-patterns-java-video`)
- *Design Patterns and Best Practices in Java* (`https://www.packtpub.com/application-development/design-patterns-and-best-practices-java`)

Section 3: New Design Patterns

3

In this section, the categories of architectural, functional, and reactive will be explored. For each of these categories, their design patterns will be explained, along with step-by-step instructions on how to solve the underlying design challenge. The architectural category contains 16 design patterns, the functional category contains 7 design patterns, and the reactive category contains 15 design patterns.

The following chapters will be covered:

Architectural Patterns - Part I

6

Architectural patterns are important to system designers as a system's architecture is one of the building blocks for creating a system. These patterns can teach us a lot about the principles behind the application of software design and, in some cases, hardware connectivity.

In this chapter, we will explore what constitutes an architectural design pattern and will look at several specific architectural design patterns. We will cover additional architectural patterns in the next chapter, *Architectural Patterns – Part II*.

Specifically, in this chapter, we will start with an introduction to architectural design patterns, and look at the patterns in the following list, along with their pattern diagrams and use cases to demonstrate their applicability and implementation:

- Introducing architectural patterns
- Blackboard pattern
- Broker pattern
- Client-server pattern
- Event-driven pattern
- Extract-transform-load pattern
- Layered pattern
- Master-slave pattern
- Microkernel pattern

There are no technical requirements associated with this chapter, so we will start directly with the first topic.

Introducing architectural patterns

Traditional design patterns, which have been categorized as behavioral, creational, and structural, remain valid in modern programming, including with Java. Architectural patterns differ from design patterns in scope—architectural patterns, as you might surmise from its name, has a broader scope. Generally speaking, architectural patterns take a holistic view of systems and group components for illustrative purposes. The visual depiction of architectural patterns does not use UML class diagrams like the aforementioned design patterns do. Instead, a nonprescriptive approach is taken for visually documenting architectural patterns.

Architectural patterns work at the system level, and it is common for *design* to be dropped from the architectural design pattern title. Regardless of which label is used, *architectural patterns* or *architectural design patterns*, provide the design of an entire system or group of system components.

We will cover eight architectural patterns in this chapter. They have been presented alphabetically, as there is no order of importance. Let's begin with the first one.

Understanding the blackboard pattern

The blackboard architectural pattern is used for large systems that do not have a definitive solution. This pattern is often used to design frameworks for speech recognition, computer games, and dynamic systems with artificial intelligence or machine learning.

We will now look at the following implementations of the blackboard architectural pattern:

- Coffee shop automation
- Warehouse security bot

Coffee shop automation example

Our first example of the blackboard architectural pattern features coffee shop automation. Let's say that we want to program an android (robot) to run a coffee shop. This android will be on duty for 24 hours each day and will have multiple tasks, as shown in the following list:

- Taking and filling customer orders
- Handling payments
- Bussing tables

- Washing dishes, cups, and so on
- Inventory, ordering, receiving, and stocking supplies
- Opening and closing the coffee shop
- Night-time deep cleaning

In order for the android to perform its functions, it will need access to acknowledge systems. It will also need to be able to learn from its interactions with the environment and the coffee shop customers. A high-level view of the system is shown here:

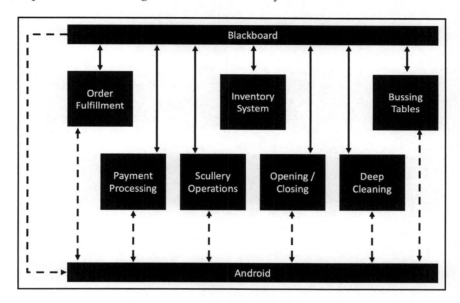

Blackboard pattern - coffee shop automation

As illustrated in this blackboard pattern diagram, the android has access to seven distinct knowledge sources. This access is depicted with double arrows to signify that the knowledge systems will learn from the android's interactions with customers and the environment. Examples of this could include learning a custom drink, remembering the orders of repeat customers, knowing how to clean the mugs, and so on.

In this implementation of the blackboard architectural pattern, the blackboard resides in memory and has read and write access to the knowledge systems.

The following UML class diagram indicates the significance of the knowledge sources in the blackboard pattern:

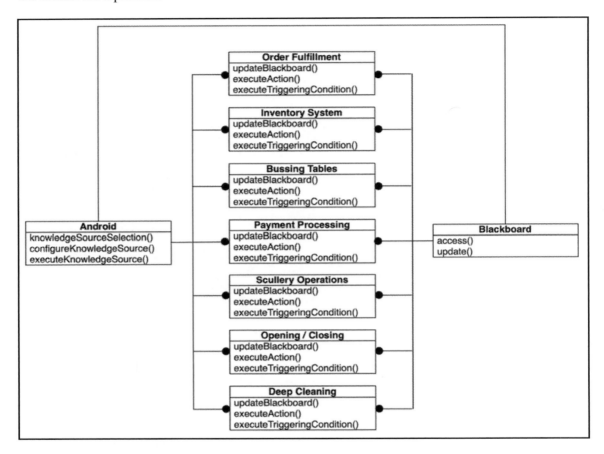

UML class diagram - coffee shop automation

The **Android** component illustrated in the UML class diagram is referred to as the control component in the blackboard architectural pattern.

Warehouse security bot example

In this example of the blackboard architectural pattern, we will consider an automated warehouse security bot. This bot will use a stun gun to shoot intruders. Our bot will have three basic responsibilities:

- Correctly identify intruders and authorized warehouse workers
- Navigate the warehouse
- Move to within the stun gun's effective range

Each of these responsibilities can be viewed as a component in our system. These components will be **Intruder Identification**, **Navigation**, and **Ballistics**. The following UML class diagram illustrates the relationship between the **Bot**, the control component, and the rest of the system:

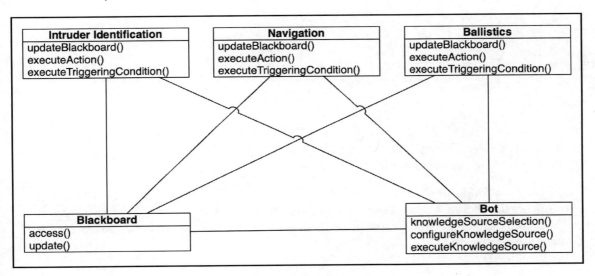

UML class diagram - warehouse security bot

The **Intruder Identification**, **Navigation**, and **Ballistics** components in the UML class diagram are the knowledge sources in the warehouse security bot implementation.

This section provided two implementation examples of the blackboard architectural pattern.

Understanding the broker pattern

The broker architectural pattern is used to architect distributed systems. These systems make use of a middleman component to coordinate and communicate between components. This decoupling of components removes dependencies and can result in greater system-wide efficiencies.

The middleman component's mission means that it is essential for it to be able to receive requests and broker the proper service or request. As illustrated by the following diagram, the middleman brokers requests from both the **Server** and the **Client**:

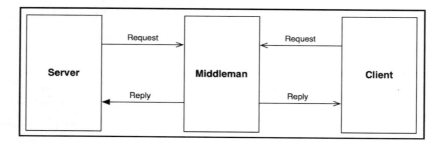

Broker pattern overview

The broker architectural pattern is similar to the facade design pattern covered in `Chapter 5`, *Structural Design Patterns*. The facade design pattern established an interface to serve as a medium between the system and its subsystems.

There is an option in the broker architectural pattern for the middleman to permit direct communication between the **Client** and the **Server**. As shown in the following diagram, the middleman still manages the communication, but the two components (**Client** and **Server**) communicate directly:

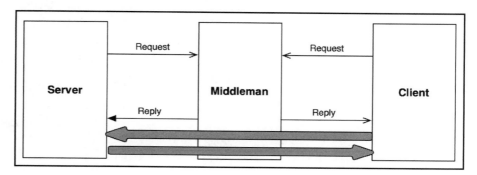

Broker pattern alternative

We will look at the following implementations of the broker architectural pattern:

- University enterprise information system
- Luxury cruise reservation system

University enterprise information system example

Let's consider an example of a university enterprise information system design using the broker architectural pattern. The university will operate two campuses, each with their own servers. All servers can send and receive requests. The **Bridge** is used to encapsulate processes between multiple brokers, typically local and remote. This setup is shown in the following diagram:

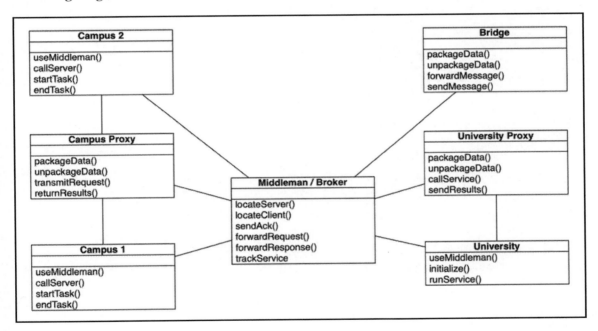

Broker pattern- university enterprise information system

As you can see in the preceding diagram, proxies are used to protect implementation details, memory addresses, and other information from other system components.

Luxury cruise reservation system example

Another implementation of the broker architectural pattern is a luxury cruise reservation system. In this example, the cruise lines each have their own server, and there is a **Cruise Line Proxy**. The **Middleman / Broker** component brokers reservations based on requests from clients and responses from the cruise lines. The following diagram provides an overview of the reservation system, highlighting the interconnectivity component:

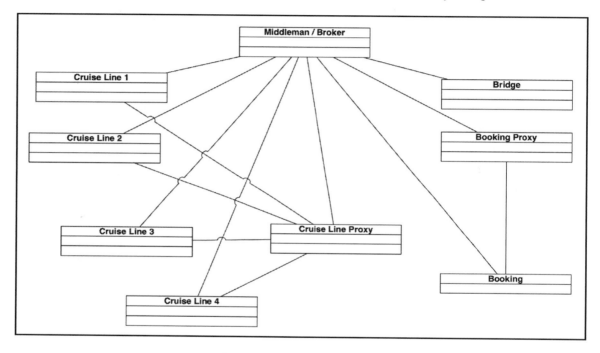

Broker pattern - luxury cruise reservation system

This section provided two implementation examples of the broker architectural pattern.

Understanding the client-server pattern

The client-server architectural pattern is one of the more commonly known architectural patterns, especially with network architectures. This architectural pattern consists of two component types—client components and server components. Simply stated, the server listens to requests from clients and provides the requested services.

The following diagram provides a high-level view of the client-server pattern. The connections between clients and the server can vary and include common connections such as TCP/IP:

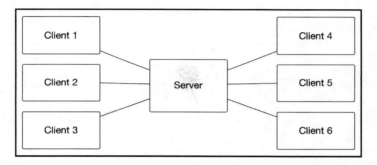

Client-server pattern

(handwritten margin notes:)
instant access
single instance
same info.
stored info on
server
(images)

We will look at the following implementations of the client-server architectural pattern:

- Coffee shop
- Three-tier network

(handwritten margin note:) Client, web browser

Coffee shop example

The following diagram depicts a simple coffee shop architecture to demonstrate the client-server architectural pattern. The **Client** has local connections to their **POS** (short for **point of sale**) system and inventory system. The **Client** communicates with the **Server**, which has its own external connections.

The architecture illustrated highlights the connectivity of the system's components, specifically the separation between the **Client** and **Server**, as well as how the **Client** accesses the **Database** via the **Server**:

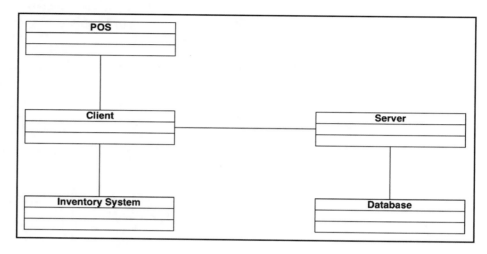

Client-server pattern - coffee shop example

In the preceding diagram, the **Client** and **Server** would likely communicate via TCP/IP.

Three-tier example

In networking, there are several client-server architectures. The one depicted next is a three-tier client-server architecture. The first tier is the **Client**, which has direct communication with two **Application Servers**. These **Application Servers** have direct communication with the **Database Server**. The example given in the following diagram shows a typical client-server structure, using a three-tiered approach:

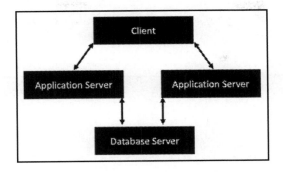

Client-server pattern example - three-tier example

This section provided two implementation examples of the client-server architectural pattern.

Understanding the event-driven pattern

The event-driven architectural pattern is for highly adaptable, distributed systems. It is used to implement applications that involve transmitting events in a decentralized system. With this pattern, events have publishers and consumers. Using this pattern allows for more efficient development of large distributed systems.

This pattern can be used for web systems, business processes, games, and almost any application you can think of that has events. Events can be button-clicks, inputs via a stream, automated analysis results, in-game conditions, such as collision detection, and so on.

The event-driven architectural pattern comes in two forms—broker and mediator. We will look at both of these pattern forms in the following sections.

Event-driven architectural pattern – broker

The broker form of the event-driven architectural pattern uses a sequence of mediated events instead of a central mediator. This form involves an initial event followed by a series of processing steps.

As illustrated in the following diagram, there is no mediator that controls the **Initiating Event**. The **Event Processors** are each responsible for processing events and then initiating new events when processing is completed:

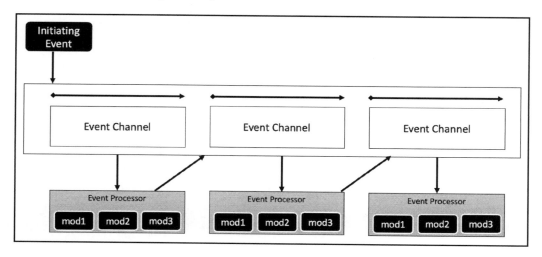

Event-driven pattern - broker form

An initiating event starts the process, and the chain of events continues until there are no published events that exist for that specific initiating event.

Event-driven architectural pattern – mediator

The mediator form of the event-driven architectural pattern is usually employed for multiple-step events, with each step requiring coordination.

The following diagram shows the mediator form of the event-driven architectural pattern. The **Initiating Event** is what starts the process. The events listed in the **Event Mediator** section are the steps that must be taken for the given process. The straight line to the left of **Event 2** and **Event 3** signify that those steps can take place simultaneously. The **Event Mediator** creates a **Processing Event** for each of the initial event steps:

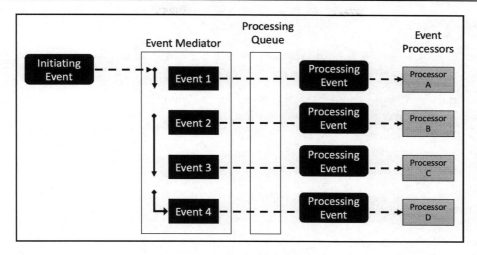

Event-driven pattern - mediator form

The processing event is sent to an event queue awaiting processing by the event processor.

This section provided both forms of the event-driven architectural pattern.

Understanding the extract-transform-load pattern

The extract-transform-load architectural pattern, as the name suggests, has the following three stages:

1. Extract data from external sources
2. Transform the extracted data as needed
3. Load the newly transformed data into a repository specific to the current system

The most common uses of the extract-transform-load pattern is in business intelligence, data warehousing, knowledge management systems, and customer relationship management systems.

We will look at the extract, transform, and load steps as they apply to the similarly-named architectural pattern in the next sections. We will use the example of a sales tool that mines various sources of customer leads, transforms that data into a common form, and then loads the data into a central database.

Extract

For our sales tool example, let's obtain data from two sources that have different formatting.

Our first data source is from an XML file provided by an affiliate insurance company's salesforce. That file has the following encoding:

```
.  .  .
<CUSTID>350032</CUSTID>
<POLICY_TYPE>term</POLICY_TYPE>
<NAME>Neo Anderson</NAME>
<STREET>1 White Rabbit Trail</STREET>
<CITY>Zion</CITY>
<STATE>MZ</STATE>
<ZIP>00000</ZIP>
<EMAIL>neo.anderson@matrix.net</EMAIL>
<PHONE>000-000-0000</PHONE>
.  .  .
```

As the ellipsis indicates, there would be far more data elements for each record in the XML document.

A secondary data source might come from a purchased list of sales leads. This might come in a **Comma Separated Values (CSV)** format, as shown in the following code:

```
350032,term,Neo
Anderson,Zion,MZ,00000,neo.anderson@matrix.net,000-000-0000,.  .  .
```

For our example, we can assume that we have several thousands of names captured from each of the data sources defined. Our next step is to transform this data into a common form that is compatible with our system and the implemented data storage solution.

Transform

With the extracted data now accessible to us, we can implement the second step and transform the data into our desired form. A real-world implementation would include source code to convert the data. The transformation process would include the following sequential steps:

1. Determine how to chunk data.
2. Grab chunk.

3. Process records:
   - Convert fields as necessary.
   - Add default values as necessary.
   - Flag incomplete records.
4. Continue step 3 until all records in the current chunk are completed.
5. Repeat step 2 until all chunks have been processed.

The first step, *determine how to chunk data*, is important because the datasets are very large and server-side scripting would most certainly time out. You might, as an example, process 100 records at a time. With this as our example, step 2 would simply involve reading the first 100 records.

The third step is where we process records, one at a time. We will want to convert data fields as needed. For example, say that the name *Neo Anderson* is provided and we want to convert it to *Anderson, Neo* or break the data up into two separate fields for first and last name. Also in step three, we will assign default values for any blank fields. This will be determined by our policy. Another important processing part of step three is to flag incomplete records. If, for example, you are processing sales leads and your sales force requires phone numbers, then records with no phone numbers might be flagged. In one case, they might be flagged as *inquire by email*, provided an email address is given. In the case that both the phone number and email address are not provided, the record might be flagged for deletion.

Converting CSV data to a MySQL database, for example, is somewhat complex. As an example, a method would need to be written to parse the CSV file one line at a time and that record processed, and when completed, this would generate an SQL INSERT query. You will use that query as part of the Load step, which will be covered in the next section.

Load

The loading process is usually straightforward. The specifics will be unique to the system and the selected core database or other data repository. Typically, this will involve the following steps:

1. Open the database
2. Write new records
3. Close the database

Here is an example statement for step 1, *Open the database*:

```
. . .
Connection con = null;
con =
csvParser.getConnection("jdbc:oracle:thin:PACKT/ETL@localhost:1500:leadsDB"
);
. . .
```

Writing the records involves the process of inserting them into the current database. Here is an example:

```
. . .
INSERT INTO Leads (leadName, leadPhone, leadEmail, leadAddress, leadCity,
leadState, leadZip) VALUES ('Neo Anderson', '000-000-0000',
'neo.anderson@matrix.net', '1 White Rabbit Trail', 'Zion', 'MZ', '00000');
. . .
```

The actual field values are displayed. A real implementation would use variable names.

Closing the database would involve a statement such as the following:

```
. . .
con.close();
if (con.isClosed()) {
  System.out.println("Database successfully closed.");
}
. . .
```

This section detailed the steps involved in implementing the extract-transform-load architectural pattern.

Understanding the layered pattern

The layered architectural pattern composes a system so that it is layered into subtasks. A system's layers have a defined set of responsibilities, specific to the implementation. This is a commonly used pattern and can be found in most robust systems, especially those that take advantage of distributed computing, such as cloud computing or cloud storage.

The layered pattern is core to much modern computing infrastructure. The **International Standards Organization (ISO) Open Systems Interconnection (OSI)** has a seven-layer model. This OSI model has been widely implemented and remains relevant in modern software architectures.

 You can learn more about the ISO OSI seven-layer model from Microsoft's online documentation at `https://docs.microsoft.com/en-us/windows-hardware/drivers/network/windows-network-architecture-and-the-osi-model`.

The seven-layer model consists of two parallel stacks, each with seven layers. The bottom-most layer is a physical layer with direct communication between the two stacks. The stacks in the following list, in top-down order, represent the communication between two computers:

- Application
- Presentation
- Session
- Application
- Network
- Data link
- Physical

Here are a few key concepts about these layers:

- A change to one layer does not impact other layers
- Layers can have different protocols
- Each layer has unique responsibilities
- Calls between layers flow downward

We will look at the following implementations of the layered architectural pattern:

- Traditional operating system layers
- Mobile operating system layers
- Business application layers

Traditional operating system layers example

One of the great benefits of the layered architectural pattern is that changes to one layer do not negatively impact the other layers. For example, if you purchased a new color printer for your computer, you would merely need to update the **Hardware Device Drivers** layer by adding the new driver. The operating system layers are shown in the following diagram:

User Interface
Application
Middleware
Operating System Interface
Operating System Kernel
Hardware Device Drivers
Hardware

Traditional operating system layers

This operating system layer diagram depicts the use of the layered architectural pattern. As you will see in the next example, there do not have to be seven layers to implement this architectural pattern.

Mobile operating system layers example

Modern mobile operating systems have a different architectural pattern. We will look at the layers of iOS as an example. As illustrated in the following diagram, the five iOS layers include a touch layer that the user interacts with:

Cocoa Touch Layer
Media Layer
Core Services Layer
Core OS Layer
Hardware

Mobile operating system layers

Let's look at this in detail:

- The communication path is downward, flowing all the way down to the **Hardware** layer.
- Immediately above the **Hardware** layer is the **Core OS Layer**. This layer has several responsibilities that include memory management, Bluetooth, security services, local authentication, and more.
- This includes responsibilities such as iCloud storage, HealthKit, HomeKit, address book, accounts, social media interfaces, peer-to-peer services, and file-sharing.
- The **Media Layer** is segmented into three frameworks:
  - **Graphics**: The graphics framework includes UI graphics, core graphics, animation optimization, advanced image support, and graphics rendering.
  - **Audio**: The audio framework includes a framework for accessing iTunes and handles audio and video recording and playback. It also has an advanced audio framework.
  - **Video**: The video framework provides recording and playback of video, presenting video, and interfaces for a variety of video data types.
- The top layer, the **Cocoa Touch Layer**, is the touch-based user interface that users see. There are many frameworks in the **Cocoa Touch Layer** that include the Event UI Kit, Game Kit, iAd, Map Kit, Push Kit, and the UI Kit.

Business application layers example

We use the layers architectural pattern to isolate functionality. When an event or request is initiated in one layer, one of three things can occur:

- The request is passed to the next layer
- The request is processed and then passed to the next layer
- The request is processed and then closed without being passed to the next layer

The following screenshot shows how each layer has one or more components and has the ability to close requests so they are not unnecessarily passed to additional layers:

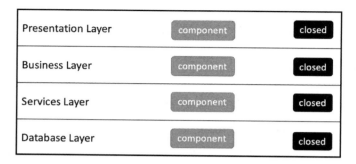

Business application layers

This section provided three implementation examples of the layered architectural pattern.

Understanding the master–slave pattern

The master–slave architectural pattern is used to improve system reliability and performance by dividing work between the master and slave components. Each component has distinct responsibilities. All slave components have identical or at least similar work, and that work must be defined prior to runtime. This pattern is not a divide-and-conquer approach to architecture; rather, it is one where the slaves' work is predefined and must be coordinated. The goal of the master–slave architectural pattern is to improve software efficiency.

The following diagram provides an overview of how the master–slave architectural pattern works. There are one or more **Clients** that can submit requests or initiate events with the **Master**:

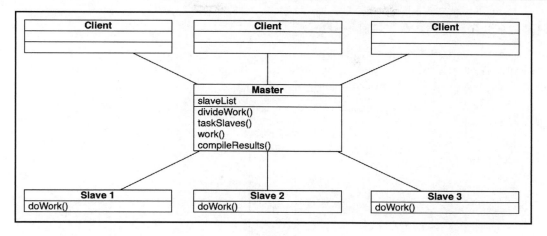

Master–slave pattern

The master performs the following functions:

- Maintains a list of slaves
- Divides the work
- Tasks slaves
- Accepts completed work from slaves
- Compiles results
- Provides feedback to clients

Distributing the workload among multiple slaves inherently results in greater efficiency. Processing multiple workloads at the same time is referred to as **parallel processing**. Another benefit of this pattern is that changes to the slaves do not impact the master. The same is true when a master needs to be updated—the slaves are not impacted.

We will now look at the following implementations of the master–slave architectural pattern:

- Single client example
- Cloud storage example

Single client example

Masters have a special relationship with clients. They receive requests from clients and then distribute the work to the slaves. As illustrated in the following diagram, the results from the slaves are combined and provided to the client:

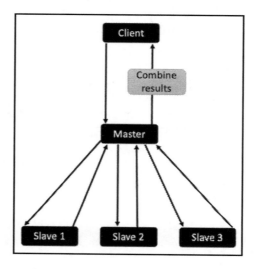

Master–slave pattern - single client example

Masters must determine how to divide the work among the slaves. There are several approaches to this to ensure that the number of components and memory size are included. Processing time is often an additional factor to consider for the division of work among the slaves in the system.

Cloud storage example

Modern applications use cloud storage for databases and other data sources. Sophisticated systems usually include data replication for the purpose of faster access times and to prevent data loss or single-source failures. The following diagram depicts a system architecture using the master–slave pattern that includes redundant data storage:

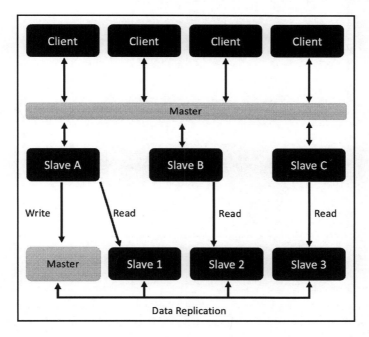

Master–slave pattern - cloud storage example

The preceding diagram shows a master–slave pattern in addition to a second master database and three database slaves. The database is replicated so that there are multiple read-only access points. This schema will result in greater efficiencies.

This section provided two implementation examples of the master–slave architectural pattern.

Understanding the microkernel pattern

The microkernel architectural pattern is also referred to as a **plug-in** architectural pattern. We typically use this pattern when we create systems with interchangeable components, illustrated in the following diagram as a **plug-in**:

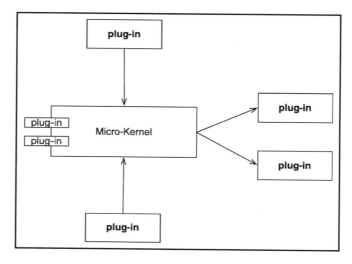

Microkernel pattern

The general framework of the microkernel architectural pattern is illustrated in the previous diagram. The microkernel contains a system's core logic and functionality. The plug-ins each have a specific functionality and contain **application programming interfaces (APIs)** for the microkernel to reference.

There are five components involved in the microkernel pattern, as shown in the following list:

- **The microkernel**: The microkernel is the core of this architectural pattern. It provides core processing and serves as the middleman between other parts of the architecture. All resources are managed by the microkernel, which also manages communications with the system's remaining components.
- **One or more clients**: The client represents the entity using the system. This can be a person or a system. The client uses external plug-ins to interface with the microkernel.

- **Internal plug-ins**: The internal plug-ins are called by the microkernel when their specific services are required. These services are internal to the microkernel, so the microkernel controls access to them.
- **External plug-ins**: The external plug-ins are external to the microkernel, which means they can be accessed directly by the clients. The microkernel API empowers the external plug-ins to process client requests.
- **Adapters**: The adapters are used to create an interface between the client and external plug-ins. As previously indicated, these adapters permit external plug-ins to process client requests directly.

This pattern results in tremendous extensibility and flexibility. Like object-oriented programming, each plug-in can be developed by different development teams, decreasing the overall development time.

We will look at the following implementations of the microkernel architectural pattern:

- Construction quote
- Optical disk player

Construction quote example

Let's assume we have an automated building construction quotation system where the microkernel receives all the inputs needed and makes calls to various plug-ins, each with a specialized quotation function. This pattern is displayed in the following diagram and indicates the inputs to the microkernel:

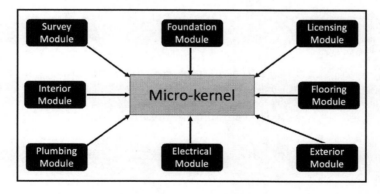

Microkernel pattern - construction quotation system

The preceding diagram shows specialized plug-ins that each perform a complex series of rules, logic, and calculations. One of the benefits of the microkernel architectural pattern is that if the **Electrical Module**, for example, changes because of new state and local codes, the rest of the system does not need to change. The associated API will still be utilized to access the **Electrical Module** and will not be aware that changes were made.

Optical disc player example

Modern optical disc players consist of hardware and software. The software is embedded on the hardware's components. These players can accept audio CDs, video CDs, DVDs, and Blu-ray discs, as shown in the following diagram. Each of these optical forms is processed differently because of the technology used to write data on the discs:

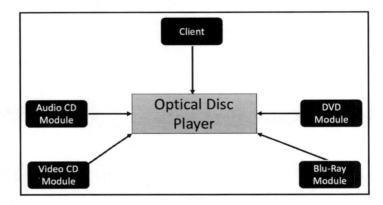

Microkernel pattern implementation - optical disc player

As illustrated, the diagram shows the external plug-ins for the **Audio CD Module**, **Video CD Module**, **DVD Module**, and **Blu-Ray Module**. This system would also include internal plug-ins to handle functionality, such as volume control, audio and video output, power settings, and more.

This section provided two implementation examples of the microkernel architectural pattern.

Summary

In this chapter, we looked at eight architectural patterns—blackboard, broker, client-server, event-driven, extract-transform-load, layered, master–slave, and microkernel. We learned that architectural patterns describe the design of an entire system or group of system components. This chapter explained how architectural patterns take a holistic view of systems and group components for illustrative purposes. In addition, the visual depiction of architectural patterns do not use UML class diagrams, as the behavioral, creational, and structural design patterns do. Instead, a nonprescriptive approach is taken for visually documenting architectural patterns. Understanding how to select and implement these patterns strengthens your ability to design and develop efficient software systems.

In the next chapter, we will continue our exploration of the architectural patterns. Specifically, we will review the microservices, model-view-controller, naked objects, peer-to-peer, pipe-filter, serverless, service-oriented, and space-based patterns.

Questions

1. What is the scope of architectural patterns?
2. What approach is taken for visually documenting architectural patterns?
3. Which pattern is used for large systems that do not have a definitive solution?
4. Which pattern uses a middleman component to coordinate and communicate between components?
5. Which pattern consists of two component types—client components and server components?
6. Which pattern has both broker and mediator forms?
7. Which pattern involves the transformation of data from external sources?
8. Which pattern is based on an OSI standard from the ISO?
9. Which pattern is used to improve system reliability and performance by dividing work?
10. Which pattern is also referred to as a plug-in architectural pattern?

Further reading

- *Java EE 8 Design Patterns and Best Practices* (https://www.packtpub.com/application-development/java-ee-8-design-patterns-and-best-practices)
- *Learn Design Patterns with Java [Video]* (https://www.packtpub.com/application-development/learn-design-patterns-java-video)
- *Design Patterns and Best Practices in Java* (https://www.packtpub.com/application-development/design-patterns-and-best-practices-java)

7
Architectural Patterns - Part II

In the previous chapter, *Architectural Patterns – Part I*, we explored the architectural pattern category and eight specific patterns—blackboard, broker, client-server, event-driven, extract-transform-load, layered, master–slave, and microkernel. Each of these eight architectural patterns was explained along with diagrams.

In this chapter, we will continue our exploration of the architectural patterns. Specifically, we will review the architectural patterns listed next, along with an examination of programming challenges and the architectural patterns to solve them:

- Microservices pattern
- Model-view-controller pattern
- Naked objects pattern
- **Peer-to-peer (P2P)** pattern
- Pipe-filter pattern
- Serverless pattern
- Service-oriented pattern
- Space-based pattern

We will cover the eight architectural patterns in this chapter. They have been presented alphabetically, as there is no order of importance.

Technical requirements

The code for this chapter can be found at `https://github.com/PacktPublishing/Hands-On-Design-Patterns-with-Java/tree/master/Chapter07`.

Understanding the microservices pattern

The microservices architectural pattern is used for breaking a system into several smaller services, or *microservices*, that have limited interdependencies. The benefits of this pattern include the following:

- The modular nature of the pattern permits individual microservices to be used elsewhere
- Processing efficiency
- Easily maintainable code

As illustrated next, there is a central point that interfaces with the microservices that comprise the system. In this example, the central point is the **System Interface**:

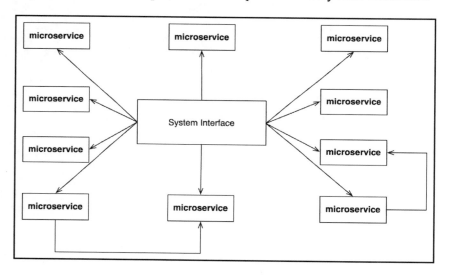

Microservices pattern

The previous diagram also indicates how some microservices can communicate with other microservices. This architectural pattern mandates that the microservices be loosely coupled, so the only true interdependency should be communications.

Software development using the microservices pattern consists of developing each microservice separately, which is a preferred approach, especially for large systems. This also permits the development of multiple microservices simultaneously by different teams, accelerating delivery time. Systems designed with this pattern are also apt to be highly scalable. Additional microservices can be added, and for those that are heavily used, they can be replicated.

In the next sections, we will explore the following example implementations of the microservices architectural pattern:

- Logistics example
- eCommerce example

Logistics example

The following diagram illustrates the implementation of the microservices architectural pattern for a logistics company. There are two interfaces, **Mobile Interface** and **Web Interface**, that serve as user gateways into the system. These interfaces receive user requests and route them to the proper microservice. Both interfaces have access to all microservices:

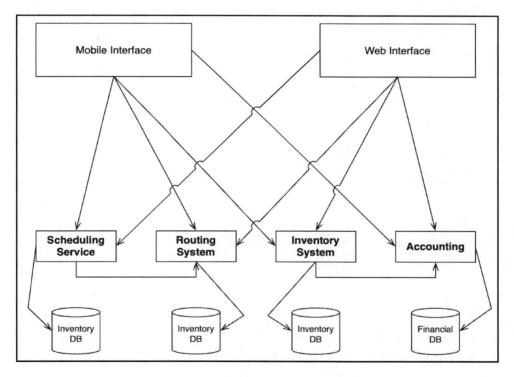

Microservices pattern—logistics example implementation

The previous diagram also indicates that some of the microservices have communication links with other microservices. For example, the **Scheduling Service** has a communication link with the **Routing System** and the **Inventory System** has a communication link with the **Accounting** microservice.

eCommerce example implementation

The eCommerce implementation example is different than the logistics example; in this, there is a **Common Gateway** that receives requests from a variety of sources, illustrated here as mobile operating systems and web browsers:

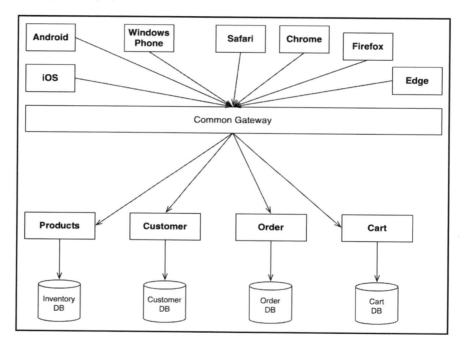

Microservices pattern—eCommerce example implementation

The **Common Gateway** interfaces between the various microservices, each of which have their own database. These microservices can work in isolation of the others.

This section provided example implementations of the microservices architectural pattern.

Understanding the model-view-controller pattern

The model-view-controller architectural pattern is one of the most commonly used patterns in modern software design and development. It is used in desktop and mobile applications. The pattern segments systems into model, view, and controller components. The model component is used to store application data and logic. The view is where visual elements are provided to the user. The controller processes input and communicates, as appropriate, to the model and view components.

 The **model-view-controller** pattern is most commonly referred to as **MVC** throughout the software industry.

The **View** is used to present data to the user. This enables the user to interact with, or use, the **Controller**. The **Controller** manipulates the **Model**, which then updates the **View**:

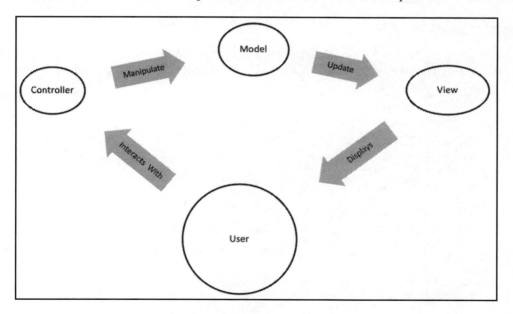

MVC pattern—overview

As illustrated, the user is viewed as the most important part of this pattern, even though it is not an official part of the MVC pattern. With a user-centric purpose, the MVC architectural pattern is often used for UI-rich applications such as mobile apps.

As with other patterns that segment systems, the MVC pattern design allows different teams to simultaneously work on the different core components—model, view, and controller. This also makes the system maintainable, since each component can be updated without impacting the others.

In the next section, we will explore the Book MVC example implementation of the MVC architectural pattern.

Book model-view-controller example implementation

To demonstrate this architectural pattern, we will use a Book class example. Our example will include a Book class, a BookView class, a BookController class, and a MVCArchitecturalPattern class. Let's look at each of these classes followed by the program's output.

Book class

The Book class establishes the class structure with three class variables: isbn, title, and year. Accessor and mutator (getters and setters) methods are provided for each of the class variables:

```
public class Book {

    private String isbn;
    private String title;
    private int year;


    // accessor methods
    public String getISBN() {
        return isbn;
    }

    public String getTitle() {
        return title;
    }

    public int getYear() {
        return year;
    }
```

```
    // mutator methods
    public void setISBN(String isbn) {
        this.isbn = isbn;
    }

    public void setTitle(String title) {
        this.title = title;
    }

    public void setYear(int year) {
        this.year = year;
    }
}
```

The Book class defined previously represents the model component of our MVC architectural pattern.

BookView class

The BookView class contains a single method for printing a book's detail to the console:

```
public class BookView {

    public void printBookData(String bookTitle, String bookISBN, int
bookYear) {
        System.out.println("\nBook Title : " + bookTitle);
        System.out.println("ISBN-13    : " + bookISBN);
        System.out.println("Pub. Year  : " + bookYear + "\n");
    }
}
```

The BookView class just shown contains the printBookData() method for providing output to the user, and represents the view component of our MVC architectural pattern.

The BookController class

The BookController class is presented next in three sections. The first section contains two private class variables: model and view. The constructor method is also provided:

```
public class BookController {
    private Book model;
    private BookView view;

    // constructor
    public BookController(Book model, BookView view) {
```

```
        this.model = model;
        this.view = view;
    }
```

The second section of the `BookController` class consists of three `accessor` methods and three `mutator` methods:

```
// accessor methods
public String getBookTitle() {
    return model.getTitle();
}

public String getBookISBN() {
    return model.getISBN();
}

public int getBookYear() {
    return model.getYear();
}

// mutator methods
public void setBookTitle(String title) {
    model.setTitle(title);
}

public void setBookISBN(String isbn) {
    model.setISBN(isbn);
}

public void setBookYear(int year) {
    model.setYear(year);
}
```

The final section of the `BookController` class contains the `updateView()` method. As you can see, the method does not accept parameters and calls the `view` object's `printBookData()` method, as shown:

```
// update view method
public void updateView() {
    view.printBookData(model.getTitle(), model.getISBN(),
model.getYear());
    }
}
```

The `BookController` class, as shown in the previous three sections of code, comprises the controller component of the MVC architectural pattern.

The MVCArchitecturalPattern class

The MVCArchitecturalPattern class contains the main() method to drive the program. This class also contains the pullBookDetails() method that gets details from the Book object instance:

```
public class MVCArchitecturalPattern {

  public static void main(String[] args) {

  Book model = pullBookDetails();

  BookView view = new BookView();

  BookController con = new BookController(model, view);

  con.updateView();

  con.setBookTitle("Mastering Java 11");
  con.setBookISBN("978-1789137613");
  con.setBookYear(2018);
        con.updateView();
    }

    private static Book pullBookDetails() {
        Book book = new Book();
        book.setTitle("Mastering Java 9");
        book.setISBN("978-1786468734");
        book.setYear(2017);
        return book;
    }
}
```

There are two sets of output, each generated from the updateView() method, as shown here:

```
Book Title : Mastering Java 9
ISBN-13    : 978-1786468734
Pub. Year  : 2017


Book Title : Mastering Java 11
ISBN-13    : 978-1789137613
Pub. Year  : 2018
```

MVC pattern—book example output

This section provided the source code and console output for the `book` implementation of the MVC architectural pattern.

Understanding the naked object pattern

The naked objects architectural pattern mandates domain object encapsulation of object data. In addition, a user interface has to be created for the following actions:

- Instantiating objects
- Object retrieval
- Object data retrieval
- Method invocation

An additional requirement of the naked objects architectural pattern is that the aforementioned user interface must be auto-generated based on the domain object definitions. The core goal is to create behaviorally complete objects, with their attributes and behaviors encapsulated, and for the view and controllers to be generic in nature:

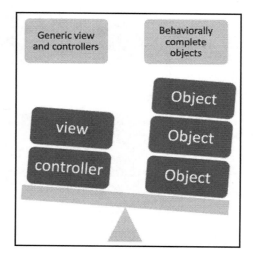

Naked object pattern—overview

The naked objects architectural pattern is relatively complex to implement and has resulted in two open source projects as listed here:

- **Naked Objects**: A .NET version with information available at this URL (`https:/ /github.com/NakedObjectsGroup/NakedObjectsFramework`)
- **Apache Isis**: A Java version of the naked objects pattern with information available at this URL (`http://isis.apache.org`)

Implementing the naked objects architectural pattern is beyond the scope of this book. The open source projects listed are suggested as a great way to delve deeper into this specific pattern.

Understanding the peer-to-peer pattern

The **peer-to-peer (P2P)** architectural pattern, consists of a series of nodes, each with the same set of functions to perform. With this pattern, there is no central controller and all nodes are created equally. The peer nodes act as both receivers and distributors of data and resources.

There are several benefits to this pattern:

- It only requires two nodes
- Additional nodes can join
- Nodes can drop out
- It's great for sharing resources
- It's great for sharing processing

However, there is also one major disadvantage:

- It's highly vulnerable to **Denial-of-Service (DoS)** attacks

In the following sections, we will explore the following example implementations of the P2P architectural pattern:

- File sharing
- Networking

File sharing example implementation

A typical file sharing P2P network would have each peer connected to two others as illustrated:

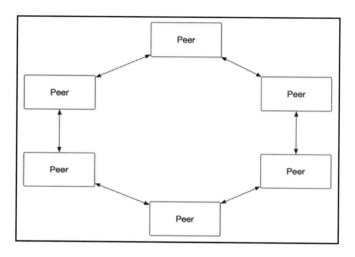

P2P pattern—file sharing example implementation

As illustrated in the next diagram, the network formation of the P2P pattern does not limit any peer from directly communicating with any other peer:

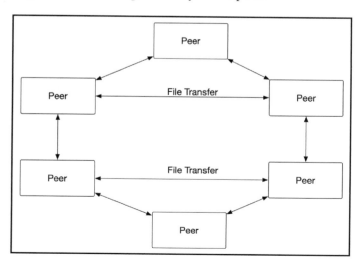

P2P pattern—additional file sharing example implementation

There are great risks associated with P2P file sharing implementations:

- Malware risks are high because of the possibility of embedding them in files
- Lack of data privacy
- Increased potential for file and software piracy

Networking example implementation

When the P2P architectural pattern is applied to physical computer networks, those networks have the following characteristics:

- There is no dedicated server on the network
- All computers on the network are considered peers
- All peers can share
- All peers are both clients and servers
- There is a lack of centralized control
- Resources are shared and not controlled centrally

Here is a diagram of a typical P2P network:

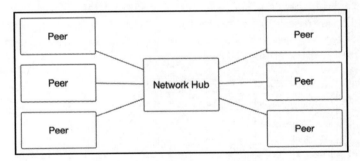

P2P pattern—networking example implementation

As illustrated next, P2P networks empower every peer to directly communicate with every other peer:

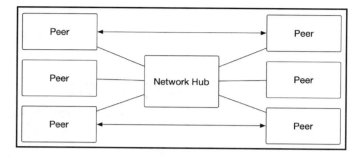

P2P pattern—additional networking example implementation

This section provided example implementations of the P2P architectural pattern.

Understanding the pipe-filter pattern

The pipe-filter, or pipe and filter, architectural pattern is a robust architecture that can contain any number of filters. The pattern starts by taking data from multiple sources and then passes them through sequential filters to transform the data from one format to another. The filters are connected via pipes. The next diagram shows an overview of the pipe-filter pattern with three sequential filters:

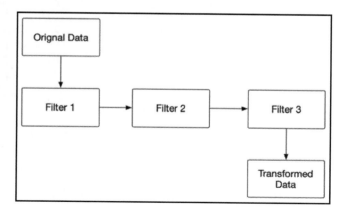

Pipe-filter pattern—overview

We can take a deeper look at this pattern with a UML sequence diagram. This diagram illustrates the data flow and the utility of the pipes connecting the filters:

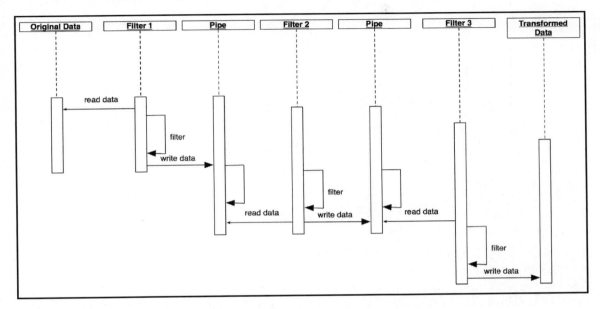

Pipe-filter pattern—UML sequence diagram

In the next sections, we will explore the following example implementations of the pipe-filter architectural pattern:

- Simple transformation
- Complex transformation

Simple transformation example implementation

A simple transformation of data might consist of collecting data from various sources, each in a different format, and passing it through two filters before the data is considered final. An example would be data sources from different systems or in different languages. In order for any business logic to process the data, it must first be transformed into a common, standard format expected by the system.

The next diagram provides a high-level look at that process:

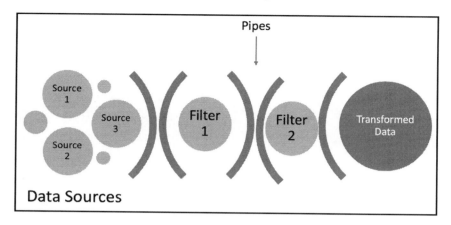

Pipe-filter pattern—simple transformation example implementation

A more complex transformation process is provided in the next section.

Complex transformation example implementation

The next diagram illustrates a complex transformation example of the pipe-filter pattern. There are three data sources, two of which can be processed by **Filter 1**. There is a **Pipe** between **Filter 1** and **Filter 2** that serves as a conduit for the data. After the data passes through **Filter 2**, the transformed data is ready to be processed by the **System Logic**. **Data Source 3** is read by **Filter A** and then piped to **Filter B**, which transforms the data for **System Logic** processing:

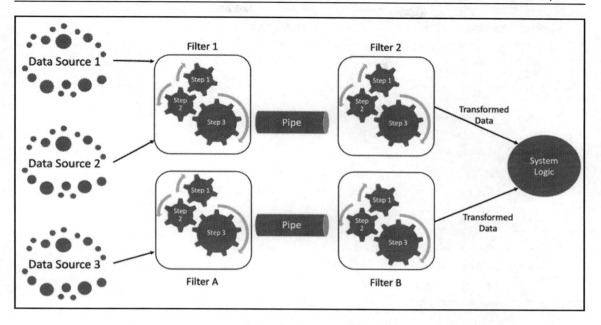

Pipe-filter pattern—complex transformation example implementation

As illustrated in the previous diagram, each filter has several processes.

This section provided example implementations of the pipe-filter architectural pattern.

Understanding the serverless pattern

The implementation of serverless architectural patterns is becoming more prevalent due to the advent of **Infrastructure as a Service (IaaS)**, **Platform as a Service (PaaS)**, **Software as a Service (SaaS)**, **Backend as a Service (BaaS)**, **Mobile Backend as a Service (MBaaS)**, and **Functions as a Service (FaaS)** cloud-based offerings. Serverless architectural patterns are simply patterns that do not incorporate dedicated on-premises servers.

The term *on-premises* refers to components that physically reside at an organization's actual location.

This does not indicate typical server-side scripting, and that functionality does not exist; rather, these components are managed by third-party services such as cloud-based services. The largest providers of these services are Amazon, Google, Microsoft, IBM, and Oracle.

The benefits of implementing a serverless architectural pattern include the following:

- Cost-effectiveness
- High scalability
- High flexibility
- Faster upgrades, changes, deployments
- Benefit from applications running closer to the end-user's region

Some of the disadvantages include the following:

- A sense of loss of control
- Inability to easily switch between cloud-service solutions (for example, Amazon AWS to Microsoft Azure)
- Potential performance issues (that is, multi-latency)

In the following sections, we will explore the following example implementations of the serverless architectural pattern.

IaaS implementation

A typical **Infrastructure as a Service (IaaS)** implementation involves a clear separation of responsibilities between the on-premises organization and the IaaS provider:

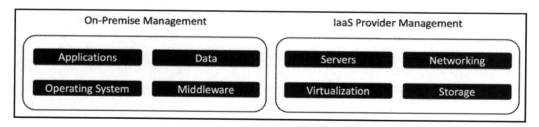

Serverless pattern—example IaaS implementation

It is important that for appropriate responsibility division that the servers and networking are taken care of by the IaaS provider.

PaaS implementation

The **Platform as a Service (PaaS)** implementation of a serverless architecture pattern involves a larger set of responsibilities for the cloud service provider compared to the IaaS implementation:

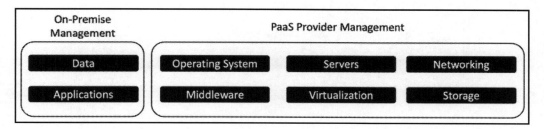

Serverless pattern—example PaaS implementation

As illustrated, the PaaS implementation only requires the on-premises staff to manage data and applications.

SaaS implementation

The **Software as a Service (SaaS)** implementation of the serverless architectural pattern involves full responsibility for the SaaS provider:

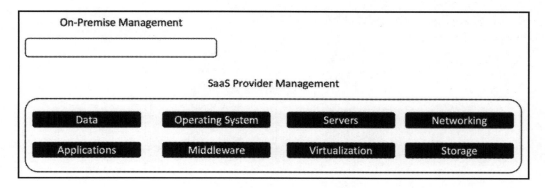

Serverless pattern—example SaaS implementation

As illustrated, the SaaS implementation only requires the on-premises use of internet browsers to access the software services.

BaaS implementation

The **Backend as a Service (BaaS)** implementation of the serverless architectural pattern involves client-side, on-premises access via a browser:

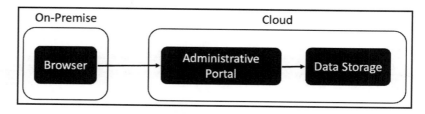

Serverless pattern—example BaaS implementation

As illustrated, the BaaS implementation only requires the on-premises use of internet browsers to access the backend administrative services.

MBaaS implementation

The **Mobile Backend as a Service (MBaaS)** implementation of the serverless architectural pattern involves client-side access to services via mobile devices and a browser. It is common to have mobile apps connect directly with backend services and a browser interface for oversight, reporting, and management:

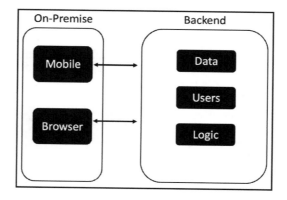

Serverless pattern—example MBaaS implementation

The MBaaS implementation is commonly used for enterprise mobile applications.

FaaS implementation

The **Functions as a Service (FaaS)** implementation of the serverless architectural pattern allows for isolated functions to run on demand. Developing with this pattern results in rapid builds because the developers focus on the functionality, and others focus on the operational environment. The key benefit to this approach is fast processing times:

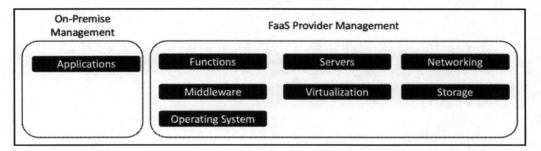

Serverless pattern—example FaaS implementation

This section provided example implementations of the serverless architectural pattern.

Understanding the service-oriented pattern

The service-oriented architectural pattern, also referred to as **Service-Oriented Architecture (SOA)**, establishes interoperable services through methodologies and rules. Web services are typically designed with an SOA pattern. These interoperable services consist of organized, deployable services with the following characteristics:

- Runs independently of other services
- Handles a specific computational task
- Has access to other services

The SOA pattern can be used to design a group of organized services to provide a cohesive set of services. There are several benefits to adopting this pattern, some of which are listed here:

- Since the architecture comprises several services, each service can be modified in isolation of the others
- Increased system flexibility and adaptability
- The system is easier to maintain because of its modularity
- Individual services can be used in multiple systems

The following diagram provides an overview of how the service-oriented architectural pattern can be implemented. The example provided starts with a **Web Interface**, which serves as the entry point to obtaining services in this pattern. A **Web Interface** is used to highlight the applicability of this architectural pattern to web services:

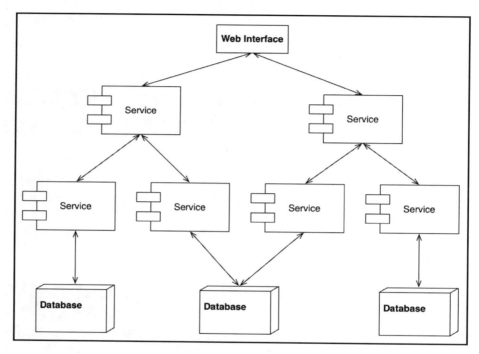

Service-oriented pattern—overview

As illustrated, the services can be gateways to other services and databases, and other resources can be shared among multiple services.

The next diagram illustrates the possible complexity of individual services within a service-oriented architectural pattern implementation. An individual service is likely to have multiple steps and business logic:

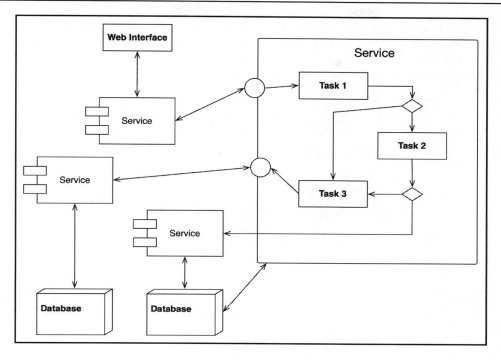

Service-oriented pattern—detailed view

This section detailed the service-oriented architectural pattern and provided both an overview diagram and a service-level detailed illustration.

Understanding the space-based pattern

The space-based architectural pattern is designed to avoid functional collapse under a high load and maximize scaling. Cloud-based architectures typically implement the space-based architectural pattern. Key to the success of this pattern is the use of distributing shared memory.

This complex approach involves the following:

- Eliminating central database constraints
- Implementing data grids
- Replicating data grids in memory
- Maintaining application data in the replicated memory

With this approach, data is replicated in memory for each processor in use. The next diagram provides an overview of the space-based architectural pattern. Each **Processing Unit** has connectivity to other processing units as well as linkage to the data grids via middleware that manages the communication between processing units and data grids:

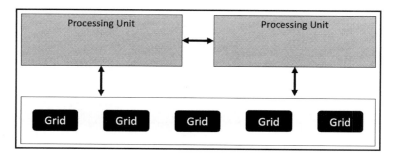

Space-based pattern—overview

The processing units can be complex and will include one or more logic modules, data, and a data replication engine.

Summary

In this chapter, we explored the eight additional architectural patterns (after the eight architectural patterns covered in `Chapter 6`, *Architectural Patterns - Part I*). The patterns covered in this chapter were microservices, model-view-controller, naked objects, P2P, pipe-filter, serverless, service-oriented, and space-based. Each of these architectural patterns was explained along with diagrams of example implementations. Having a firm understanding of the 16 architectural patterns and knowing how to implement them will broaden your ability to design and develop efficient software systems.

In the next chapter, *Functional Design Patterns*, we will explore the functional design pattern category and its individual design patterns. Specifically, we will cover the execute around, lambda, loan, MapReduce, memoization, streams, and tail call patterns. We will examine the programming challenges and creational design patterns that solve them.

Questions

1. What are three benefits of the microservices pattern?
2. How does the space-based pattern accomplish its goal?
3. Which pattern is used when breaking a system into several smaller services?
4. Which pattern segments systems into three distinct components?
5. Which pattern requires behaviorally complete objects?
6. Which pattern consists of a series of nodes, each with the same set of functions to perform?
7. Which pattern involves passing data through sequential filters to transform the data?
8. Which pattern includes a MBaaS approach?
9. Which pattern establishes interoperable services through methodologies and rules?
10. Which pattern is designed to avoid functional collapse under a high load?

Further reading

- *Java EE 8 Design Patterns and Best Practices* (https://www.packtpub.com/application-development/java-ee-8-design-patterns-and-best-practices)
- *Learning Design Patterns with Java [Video]* (https://www.packtpub.com/application-development/learn-design-patterns-java-video)
- *Design Patterns and Best Practices in Java* (https://www.packtpub.com/application-development/design-patterns-and-best-practices-java)

Functional Design Patterns

8

In the previous chapter, *Architectural Patterns – Part II*, we concluded our coverage of architectural patterns. In addition to the eight architectural patterns covered in Chapter 6, *Architectural Patterns – Part I*, the patterns covered in Chapter 7, *Architectural Patterns – Part II*, were the microservices, model-view-controller, naked objects, peer-to-peer, pipe-filter, serverless, service-oriented, and space-based architectural patterns. Each of these architectural patterns was explained along with a diagram.

In this chapter, we will explore the functional design pattern category and its individual design patterns listed next. We will examine the programming challenges and functional design patterns that solve them:

- Introducing functional design patterns
- Understanding the execute around pattern
- Understanding the lambda design pattern
- Understanding the loan design pattern
- Understanding the MapReduce design pattern
- Understanding the memoization design pattern
- Understanding the streams design pattern
- Understanding the tail call design pattern

These design patterns are important when designing systems that use functional programming.

Technical requirements

The code for this chapter can be found at https://github.com/PacktPublishing/Hands-On-Design-Patterns-with-Java/tree/master/Chapter08.

Introducing functional design patterns

Functional design patterns are not the same as functional programming. While they can both be considered programming paradigms, functional programming can be defined as an approach to structuring computer programs that model computational functionality such as mathematical functions. The term *functional design patterns* refers to the use of functional programming to solve computational problems.

The following table provides an overview of how functional programming fits into the general programming approach landscape, especially when compared to object-oriented programming:

Programming Approach	Description
Functional programming	Uses a style similar to mathematical functions.
Object oriented programming	Uses an object-centric approach. Objects contain attributes and behaviors.
Parallel-programming	Uses shared memory. Processes can be executed several times at once.

Programming approach overview

A key concept of functional design is that the individual functions have a set of rules. For example, functions in a functional programming approach honor the following:

- They do not mutate any data
- They provide consistent results, given the same set of arguments
- They exist to provide a return value

Let's look at two short examples. This first example shows how a variable is mutated:

```
void calculateAge(int years) {
  years = years + 1;
}
```

The next example accepts the same argument as the previous example but does not mutate it. Instead, it returns a value based on the argument and a calculation:

```
int calculateAge(int years) {
    return years + 1;
}
```

The advantages to using a functional approach include easier debugging and the ability to pass functions as parameters. You will explore the latter advantage in the *Understanding the lambda design pattern* section. Additional advantages include the high applicability to mathematical, statistical, concurrency, and parallelism applications.

The general disadvantages of implementing the functional design patterns include code complexity, code readability, and application performance.

The functional design patterns listed in the table you have just seen are detailed in the remaining sections of this chapter. They are presented in alphabetical order to illustrate that one is not more important than the others.

Understanding the execute around design pattern

The execute around functional design pattern is used when processes have pre- and post-processing that always occur. This allows us to focus on the core function and not on the processing that comes before or after. The pre- and post-processing code can exist once, instead of being part of each core process. This can result in a big win.

Consider a system with hundreds of individual classes that are run on an ad hoc nature based on business logic. Instead of each of those hundreds of processes including the pre- and post-processing code, that code can be located in one class.

The pre- and post-processing actions are paired and included in the object that requires those actions. This is done instead of including those actions in a class that uses the object. So, we are including the actions in the object itself, not in a class that uses the object.

Demonstrated implementation

At a high level, we can consider the following routine flow of generic operations. We start with a preProcessing() method followed by a commonTask() method, and, finally, a postProcessing() method:

```
preProcessing();
commonTask();
postProcessing();
```

Consider a system that processes electronic files, maybe for a banking application. Each of these files represents an individual transaction. There are a vast number of different types of transactions, each governed by a separate class in the system. Thousands of these files are processed every hour. Explicitly including the `preProcessing()` and `postProcessing()` methods as part of the individual classes is wasteful and should be avoided. To accomplish this, we can implement our bank transaction system with syntax as displayed here:

```
Transaction preProcessDuring: [this performBankingOperation: Transaction]
```

We can use the execute around design pattern to encapsulate a pair of actions in the actual objects that require the pair of actions instead of encapsulating the actions in a code that uses the object. The goal of this design pattern is to avoid duplicated code in classes.

This section provided an overview of the execute around functional design pattern along with representative sample implementation source code.

Understanding the lambda design pattern

Lambda functionality was introduced in Java 8 and has forever changed the landscape of programming in Java. The lambda functional design pattern uses lambda functions, also referred to as *anonymous* functions. These functions are passed as arguments to other functions.

Lambda functions have three parts:

- A single parameter: `(argument)`
- The arrow operator: `->`
- The body: `(body)`

As with anything else in Java, there are a bunch of rules associated with even this seemingly simple syntax:

- If the parameter on the left has its type explicitly stated, it and the parameter must be encased in parenthesis, for example, (String a)
- The body can only call a single method
- The body must return a result
- For bodies with only one parameter, you do not need braces or a semicolon
- For bodies with more than one parameter, you do need braces and a semicolon
- You cannot re-declare a local variable

The syntax of a lambda function is as follows:

```
(argument) -> (body)
```

An example of this syntax is this:

```
// Example 1
a->a.canHop();
```

The previous line of code does the same thing as the following line of code:

```
// Example 2
(Animal a)->{return a.canHop();}
```

When comparing the previous two examples, we see the following differences:

- There is only one parameter whose type is not explicitly stated; then parenthesis can be omitted
- We can omit braces when we have only a single statement

Accessing variables

The following syntax illustrates how to access via a lambda expression:

```
boolean varName = false;
doSomething(objectName, obj -> obj.methodName() == varName);
```

It is important to note that, when accessing local variables via lambda expressions, you cannot change their value.

Implementing lambda with a single parameter

To demonstrate use of the lambda design pattern, we will create a functional interface and a main `Driver` class. The functional interface will contain an abstract method with a single `int` parameter. Here is that interface:

```
public interface FunctionalGift {

  void abstractMethod(int number);
}
```

The FunctionalGift interface is a functional interface because it has only one abstract method.

 Of note, we can use the @FunctionalInterface annotation for code clarity.

The Driver class provided next contains the main() method for our program. That method contains a lambda expression that implements the FunctionalGift interface. The interface implements the abstractMethod() method by default. Our myObject.abstractMethod() statements call the lambda expression:

```
public class Driver {

    public static void main(String[] args) {

        System.out.println();
        FunctionalGift myObject = (int number)->System.out.println
                (number + " squared is " + (number*number));

        myObject.abstractMethod(1);
        myObject.abstractMethod(2);
        myObject.abstractMethod(3);
        myObject.abstractMethod(4);
        myObject.abstractMethod(5);
    }
}
```

The output of the previous program is provided here:

```
1 squared is 1
2 squared is 4
3 squared is 9
4 squared is 16
5 squared is 25
```

Lambda design pattern with single parameter—console output

In the next section, we will use the same FunctionalGift interface and create a new Driver class to demonstrate the use of lambda expressions with multiple arguments.

Implementing lambda with multiple parameters

Our example implementation of lambda with multiple parameters will consist of the
`FunctionalGift` interface that is provided next. We will also have a `Driver` class that
accepts user input for two types of tokens (`blue` and `red`), implements basic math, and
then provides a random gift to the user who submitted the tokens. Here is the
`FunctionalGift` interface:

```
public interface FunctionalGift {

    void abstractMethod(int number);

}
```

Our implementation's `Driver` class is presented in five sequential sections. The first
section, provided next, includes two import statements—`java.util.Random` and
`java.util.Scanner`. We will use the `Scanner` class in the second section of the code and
the `Random` class in the fifth section. This first section of code also includes two interfaces:
one that takes two `int` parameters and one that takes a single `String` parameter:

```
import java.util.Random;
import java.util.Scanner;

public class Driver {

    interface FirstFunctionalInterface {
        int calculation(int a, int b);
    }

    interface SecondFunctionalInterface {
        void displayResults(String message);
    }

    private int calculate(int a, int b, FirstFunctionalInterface
firstObject) {
        return firstObject.calculation(a, b);
    }
```

The second section of the `Driver` class code is the beginning of the `main()` method. The
method starts by obtaining user input, prompting for the number of blue and then red
tokens. We utilize the `Scanner` class to obtain this input. After the input is received, we
display a decorative output header:

```
public static void main(String[] args) {

    // Obtain user input
```

```
System.out.println();
Scanner in = new Scanner(System.in);
System.out.println("How many blue tokens do you have to exchange: ");
int blueTokens = in.nextInt();
System.out.println("How many red tokens do you have to exchange: ");
int redTokens = in.nextInt();

// Display system header
System.out.println("\n======================");
System.out.println("TOKEN-TO-GIFT EXCHANGE");
System.out.println("======================");
```

Our third section of the `Driver` class code is the second part of the `main()` method. This section of code starts with a lambda expression for calculating the sum of the tokens entered by the user. Next, a second lambda expression is used to calculate the sum of the two tokens squared. Finally, we instantiate a `firstObject` object to test our lambda expressions:

```
// add blue and red tokens
FirstFunctionalInterface sum = (int nbr1, int nbr2) -> nbr1 + nbr2;

FirstFunctionalInterface superSquare = (int nbr1, int nbr2) ->
        ((nbr1 * nbr1) + (nbr2 * nbr2));

Driver firstObject = new Driver();
```

Our fourth section of the `Driver` class code is the third and final part of the `main()` method.

In this section, we generate output to the user on six lines:

- The first two lines echo the number of `blue` and `red` tokens entered by the user.
- The third line provides the sum of the tokens using a lambda expression.
- The fourth line also uses a lambda expression and provides the sum of the individual squared token values.
- The output of line five is simply a decorative separator.
- The final output line provides the result of a `displayResults()` method call:

```
// Generate output
System.out.println(blueTokens + " blue tokens submitted");
System.out.println(redTokens + " red tokens submitted");
System.out.println(firstObject.calculate(blueTokens, redTokens, sum) +
        " total tokens submitted");

System.out.println(firstObject.calculate(blueTokens, redTokens,
superSquare) +
```

```
            " SuperSquare number result");

    System.out.println("==");
    SecondFunctionalInterface secondObject = message ->
            System.out.println("Your gift is a pound of " + message);

    secondObject.displayResults(selectGift());
}
```

The fifth and final section of our `Driver` class contains the `selectGift()` method. This method simply creates an array with five precious metal types and generates a random number between 0 and 4. The random number is used as the index of the `giftArray`. The value at that index of the array is returned:

```
public static String selectGift() {
    String[] giftArray = new String[]
            {"Gold", "Silver", "Platinum", "Titanium", "Copper"};
    Random giftNumber = new Random();
    int giftToGive = giftNumber.nextInt(4);

    return giftArray[giftToGive];
}
}
```

Here is the output of our program:

```
How many blue tokens do you have to exchange:
4
How many red tokens do you have to exchange:
5


===========================
TOKEN-TO-GIFT EXCHANGE
===========================
4 blue tokens submitted
5 red tokens submitted
9 total tokens submitted
41 SuperSquare number result
==
Your gift is a pound of Silver
```

Lambda design pattern with multiple parameters—console output

This section provided the source code and the console output for two implementations of the lambda functional design pattern.

Understanding the loan design pattern

The loan functional design pattern can be used to create resource-aware applications. With this pattern, we are not creating code that has to manage resources such as memory; rather, we want to control how the resources are used. Of key significance is ensuring that garbage collection occurs on our terms rather than waiting for Java's default garbage collection system to kick into action. In this section, we will look at an implementation example regarding file processing. Our example will include a look at file-processing source code before the loan design pattern is implemented, and then we will modify the code using the loan design pattern. We will see how the two approaches can be used with the same results.

Implementing file processing

In order to understand the power of the loan design pattern, we will implement a file-processing application demonstrating source code before and after using the loan pattern. Our application will simulate the opening and closing of a file with an additional four processing steps. The workflow is as depicted in this diagram:

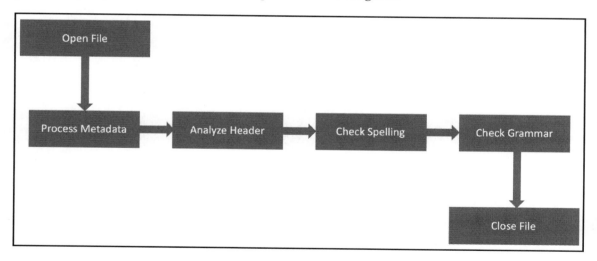

File-processing workflow

Our implementation will consist of a `FileToProcess` class and a `Driver` class. The `FileToProcess` class is provided next in two sections. This class contains a default constructor and six public methods, each providing console output to indicate that the method was called. This first section includes the class header, the constructor method, and the `openFile()` method. As you can see, the `openFile()` method simply outputs a text statement to the console, simulating that the file is open. This application is for demonstrative purposes and does not actually open or process any files:

```
public class FileToProcess {

    // constructor
    public FileToProcess() {
    }

    public FileToProcess openFile() {
        System.out.println("\nFile opened for processing");
        return this;
    }
```

The second part of the `FileToProcess` class contains the `processMetaData()`, `analyzeHeader()`, `checkSpelling()`, `checkGrammar()`, and `closeFile()` methods. Each of these methods simply outputs text to the console:

```
    public FileToProcess processMetaData() {
        System.out.println("\tProcessing metadata. . .");
        return this;
    }

    public FileToProcess analyzeHeader() {
        System.out.println ("\tAnalyzing header. . .");
        return this;
    }

    public FileToProcess checkSpelling() {
        System.out.println("\tChecking spelling. . . ");
        return this;
    }

    public FileToProcess checkGrammar() {
        System.out.println("\tChecking grammar. . . ");
        return this;
    }

    public void closeFile() {
        System.out.println("File closed");
    }
}
```

Our application's `Driver` class contains the `main()` method. That method, provided next, starts by creating an instance of a `FileToProcess` class named `myFile`. We then use method chaining to call each of the methods in the `FileToProcess` class. These six chained method calls are called and executed in the specific order we desire and as specified in the previously provided workflow:

```
public class Driver {

  public static void main(String[] args) {
  FileToProcess myFile = new FileToProcess();

  myFile.openFile().processMetaData().analyzeHeader()
            .checkSpelling().checkGrammar().closeFile();
    }
}
```

Here is the output of our application:

```
File opened for processing
    Processing metadata. . .
    Analyzing header. . .
    Checking spelling. . .
    Checking grammar. . .
File closed
```

Loan design pattern—file-processing implementation console output

Our application works well and does not yet implement the loan functional design pattern. The problem with the application, as it is currently written, is that we place the onus on the developer to ensure the six methods are called in the specific order intended by the workflow. If the application was programmed with improper logic, such as closing the file before opening it or performing a processing step after the file is closed, we will run into problems. These potential problems could be overcome with a bunch of code that tests whether specific processes were completed prior to others starting. This would be tedious and would not result in a clean code base for an application.

Let's use the loan design pattern to enforce this functionality. First, we will update the `FileToProcess` class in our previous example and rename it `FileToProcess2`. Here is the first section of that class:

```
import java.util.function.Consumer;

public class FileToProcess2 {

    // constructor
```

```
protected FileToProcess2() {
    openFile();
}

public static void processFile(final Consumer<FileToProcess2> block) {
    final FileToProcess2 theFile = new FileToProcess2();

    block.accept(theFile);

    theFile.closeFile();
}
```

We changed the constructor so that a call is made to the openFile() method when a FileToProcess2 object is instantiated. This gives the object the responsibility for opening the file.

As you can see from the previous code segment, we import Java's Consumer class, which is used to implement functional programming.

The remaining portion of the FileToProcess2 class simply contains the individual processing methods along with the closeFile() method, each providing contextual output to the console. Here is that code:

```
public FileToProcess2 openFile() {
    System.out.println("\nFile opened for processing by constructor");
    return this;
}

public FileToProcess2 processMetaData() {
    System.out.println("\tProcessing metadata. . .");
    return this;
}

public FileToProcess2 analyzeHeader() {
    System.out.println ("\tAnalyzing header. . .");
    return this;
}

public FileToProcess2 checkSpelling() {
    System.out.println("\tChecking spelling. . . ");
    return this;
}

public FileToProcess2 checkGrammar() {
    System.out.println("\tChecking grammar. . . ");
    return this;
}
```

```
        public void closeFile() {
            System.out.println("File closed");
        }
    }
```

Next, we can modify the `Driver` class from the previous example and rename it `Driver2`. Here is the updated `Driver2` class source code:

```
public class Driver2 {

    public static void main(String[] args) {

        FileToProcess2.processFile(theFile -> theFile.processMetaData()
                .analyzeHeader().checkSpelling().checkGrammar());
    }
}
```

The output for our application is the same as with our previous example with one small difference. We updated the `openFile()` method to indicate that the simulated file was opened for processing by the constructor. Here is the updated console output from our application:

```
File opened for processing by constructor
    Processing metadata. . .
    Analyzing header. . .
    Checking spelling. . .
    Checking grammar. . .
File closed
```

Loan design pattern—updated file-processing implementation console output

This section provided the source code and the console output for our file-processing implementation of the loan functional design pattern.

Understanding the MapReduce design pattern

The MapReduce functional design pattern is used for large-scale parallel-programming. Google developed this functional design pattern to take large tasks and break them up into smaller tasks. These smaller tasks are then run in parallel and produce a consolidated result. The goal of the MapReduce functional design pattern was for performance gains when processing large datasets, also referred to as *big data*.

Big-data processing and detailed analysis of the MapReduce functional design pattern are complex concepts and are beyond the scope of this chapter. In order to appreciate the MapReduce design pattern, we will briefly cover the following implementation approaches:

- Input-Map-Output
- Input-Map-Reduce-Output
- Input-Multiple Maps-Reduce-Output
- Input-Map-Combiner-Reduce-Output

Input-Map-Output

The Input-Map-Output form of the MapReduce functional design pattern can be used without the `reduce` component. This will be implemented when there is a need to change data formats and not perform aggregate calculations. An overview of the process is provided in the following diagram:

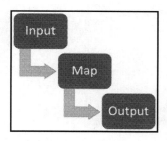

MapReduce design pattern—Input-Map-Output

To demonstrate this approach, we will use the scenario of a faculty registry system that is being cleaned up. We will handle each step in this pattern in the subsections that follow.

Input

For our example, let's assume that we have a faculty registry containing over 4,000 full-time and adjunct instructors for a non-specific university. The registry names have become corrupted over the years, mostly due to poor data entry controls. For example, here are several different forms of current faculty entries (displayed here for a single faculty member for comparison). The faculty member listed next has the full name `Thomas A. Anderson` and a nickname of `Neo`:

```
Thomas Anderson
Thomas A. Anderson
```

```
Anderson, Thomas
Anderson, T. A.
Anderson, Thomas A.
Neo Anderson
Anderson, Neo
N. Anderson
T. Anderson
T. A. Anderson
```

Having these many possible variations makes the faculty look up and search for problems. In addition to the different forms, capitalization might be inconsistent.

Map

The map component might consist of creating keys based on the last name. Given our scenario, we might need to reference an additional data field to ensure we properly identify the last name.

We would do the same for the first name. For the middle name, we might allow middle initials as well as middle names, as it might be difficult to obtain any missing data.

Output

Our final output would be a list of names in the proper format to include capitalization. Our selected format might be this:

```
Last name, First Name <Middle initial OR Middle name>
```

The final results would be an updated faculty registry with each entry in the same format.

Input-Map-Reduce-Output

To illustrate the Input-Map-Reduce-Output form of the MapReduce functional design pattern, we will use the scenario of student grade-point averages by school year. An overview of the process is provided in this diagram:

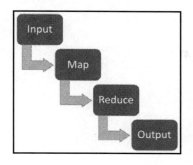

MapReduce design pattern—Input-Map-Reduce-Output

We will handle each step of this pattern in the subsections that follow.

Input

Here is the data used for the Input-Map-Output scenario:

Student	Grade	Grade-Point Average
Tom Zarek	Freshman	3.8
William Adama	Senior	4.0
Galen Tyrol	Senior	2.7
Gaius Baltar	Sophomore	3.1
D'Anna Biers	Junior	3.9
Kara Thrace	Junior	2.6
Sharon Valeri	Sophomore	3.2
Laura Roslin	Senior	3.9
Saul Tigh	Freshman	3.3
Felix Gaeta	Freshman	3.4
Tory Foster	Junior	2.8
Anastasia Dualla	Sophomore	3.0

As you can see, we have several students in each of the grade categories.

Map

Looking at the representative data in the previous section, we know we create a data grade key and then key-value pairs. Here is how that would look given our previous dataset:

```
{ (Freshman, 3.8), (Senior, 4.0), (Senior, 2.7),
  (Sophomore, 3.1), (Junior, 3.9), (Junior, 2.6),
  (Sophomore, 3.2), (Senior, 3.9), (Freshman, 3.3),
  (Freshman, 3.4), (Junior, 2.8), (Sophomore, 3.0) }
```

The next step will be `reduce`.

Reduce

Give your key-value pair maps; we can reduce that data into an intermediate form as indicated:

```
{
  ( Freshman [3.8, 3.3, 3.4] ),
  ( Sophomore [3.1, 3.2, 3.0] ),
  ( Junior [3.9, 2.6, 2.8] ),
  ( Senior [ 4.0, 2.7, 3.9] )
}
```

Our last step is the output from the `reduce` process.

Output

The final output of the Input-Map-Reduce-Output implementation is provided here:

```
{
  ( Freshman, 3.5 ),
  ( Sophomore, 3.1 ),
  ( Junior, 3.1 ),
  ( Senior, 3.5 )
}
```

The results provided are the aggregate grade-point averages based on the school year.

Input-Multiple Maps-Reduce-Output

The Input-Multiple Maps-Reduce-Output implementation of the MapReduce functional design pattern is similar to the Input-Map-Reduce-Output implementation. With multiple maps, there would be multiple sources of input, each with different formats.

An overview of the workflow is illustrated in this diagram:

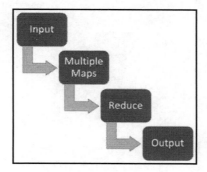

MapReduce design pattern—Input-Multiple Maps-Reduce-Output

We will handle each step in this pattern in the subsections that follow.

Input

To extend our university faculty registry example, we might be combining two registries: one for the full-time faculty and one for the adjunct faculty. This scenario is relevant for multiple data sources, with different formatting schemas, that can be aggregated into a single output.

Multiple maps

The following diagram shows how more than one map component can exist, each with a separate input stream, database source, or data file:

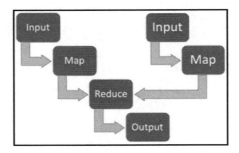

MapReduce design pattern—multiple maps

The last two components of this approach are `reduce` and `output`, which work as with the Input-Map-Reduce-Output implementation detailed earlier.

Input-Map-Combiner-Reduce-Output

The Input-Map-Combiner-Reduce-Output approach introduces the combiner into the process. A combiners is a smaller version of a reducer. This diagram illustrates where combiners fall within the workflow:

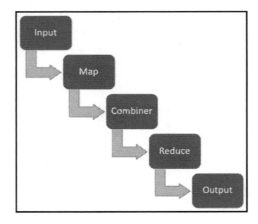

MapReduce design pattern—Input-Map-Combiner-Reduce-Output

The combiners reside after the `map` component and before the `reduce` component. Referencing this from a code perspective, the `Combiner` class would receive input from the `Map` class and pass the results to the `Reduce` class.

This section provided an overview of four implementations of the MapReduce functional design pattern.

Understanding the memoization design pattern

The memoization functional design pattern stores the results of key functions so that overall processing efficiency is increased. When there are specific processes that have the same output each time they are invoked, it is less costly, from a processing time perspective, to cache the results instead of recalculating them each time.

The Fibonacci sequence is often used to demonstrate memoization, so it shall be used here as well.

 Fibonacci numbers are a mathematical construct where each number is the sum of the two preceding numbers. The Fibonacci sequence starts with the numbers 0 and 1.

Let's start by looking at a standard implementation of the Fibonacci sequence. Here is the source code:

```
public class FibonacciTest1 {

    public static int computeFibonacciNumber(int number) {

        // this checks for the fibonacci base of 0 and 1
        if ( (number == 0) || ( number == 1) ) {
            return number;
        }

        System.out.println("Computing computeFibonacciNumber(int " + number
+ ")...");

        return (computeFibonacciNumber(number - 1)) +
(computeFibonacciNumber(number - 2));
    }

    public static void main(String[] args) {
```

```
        System.out.println();
        computeFibonacciNumber(7);
    }
}
```

Next, let's show an example of the output of the `FibonacciTest1` class. As you can see, there were several duplicate-processing steps that took place:

```
Computing computeFibonacciNumber(int 7)...
Computing computeFibonacciNumber(int 6)...
Computing computeFibonacciNumber(int 5)...
Computing computeFibonacciNumber(int 4)...
Computing computeFibonacciNumber(int 3)...
Computing computeFibonacciNumber(int 2)...
Computing computeFibonacciNumber(int 2)...
Computing computeFibonacciNumber(int 3)...
Computing computeFibonacciNumber(int 2)...
Computing computeFibonacciNumber(int 4)...
Computing computeFibonacciNumber(int 3)...
Computing computeFibonacciNumber(int 2)...
Computing computeFibonacciNumber(int 2)...
Computing computeFibonacciNumber(int 5)...
Computing computeFibonacciNumber(int 4)...
Computing computeFibonacciNumber(int 3)...
Computing computeFibonacciNumber(int 2)...
Computing computeFibonacciNumber(int 2)...
Computing computeFibonacciNumber(int 3)...
Computing computeFibonacciNumber(int 2)...
```

Fibonacci processing output—without memoization design pattern

As you can see, there is great computational waste. With this example, there are 20 output lines, signifying 20 calls to the `computeFibonacciNumber()` method. A review of this table highlights the duplicative nature of the method calls:

Method Call	Times Processed
computeFibonacciNumber(int 7)	1
computeFibonacciNumber(int 6)	1
computeFibonacciNumber(int 5)	2
computeFibonacciNumber(int 4)	3
computeFibonacciNumber(int 3)	5
computeFibonacciNumber(int 2)	8

As you can see, there is a lot of processing waste. If we started with a larger number, the amount of waste would skyrocket. For example, if we started with `computeFibonacciNumber(300)`, there would be a total of 24,372 output lines. As you can see from the next table, `computeFibonacciNumber(int 3)` would be processed 5,757 times and `computeFibonacciNumber(int 2)` would be processed 9,315 times:

Method Call	Times Processed
computeFibonacciNumber(int 7)	839
computeFibonacciNumber(int 6)	1,358
computeFibonacciNumber(int 5)	2,198
computeFibonacciNumber(int 4)	3,558
computeFibonacciNumber(int 3)	5,757
computeFibonacciNumber(int 2)	9,315

The previous table is abbreviated for representative brevity and only shows `int` values of 7 and below.

If you are running this test on your computer, please note that it can take a long time to process large Fibonacci numbers.

Let's now try this same application using the memoization design pattern. We will use a hash map in our solution. The first section of our `FibonacciTest2` class is displayed next. The class imports two classes (`java.util.Map` and `java.util.HashMap`) in order to implement the `HashMap` instance. The start of the `computeFibonacciNumber()` method is also in this section and checks to see whether the number is equal to one of the Fibonacci base numbers (0 or 1):

```java
import java.util.Map;
import java.util.HashMap;

class FibonacciTest2 {

    private static Map<Integer, Integer> memoization = new HashMap<>();

    public static int computeFibonacciNumber(int number) {

        // this checks for the fibonacci base of 0 and 1
        if ( (number == 0) || ( number == 1) ) {
            return number;
        }
```

The second section of our `FibonacciTest2` class is the final section of the
`computeFibonacciNumber()` method and shows three steps. The first step is to check
whether a calculation has already been made. If it has, then we retrieve the result from our
`HashMap` instead of performing the calculation. The second step performs the calculation if
it has not already been calculated. The third step is to add the result to the `HashMap`, the
first time the calculation is performed:

```
// Step 1: Check if calculation has already been made
if (memoization.containsKey(number)) {
    System.out.println("First time computing memoization " + number);
    return memoization.get(number);
}

// Step 2: Calculate if not already calculated
System.out.println("Computing computeFibonacciNumber(int " + number +
")...");
    int fibonacciResult = (computeFibonacciNumber(number - 1)) +
(computeFibonacciNumber(number - 2));

// Step 3: Add result to Map
memoization.put(number, fibonacciResult);

    return fibonacciResult;
}
```

The final section of our `FibonacciTest2` class is the `main()` method, which prints a blank
line and then invokes the `computeFibonacciNumber()` method, passing 7 as the
parameter:

```
public static void main(String[] args) {

    System.out.println();
    computeFibonacciNumber(7);
}
}
```

The result of the application is provided in the following screenshot of the console output:

```
Computing computeFibonacciNumber(int 7)...
Computing computeFibonacciNumber(int 6)...
Computing computeFibonacciNumber(int 5)...
Computing computeFibonacciNumber(int 4)...
Computing computeFibonacciNumber(int 3)...
Computing computeFibonacciNumber(int 2)...
First time computing memoization 2
First time computing memoization 3
First time computing memoization 4
First time computing memoization 5
```

Fibonacci processing output—with memoization design pattern

This section provided the source code and the console output for our implementations of the memoization functional design pattern.

Understanding the streams design pattern

The streams functional design pattern presents a pipeline functionality used to transform data. In this sense, transforming data is different from mutating data. Data is transformed in the stream, but not mutated. In order to obtain the transformed data, a call must be made to the terminal operation. Once a stream is closed, it can no longer be accessed, nor can the transformed data.

The following table provides a lexicon of terminology relevant to the streams functional design pattern:

Term	Explanation
Stream	A pipeline of functionality.
Transform	Changing data in the stream.
Mutation	Permanently changing data.
Creator	Creating a stream generates an infinite sequential unordered stream.
Intermediate operation	Returns a stream and supports querying when a terminal operation is executed.
Terminal operation	Provides a non-stream result.

The following diagram depicts how the streams functional design pattern workflow is implemented:

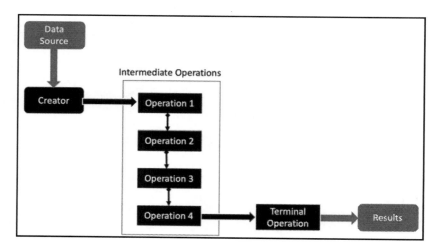

Streams functional design pattern—overview

We will next take a closer look at the intermediate operations followed by the terminal operation.

Stream intermediate operations

There are eight intermediate operations for streams. These operations are methods and are listed next, separated by their return type:

Stream	IntStream	LongStream	DoubleStream
district()	flatMapToInt()	flatMapToLong()	flatMapToDouble()
filter()	maptoInt()	mapToLong()	mapToDouble()
flatMap()			
limit()			
map()			
peek()			
skip()			
sorted()			

Understanding the return type of these stream operations will help with their implementation.

Stream terminal operations

There are 13 terminal operations for streams. These operations are methods and are listed in alphabetical order next:

- allMatch()
- anyMatch()
- collect()
- count()
- findAny()
- findFirst()
- forEach()
- forEachOrdered()
- max()
- min()
- noneMatch()
- reduce()
- toArray()

Programming the streams design pattern

The StreamExample class provided next demonstrates the streams design pattern. The class imports the Stream class, which is part of the java.util.stream package. There are three chained calls made to the peek(), limit(), and forEach() methods:

```
import java.util.stream.Stream;

public class StreamExample {

    public static void main(String[] args) {

        System.out.println();

        Stream.iterate(0, x->x+3)
 .peek(number -> System.out.print("\nPeeked at: "))
 .limit(7)
 .forEach(System.out::println);
    }
}
```

The output of the `StreamExample` class is provided here:

```
Peeked at: 0

Peeked at: 3

Peeked at: 6

Peeked at: 9

Peeked at: 12

Peeked at: 15

Peeked at: 18
```

Streams design pattern implementation—console output

This section provided the source code and the console output for our `streamSample` implementation of the streams functional design pattern.

Understanding the tail call design pattern

The tail call functional design pattern is a subroutine, or a tail-recursive function, that is executed at the end of a procedure. This design pattern is also referred to as the **Tail Call Optimization** (**TCO**). The concept of this pattern is straightforward. The tail call is the last call performed by a method.

In the next section, we will implement the tail call functional design pattern.

Programming the tail call design pattern

To demonstrate the tail call functional design pattern, we will implement a `Lucky 7` application consisting of a single `TailCallExample` class. This class will prompt the user for a number and perform multiple mathematical on the number that will result in 7, regardless of the input.

The first section of code starts with the `import` statement. We will use the `Scanner` class to obtain user input from the console window. The following code also contains `theInitialNumber`, an `int` class variable. Next is the first section of the `main()` method, which simply prompts the user for input and stores the result in the `theInitialNumber` class variable. This value will be used throughout our application:

```java
import java.util.Scanner;

public class TailCallExample {

    public static int theInitialNumber;

    public static void main(String[] args) {

        Scanner in = new Scanner(System.in);
        System.out.println("\n\nI can turn your number into 7.");
        System.out.print("Enter a number: ");
        theInitialNumber = in.nextInt();
```

The second section of the `TailCallExample` class is provided next and completes the `main()` method. This section of code prints a decorative header to the console window. It also prints the value of `theInitialNumber` to the console window for reference. Next, the result label is printed along with the results based on the `executeThisMethod(theInitialNumber)` method call. This method call is the last call for this method and is therefore the tail call:

```java
        // Display system header
        System.out.println("\n=========================");
        System.out.println("ANY NUMBER CAN BE LUCKY 7");
        System.out.println("=========================");

        System.out.println("\nThe initial number: " + theInitialNumber);

        System.out.println("The tail call sent this as the result: " +
                (excecuteThisMethod(theInitialNumber))); // tail call
    }
```

The next section of the `TailCallExample` class is the `executeThisMethod()` method. As you will see in the next code block, the method has a local `funWithNumbers` variable. The method also invokes the following methods in sequential order—`operation1()`, `operation2()`, `operation3()`, `operation4()`, and `operation5()`. Finally, the `return(funWithNumbers)` statement is executed. The `operation5()` method call is the last one called in the `executeThisMethod()` method, making it the tail call. It might be tempting to assume the `return` statement is the tail call, but it is not a method, so it cannot be the tail call for this or any method:

```
private static int excecuteThisMethod(int theNumber) {

    int funWithNumbers;

    funWithNumbers = operation1(theNumber);

    funWithNumbers = operation2(funWithNumbers);

    funWithNumbers = operation3(funWithNumbers);

    funWithNumbers = operation4(funWithNumbers);

    funWithNumbers = operation5(funWithNumbers); // tail call

    return(funWithNumbers);
}
```

The final segment of the `TailCallExample` class is provided next and contains the `operation1()`, `operation2()`, `operation3()`, `operation4()`, and `operation(5)` methods. Each one of those methods makes a call to the `println()` method, which is, in each case, the tail call for those methods:

```
private static int operation1(int theNbr) {
    System.out.println("\t+ 9 = " + (theNbr + 9)); // tail call
    return theNbr + 9;
}
private static int operation2(int theNbr) {
    System.out.println("\t* 2 = " + (theNbr * 2)); // tail call
    return theNbr * 2;
}
private static int operation3(int theNbr) {
    System.out.println("\t- 4 = " + (theNbr - 4)); // tail call
    return theNbr - 4;
}
private static int operation4(int theNbr) {
    System.out.println("\t/ 2 = " + (theNbr / 2)); // tail call
    return theNbr / 2;
```

```
    }
    private static int operation5(int theNbr) {
        System.out.println("\t- initial number = " + (theNbr -
theInitialNumber)); // tail call
        return (theNbr - theInitialNumber);
    }
}
```

The output for our application is provided here:

```
The intial number: 4500
    + 9 = 4509
    * 2 = 9018
    - 4 = 9014
    / 2 = 4507
    - initial number = 7
The tail call sent this as the result: 7
```

Tail call design pattern implementation—console output

This section provided the source code and the console output for our `Lucky 7` implementation of the tail call functional design pattern.

Summary

In this chapter, we examined the functional design pattern category and eight specific design patterns. We learned that functional design patterns are not the same as functional programming and that they are both considered programming paradigms. The term *functional design patterns* refers to the use of functional programming to solve computational problems. The functional design patterns covered in this chapter were the execute around pattern, the lambda pattern, the loan pattern, the MapReduce pattern, the memoization pattern, the streams pattern, and the tail call pattern.

In the next chapter, *Reactive Design Patterns*, we will explore the reactive design pattern category and its individual design patterns of asynchronous communication, autoscaling, bounded queue, bulkhead, caching, circuit breaker, event-driven communication, fail fast, failure handling, fan-out and quickest reply, idempotency, monitoring, publisher-subscriber, self-containment, and stateless.

Questions

1. What are the three rules for functions using a functional design approach?
2. List seven functional design patterns.
3. What functional model is used by functional programming?
4. Which design pattern encapsulates a pair of actions in the actual objects that require the pair of actions?
5. Which design pattern uses anonymous functions?
6. Which design pattern can be used to create resource-aware applications?
7. Which design pattern is used for large-scale parallel-programming?
8. Which design pattern stores the results of key functions so that the overall processing efficiency is increased?
9. Which design pattern presents a pipeline functionality used to transform data?
10. Which design pattern is a subroutine that is executed at the end of a procedure?

Further reading

- *Java EE 8 Design Patterns and Best Practices* (https://www.packtpub.com/application-development/java-ee-8-design-patterns-and-best-practices)
- *Learn Design Patterns with Java [Video]* (https://www.packtpub.com/application-development/learn-design-patterns-java-video)
- *Design Patterns and Best Practices in Java* (https://www.packtpub.com/application-development/design-patterns-and-best-practices-java)
- *Learning Big Data with Amazon Elastic MapReduce* (https://www.packtpub.com/virtualization-and-cloud/learning-big-data-amazon-elastic-mapreduce)

9
Reactive Design Patterns

In the previous chapter, *Functional Design Patterns*, we examined the functional design pattern category and compared functional design to functional programming. We reviewed and implemented the execute around pattern, lambda pattern, loan pattern, MapReduce pattern, memoization pattern, streams pattern, and tail call pattern.

In this chapter, we will explore the reactive design pattern category and its individual design patterns of asynchronous communication, autoscaling, bounded queue, bulkhead, caching, circuit breaker, event-driven communication, fail fast, failure-handling, fan-out and quickest reply, idempotency, monitoring, publisher-subscriber, self-containment, and stateless. Our exploration of the reactive design patterns is fueled by the desire to design and develop systems that have characteristics of resilient, reliable, scalable, and message-driven. Implementing the design patterns can help us achieve those system characteristics.

Specifically, we will cover the following in this chapter:

- Introducing reactive design patterns
- Asynchronous communication design pattern
- Autoscaling design pattern
- Bounded queue design pattern
- Bulkhead design pattern
- Caching design pattern
- Circuit-breaker design pattern
- Event-driven communication design pattern
- Fail-fast design pattern
- Failure-handling design pattern
- Fan-out and quickest-reply design pattern
- Idempotency design pattern
- Monitoring design pattern

- Publisher-subscriber design pattern
- Self-containment design pattern
- Stateless design pattern

Technical requirements

The code for this chapter can be found at
`https://github.com/PacktPublishing/Hands-On-Design-Patterns-with-Java/tree/master/Chapter09`.

Introducing reactive design patterns

Reactive design patterns exist to provide system architects, engineers, and developers with the ability to create systems that are, at their core, responsive and scalable. Using a reactive design pattern helps ensure that a system will be both maintainable and able to react to external changes such as resource changes and new connectivity. One of the goals of creating systems with one of these design patterns was to avoid redesigning the system because it was not responsive to change.

The concept of designing systems that are reactive to change can be considered an approach to future-proofing a system. We want, as much as possible, to design our systems so they can react to events and changes for the foreseeable future.

Reactive design patterns were generated from reactive programming and documented in the form of a *Reactive Manifesto*. This is a document that outlines rules and approaches to using reactive programming and reactive design patterns. This manifesto establishes four characteristics:

- Responsive
- Resilient
- Elastic
- Message-driven

Each of these characteristics is explained in the sections that follow.

Responsive

When a system is responsive, it is said to be able to respond to events quickly. This does not simply refer to processing data or objects; it is more significant than that. The desired level of responsiveness includes rapid identification of issues, a determination of what type of response is necessary, and then the actual response.

We will highlight the responsive nature of the reactive design patterns featured in this chapter.

Resilient

Resilient systems are ones that have a tremendous up-time and are impervious to errors. Designing a system to be resilient involves extensive error-handling, data redundancy, distributed processing, and other concepts that will be further explored in this chapter. Resilient systems do not have a single point of failure. For example, instead of having a single database, a resilient system might employ replication of a database. Labeling a system as resilient not only signifies that the overall system is resilient but that the components and sub-components are as well.

We will highlight the resilient nature of the reactive design patterns featured in this chapter.

Elastic

An elastic system has the ability to upscale and downscale based on system needs. An example of this might be when an eCommerce site needs additional servers, gateways, and other system components to react to an exponential increase in site visits during a holiday season.

It is important to highlight that the elasticity of a system includes the ability to both upscale and downscale system resources. Depending on the system used, this elasticity can be controlled using predictive analysis and specialized algorithms to detect when specific system components reach specific high and low levels.

We will highlight the elastic nature of the reactive design patterns featured in this chapter.

Message-driven

The fourth characteristic of reactive design patterns is that they are message-driven. This characteristic means that reactive systems have a reliance on the messages that are passed between system components. This message passing is asynchronous and enables a system to isolate system failures. The strong reliance on message passing enables elasticity, node-control, and processing load control.

We will highlight the message-driven nature of the reactive design patterns featured in this chapter.

 The four characteristics of reactive design patterns (responsive, resilient, elastic, and message-driven) are also the four principles of reactive programming and reactive design patterns.

Each of the reactive design patterns in this chapter can be assigned to one or more of the four characteristics defined previously.

The following table provides that categorical grouping:

Responsive	Resilient	Elastic	Message-driven
Asynchronous communication	Bounded queue	Autoscaling	Event-driven communication
Caching	Bulkhead	Self-contained	Idempotency
Fail-fast	Circuit breaker	Stateless	Publisher-subscriber
Fan-out and quickest reply	Failure-handling		
	Monitoring		

Reactive design pattern groupings

The reactive design features in the remainder of this chapter are presented in alphabetical order to illustrate that one is not more important than the others.

Understanding the asynchronous communication design pattern

Earlier in this chapter, we identified one of the reactive design principles as asynchronous message-driven communication. That principle is core to the asynchronous communication design pattern:

1. First, the client sends a request message to a server
2. Next, the server sends an acknowledgement message to the client immediately and then takes whatever time is necessary to process the request
3. Once the request is fully processed, the response message is sent from the server to the client

This diagram illustrates three components of asynchronous communication:

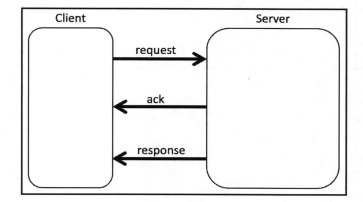

Asynchronous communication design pattern implementation—overview

This method of communication is efficient because it allows the client to send multiple request messages to the server and not dedicate processing resources, and anticipate a response message from the server. The client understands that the server will eventually send the response message and it can allocate the processing resources at that time.

Implementing the asynchronous communication design pattern

The most common approach to implementing the asynchronous communication reactive design pattern is with asynchronous callbacks. The basic process of implementing asynchronous callbacks is illustrated next. The process starts with the client authenticating itself to the server. The client sends the request message to the server and subscribes to the server. The server sends an immediate acknowledgement message, processes the request, and then sends a response message. The client receives the response and conducts any follow-on processing:

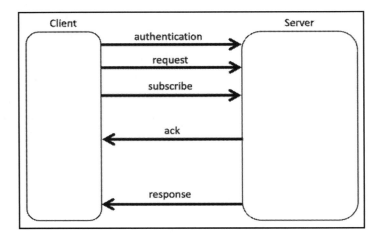

Asynchronous communication design pattern implementation—details

The next UML diagram depicts the class structure of an implementation example. The solution includes a `CallbackListener` interface and `CallerOne` and `CallerTwo` classes. Only the `CallerOne` class implements the `CallbackListener` interface:

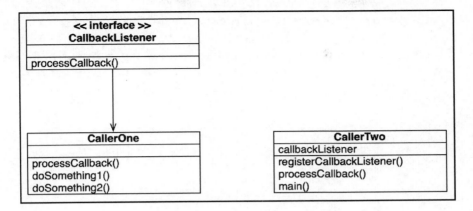

UML class diagram—asynchronous communication design pattern implementation

Let's take a look at an example of this design pattern in code. The first segment of code is the CallbackListener interface. It contains a simple processCallback() method that the CallerOne class will override. The CallerTwo class will not override the method, but will still contain its own processCallback() method as it does not implement the CallbackListener interface:

```
package CH9AsynchronousCommunication;

public interface CallbackListener {

    void processCallback();
}
```

The CallerOne class is provided next in four sequential sections. The first section, provided next, contains the package declaration as well as four import statements. The classes imported will support the doSomething2() method:

```
package CH9AsynchronousCommunication;

import java.util.ArrayList;
import java.util.Collections;
import java.util.List;
import java.util.ListIterator;

public class CallerOne implements CallbackListener {
```

The second section of the `CallerOne` class is provided next. The `CallerOne` class has three methods; the first of them, the `processCallback()` method, is shown here. When called, this method prints to the console window to simulate processing messages. Two method calls, one each to `doSomething1()` and `doSomething2()`, are made for further message processing simulation:

```
@Override
public void processCallback()
{
    System.out.println("\nAsynchronous Task Completed Followed by
Callback.");

    System.out.println("\tSimulated processing from Caller One . . . ");
    doSomething1(34, 12);

    System.out.println("\tSimulated processing from Caller Two . . . ");
    doSomething2("nrettaP ngiseD noitacinummoC suonorhcnysA");
    System.out.println();
}
```

The third section of the `CallerOne` class contains the `doSomething1()` method and is provided next. This method simply determines the larger of the two `int` arguments and provides output to the console window. The `doSomething1()` method was included in the example implementation of the asynchronous communication reactive design pattern to simulate additional processing:

```
public void doSomething1(int x, int y) {

    // determine and output max value
    System.out.println("\t\tThe largest number is " + Math.max(x, y));
}
```

The fourth and final section of the `CallerOne` class is provided next and contains the `doSomething2()` method. This method simply takes the `String` argument and prints the same `String`, in reverse character order, to the console window. This is accomplished using an `ArrayList`, and a `ListIterator`. The `doSomething2()` method was included in the example to simulate additional processing of our implementation of the asynchronous communication reactive design pattern:

```
    public void doSomething2(String backwardsPhrase) {

        // reverse a string
        char[] phrase = backwardsPhrase.toCharArray();
        List<Character> newPhrase = new ArrayList<>();

        for (char character: phrase)
```

```
                newPhrase.add(character);

            Collections.reverse(newPhrase);
            ListIterator myInterator = newPhrase.listIterator();

            System.out.print("\t\tResultant Phrase: ");
            while (myInterator.hasNext())
                System.out.print(myInterator.next());
        }
    }
```

The `CallerTwo` class is presented in three sections. The first section, provided next, creates a `callbackListener` object. The next operation performed by this class is to register `callbackLister`. This is done with the `registerCallbackListener()` method:

```
    package CH9AsynchronousCommunication;

    public class CallerTwo {

        // create callbackListener object
        private CallbackListener callbackListener;

        // setting up the callbacklistener
        public void registerCallbackListener(CallbackListener callbackListener)
        {
            this.callbackListener = callbackListener;
        }
```

The second section of the `CallerTwo` class includes the `processCallback()` method. This is an asynchronous operation for the `CallerTwo` class. We accomplish this by creating a new thread for the operation and using a lambda expression.

 More information on lambda expressions can be found in `Chapter 8`, *Functional Design Patterns*.

As you can see from the following code, we must check to see whether the `callbackListener` is registered. If it does not exist, we call the `processCallback()` method from the `CallerOne` class:

```
    // asynchronous operation for CallerTwo
    public void processCallback()
    {
        // a new thread for the asynchronous operations using lambda
        new Thread(() -> {
```

```
        // simulated processing
        System.out.println("\nAsynchronous operations taking place . . .");
        System.out.println("\tSimulated processing from Caller Two. . . ");

        // check if callbackListener exists
        if (callbackListener != null) {

            // use processCallback() method of CallerOne
            callbackListener.processCallback();
        }
    }).start();
}
```

The final section of the `CallerTwo` class is the `main()` method. As you can see from the following code, there are only four lines of code. The first line creates an instance of `CallerTwo` named `asynchronousMessage`. The second line creates a `CallbackListener` instance and calls it `callbackListener`. Our third line calls the `registerCallbackListerner()` method of the `asynchronousMessage` object, passing the `callbackListener` created on the second line as the parameter. The fourth line calls the `processCallback()` method of the `asynchronousMessage` object:

```
    public static void main(String[] args)
    {
        CallerTwo asynchronousMessage = new CallerTwo(); // line 1

        CallbackListener callbackListener = new CallerOne(); // line 2

        asynchronousMessage.registerCallbackListener(callbackListener); //
line 3

        asynchronousMessage.processCallback(); // line 4
    }
}
```

The output of our program, using the `CallerTwo` class as our `Driver` class, is provided here:

```
Asynchronous operations taking place . . .
    Simulated processing from Caller Two. . .

Asynchronous Task Completed Followed by Callback.
    Simulated processing from Caller One . . .
        The largest number is 34
    Simulated processing from Caller Two . . .
        Resultant Phrase: Asynchronous Communication Design Pattern
```

Asynchronous communication design pattern implementation—console output

This section provided the source code and the console output for our implementation of the asynchronous communication reactive design pattern.

Understanding the autoscaling design pattern

The autoscaling design pattern typically refers to the ability to auto-scale processing and storage capacity, both by increasing and decreasing assets. This is one of the greatest benefits of using a cloud-based **Infrastructure as a Service (IaaS)**. The concept is simply that when you need additional capacity, your system is automatically scaled. Using the autoscaling reactive design pattern, our systems can automatically react to increases and decreases of system events such as increased or decreased web page visits, number of transactions, larger datasets, and so on.

As an example, we might have designed an online store with the ability to support 100 simultaneous potential customers. What if, during the holiday season, we receive 1,000 simultaneous users all querying our product catalog and processing orders? Our system might not be able to handle it. So, let's plan for 1,000 simultaneous users. If our site receives 10,000 simultaneous users, we still have a problem. If we decide to plan for 100,000 simultaneous users, our online store might perform well. The downside of that approach is that we do not want to waste capacity, because it is expensive.

The ideal solution is to design a system that is auto-scalable, but up and down. The following diagram shows the large divide between the low usage and high usage for a given system. As you can see, if our system was designed for low usage or even slightly higher usage, such as 20 or 30 million simultaneous users, the system would still fall short at least four months of the year. If we designed our system for high usage, 100 million simultaneous users, our system would perform well, but would have excess capacity 11 of the 12 months:

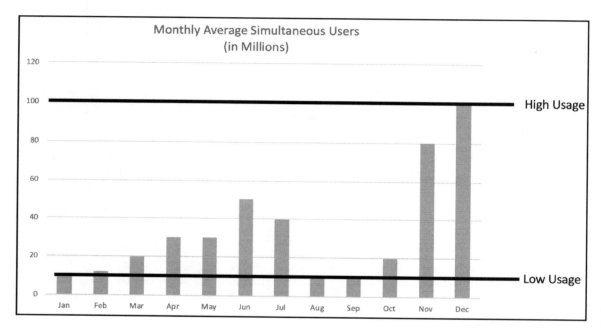

Autoscaling design pattern—usage disparity

Let's look at the same diagram but with a graph that shows the ideal capacity based on the usage. Here you can see that capacity is slightly above the usage. When we employ autoscaling, we always want a bit more capacity than we are using so there are no access- or system-related issues:

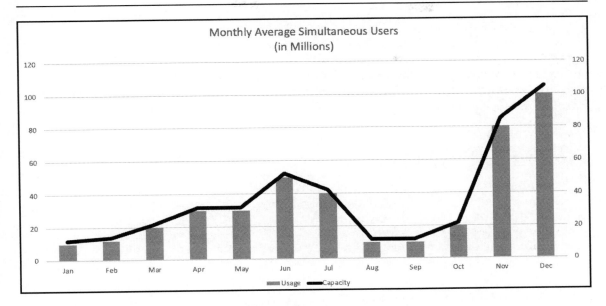

Autoscaling design pattern—ideal capacity-usage ratio

Now that we have some knowledge of autoscaling, let's look at the two types of autoscaling:

- Horizontal scaling
- Vertical scaling

We will review both of these autoscaling types in the next two sections.

Horizontal scaling

An example of horizontal scaling is when we increase or decrease our processing load such as with more servers or database servers. Since we only scale when our system requires it, we only pay for what we use. This underscores the importance of never having too much nor too little processing capability.

When we horizontally scale, we are scaling out. An easy way to remember this is that you would need to zoom out of your system's diagrams to see the additional servers on the same horizontal level.

Vertical scaling

Vertical scaling, also referred to as scaling up, involves adding increasing capacity with additional hardware. Examples include faster or more processors and adding memory capacity. Another example of vertical scaling would be to increase a database instance with larger RAM allocation.

Implementing autoscaling

To implement autoscaling, we would need to consult the operating instructions for our cloud-based service such as **Amazon Web Services (AWS)**, Microsoft Azure, Google Cloud Platform, IBM Cloud, Oracle Cloud, and so on.

This section provided an overview of the autoscaling reactive design pattern.

Understanding the bounded queue design pattern

Bounded queues are those that have a fixed number of elements. To implement a bounded queue in Java, we need to use the `java.util.concurrent` package. If we used the `java.util` package, our queues would not be bounded.

Let's implement the bounded queue reactive design pattern with a two-class program. Our implementation will consist of a `Bounded` class that extends the `Thread` class. We will also add a `Driver` class to contain our solution's `main()` method.

This first segment of code is the beginning of the `Bounded` class. It contains the `import` statement for the `java.util.concurrent.BlockingQueue` class. It also contains the class definition showing that it extends the `Thread` class. There is an `inputValue` class variable of a `BlockingQueue` type. Next, we have the class constructor method that takes a `BlockingQueue` object as an argument:

```
package CH9BoundedQueue;

import java.util.concurrent.BlockingQueue;

public class Bounded extends Thread {

    private BlockingQueue<Integer> inputValue;
```

```
Bounded(BlockingQueue<Integer> blockingQueue) {
    this.inputValue = blockingQueue;
}
```

The segment of the next code is the remaining portion of the `Bounded` class. It contains the `run()` method, which contains a `try` / `catch` statement. If the input value is not `null`, then the number will be squared and the appropriate results sent to the console:

```
public void run() {
    try {
        while (true) {
            Integer myInteger = inputValue.take();

            if (myInteger == null) {
                break;
            }
            System.out.println(myInteger + " squared is " +
                    (myInteger * myInteger));
        }
    } catch (InterruptedException e) {
        System.out.println("Interrupted Exception Encountered.");
    }
}
}
```

The next two segments of code comprise the `Driver` class. The first section, shown next, imports `ArrayBlockingQueue` and `BlockingQueue`. The `main()` method is declared and, as indicated, it throws the `InterruptedException` exception error. Lastly, the `boundedSize` int variable is set to `10`:

```
package CH9BoundedQueue;

import java.util.concurrent.ArrayBlockingQueue;
import java.util.concurrent.BlockingQueue;

public class Driver {

    public static void main(String[] args) throws InterruptedException {

        int boundedSize = 10;
```

The second portion of our `main()` method creates a `BlockingQueue` named `blockingQueue`. The `boundedThread` int is also created, as is the `bounded` array of the `Bounded` type. After a blank line is printed to the console, we have two `for` loops. The first `for` loop populates the `bounded` array and calls the `Thread start()` method. The second `for` loop puts elements into the `blockingQueue` queue:

```
        BlockingQueue<Integer> blockingQueue = new
    ArrayBlockingQueue<>(boundedSize);

        int boundedThread = 2;

        Bounded[] bounded = new Bounded[boundedThread];

        System.out.println();

        for (int i=0; i < bounded.length; i++) {
            bounded[i] = new Bounded(blockingQueue);
            bounded[i].start();
        }

        for (int i=1; i < 11; i++) {
            blockingQueue.put(i);
        }
    }
}
```

The output of our implementation is illustrated next:

```
1 squared is 1
2 squared is 4
3 squared is 9
4 squared is 16
5 squared is 25
6 squared is 36
7 squared is 49
8 squared is 64
9 squared is 81
10 squared is 100
```

Bounded queue design pattern implementation—console output

This section provided the source code and the console output for our implementation of the bounded queue reactive design pattern.

Understanding the bulkhead design pattern

Bulkheads on ships help isolate areas of the ship so that damage such as flooding, fire, or explosion impacts only one section of the ship and is not spread to other sections. Bulkheads also establish the stability of the overall ship. The bulkhead design pattern is based on the ship example. Instead of a ship, we are protecting the system.

Most non-trivial systems will involve multiple components. When those components are implemented in a manner that they are interdependent, systems can fail. As an example, review the system design illustrated next. As you can see, there are several points of failure. If the **Server** fails, nothing is accessible. Also, if one of the three modules fails, the connected database is inaccessible. These scenarios would make the entire system unusable:

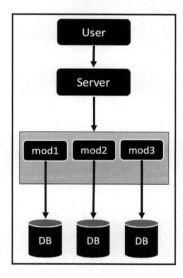

System without the bulkhead design pattern

Now let's take a look at what this same system would look like with the bulkhead design pattern implemented. Here, you can see a simulated bulkhead between the load balancers. These load balancers will determine to which server requests get routed. This provides isolation from server errors; when one server goes down, the other can be used. Also, in a dynamic cloud-computing environment, you would likely have a fail-safe set up to automatically spin up a new server instance as soon as one goes down. This would help ensure consistent up-time:

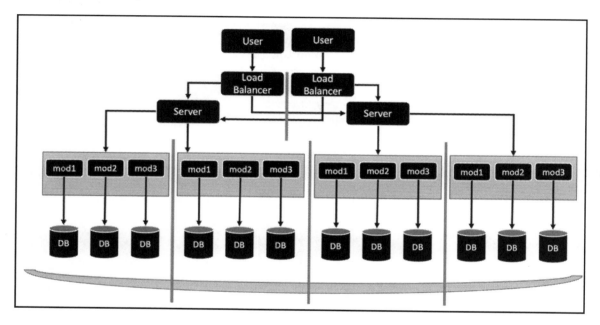

System with bulkhead design pattern

The preceding diagram also depicts how bulkheads can separate replicated processing models.

The bulkhead reactive design pattern is applied at the architectural level and most frequently when implementing cloud-based solutions.

This section provided an overview of the bulkhead reactive design pattern.

Understanding the caching design pattern

The concept of caching is to temporarily store data that makes accessing it faster. Caching is employed to help save on the use of resources. When we retrieve data, it should be made available for future requests for the same data. Implementing this saves on the processing time required for continual retrieval of the same data.

The next diagram provides a conceptual view of how caching is architected into a system. As you can see, there are several caches and a cache-management system that controls what is in a cache and how it is accessed. The diagram illustrates how redundancy can also be built into a caching system:

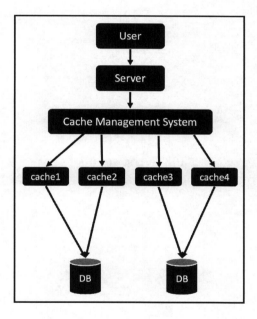

Conceptual view of caching

There is no single method of implementing caching in Java. In the next section, we will review one possible approach for implementing this design pattern.

Implementing the caching design pattern in Java

We will demonstrate the implementation of the caching design pattern with a simple example. We will create a `Player` class that is used to record a basketball team's all-time top scorers. We will create a pairing with jersey numbers and total points. We will also have an `ExampleCache` class and a `ClassDriver` class.

The `Player` class is provided next. It has four class variables and a `constructor` method:

```java
public class Player {

    int playerJersey;
    int playerPoints;
    Player before;
    Player next;

    // constructor
    public Player(int jersey, int points) {
        this.playerJersey = jersey;
        this.playerPoints = points;
    }
}
```

The `ExampleCache` class is presented in five sequential segments. The first segment contains the `import` statement for the `HashMap` class and the five class variables:

```java
import java.util.HashMap;

public class ExampleCache {

    // class variables
    private HashMap<Integer, Player> map;
    private int cacheCapacity;
    private int cacheCount;
    private Player playerHead;
    private Player playerTail;
```

The second segment of the `ExampleCache` class contains the `constructor` method. Here, you can see we are taking the cache's capacity as an argument:

```java
// constructor
public ExampleCache(int cCapacity) {
    this.cacheCapacity = cCapacity;

    map = new HashMap<>();
    playerHead = new Player(0,0);
    playerTail = new Player(0,0);
```

```
    playerHead.next = playerTail;
    playerTail.before = playerHead;
    playerHead.before = null;
    playerTail.next = null;
    cacheCount = 0;
}
```

The third segment of the `ExampleCache` class is provided next. Here, we have the `addToPlayerHead()` and `deletePlayer()` methods, each taking a `Player` object as an argument:

```
public void addToPlayerHead(Player player) {
    player.next = playerHead.next;
    player.next.before = player;
    player.before = playerHead;
    playerHead.next = player;
}

public void deletePlayer(Player player) {
    player.before.next = player.next;
    player.next.before = player.before;
}
```

The next code is the fourth segment of the `ExampleCache` class. It contains the `retrieve()` method. This method works by receiving a `playerJersey` int. If the jersey number is found in the cache, the matching total points score is provided; otherwise, an appropriate message is displayed on the console:

```
public int retrieve(int playerJersey) {
    if (map.get(playerJersey) != null) {
        Player player = map.get(playerJersey);
        int result = player.playerPoints;
        deletePlayer(player);
        addToPlayerHead(player);
        System.out.println("\t\t\t\t\t\t\t\t\tRETRIEVED: jersey -> " +
playerJersey +
                "\tPoints-> " + result);
        return result;
    }
    System.out.println("\t\t\t\t\t\t\t\t\tRETRIEVED: jersey-> " +
playerJersey +
                "\tPoints-> " + " no value");
    return -1;
}
```

The fifth and final segment of the `ExampleCache` class is provided next. It is used to set the jersey and total points pair so they can be added to the cache:

```java
public void put(int jersey, int points) {
    System.out.println("SETTING: " + jersey + " (jersey) & " +
            points + " (points)");
    if (map.get(jersey) != null) {
        Player player = map.get(jersey);
        player.playerPoints = points;
        deletePlayer(player);
        addToPlayerHead(player);
    } else {
        Player player = new Player(jersey, points);
        map.put(jersey, player);
        if (cacheCount < cacheCapacity) {
            cacheCount++;
            addToPlayerHead(player);
        } else {
            map.remove(playerTail.before.playerJersey);
            deletePlayer(playerTail.before);
            addToPlayerHead(player);
        }
    }
}
```

The `CacheDriver` class is provided in two sections. This first section is the first half of the `main()` method. It creates the `ExampleCache` instance and puts six pairs of jersey numbers and total points in the cache:

```java
public class CacheDriver {

    public static void main(String[] args) {

        System.out.println("\nChapter 9 Caching System.");

        ExampleCache myCache = new ExampleCache(5);

        myCache.put(8, 33643);  // K.Bryant
        myCache.put(14, 25192); // J.West
        myCache.put(22, 23149); // E.Baylor
        myCache.put(24, 33643); // K.Bryant
        myCache.put(32, 17707); // E.Johnson
        myCache.put(33, 24176); // K.Jabbar
```

The second half of the `main()` method is provided next. Here, we simply print six lines, one for each player, to the console. This output includes text and the results of the `retrieve()` method calls:

```
System.out.println("From Cache Driver: Jersey->  8\tPoints-> " +
    myCache.retrieve(8));
System.out.println("From Cache Driver: Jersey-> 14\tPoints-> " +
    myCache.retrieve(14));
System.out.println("From Cache Driver: Jersey-> 22\tPoints-> " +
    myCache.retrieve(22));
System.out.println("From Cache Driver: Jersey-> 24\tPoints-> " +
    myCache.retrieve(24));
System.out.println("From Cache Driver: Jersey-> 32\tPoints-> " +
    myCache.retrieve(32));
System.out.println("From Cache Driver: Jersey-> 33\tPoints-> " +
    myCache.retrieve(33));
    }
  }
```

The output of our program is displayed next. As you can see, our six calls to the `put()` method resulted in six output lines indicating that the `jersey points` pairs were added to the cache. Next are pairs of lines initiated by the `myCache.retrieve()` calls in the `main()` method, located in the `CacheDriver` class. The `RETRIEVED` line is generated from the `retrieve()` method in the `ExampleCache` class and the `From Cache` lines are printed to the console from within the `main()` method. As you can see, although we had six pairs, only five of them were stored in the cache. This was because our cache was too small for all the data. To make space, the cache removed the last recently used entry:

```
Chapter 9 Caching System.
SETTING: 8 (jersey) & 33643 (points)
SETTING: 14 (jersey) & 25192 (points)
SETTING: 22 (jersey) & 23149 (points)
SETTING: 24 (jersey) & 33643 (points)
SETTING: 32 (jersey) & 17707 (points)
SETTING: 33 (jersey) & 24176 (points)
                          RETRIEVED: jersey-> 8    Points-> no value
From Cache Driver: Jersey-> 8   Points-> -1
                          RETRIEVED: jersey -> 14 Points-> 25192
From Cache Driver: Jersey-> 14  Points-> 25192
                          RETRIEVED: jersey -> 22 Points-> 23149
From Cache Driver: Jersey-> 22  Points-> 23149
                          RETRIEVED: jersey -> 24 Points-> 33643
From Cache Driver: Jersey-> 24  Points-> 33643
                          RETRIEVED: jersey -> 32 Points-> 17707
From Cache Driver: Jersey-> 32  Points-> 17707
                          RETRIEVED: jersey -> 33 Points-> 24176
From Cache Driver: Jersey-> 33  Points-> 24176
```

Caching design pattern implementation—console output

This section provided the source code and the console output for our implementation of the caching reactive design pattern.

Understanding the circuit-breaker design pattern

The circuit-breaker design pattern is based on the same concept as an electrical circuit. As you can see in the following diagram, when the circuit is open, the flow of electricity is impeded and cannot flow between the two points—the power source and light bulb in our example. When the circuit is closed, electricity is unimpeded and the light bulb can receive power:

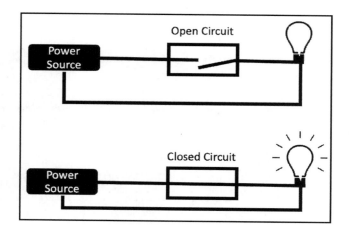

Circuit breaker—light-switch example

The circuit-breaker design pattern is modeled after electrical circuits. This design pattern has three possible states:

- **Open**: If the state is open, then an error will be returned.
- **Closed**: This is the preferred state where functionality is permitted.
- **Half-Open**: This state is used after an open state error and a wait period. The function will allow one use as a test.

If the test is successful, the circuit will be closed and processing will resume. If the test fails, then the circuit will remain open.

Use case

Systems that have a high volume of method calls that are susceptible to failure can benefit from using the circuit-breaker design pattern. These failures can be caused by intermittent access, timeouts, and so on. In order to implement the circuit-breaker pattern, we encase a method or a set of functionality in a circuit breaker. The next diagram illustrates this approach:

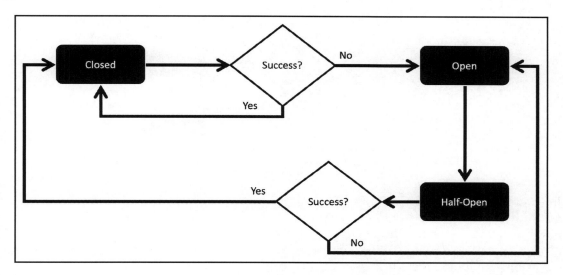

Circuit breaker design pattern—overview

This design pattern can help systems achieve the resilient component of reactive design patterns.

This section provided an overview of the circuit-breaker reactive design pattern.

Understanding the event-driven communication design pattern

The event-driven communication design pattern is based on initiating events such as a query or node request. This event initiates communication between multiple components. The communications between system components can be managed as messages.

To manage these messages, we implement a scheduler to listen to the initiating events and then process the necessary communication via handlers. As illustrated next, the scheduler plays a critical role in the overall communication management system, so care should be taken to make sure it catches exceptions and processes them appropriately:

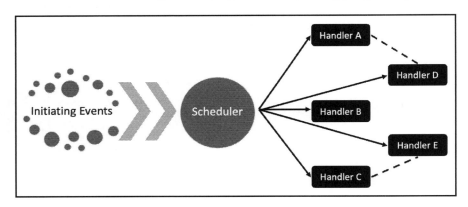

Event-drive communication design pattern implementation—overview

The handlers illustrated in the preceding diagram represent a module of code that is generally short with respect to the amount of functionality that it provides. So, you can see that there can be a lot of handlers in a system. Moreover, there can be a plethora of initiating events happening at the same time. This underscores the significance of ensuring exceptions are handled so processes do not fail.

This section provided an overview of the event-driven communication reactive design pattern.

Understanding the fail-fast design pattern

The fail-fast reactive design pattern stipulates that if something is going to fail, let it happen as fast as possible. The intention is not to perform any unnecessary processing because something is going to fail. We should also be mindful of wasting user time. A scenario would be if a user was given the opportunity to complete a survey and receive a gift card for completing it. If the user answered the first 25 questions and then the survey indicated the user was not eligible for the survey or the gift card, the result would be dreadful. In this scenario, the disqualifying determination should be made much earlier.

Programming the design pattern

Let's take a look at an example. The FailFastImplementation1 class code is provided next in two sections. This class demonstrates the use of Iterator to catch an exception. The first section of our code consists of the import statements and the start of the main() method. The main() method starts by printing a blank line and then creates a HashMap of first and last names. Four key-value pairs are added using the put() method:

```java
package CH9FailFast;
import java.util.ConcurrentModificationException;
import java.util.HashMap;
import java.util.Iterator;
import java.util.Map;

public class FailFastImplementation1 {

    public static void main(String[] args) throws
ConcurrentModificationException {

        System.out.println();

        Map<String, String> firstLast = new HashMap<String, String>();
        firstLast.put("Kay", "Brentwood");
        firstLast.put("Daisy", "Jinsen");
        firstLast.put("Frank", "Corsack");
        firstLast.put("Hugo", "Trapleton");
```

The next section of code completes the main() method and the FailFastImplementation1 class. Here, we create an Iterator instance and then use a while loop, checking to see whether the iterator has a next element using the hasNext() method. Inside the while loop, we use a try-catch block to catch the ConcrrentModificationException error:

```java
        Iterator iterator = firstLast.keySet().iterator();

        while (iterator.hasNext()) {

            try {
                System.out.println(firstLast.get(iterator.next()));
            } catch (ConcurrentModificationException e) {
                System.out.println("Encountered Exception: Failing Fast!");
                return;
            }
        }
    }
}
```

The program's output is provided next. No exceptions were found and the program did not fail-fast or even fail at all:

```
Brentwood
Trapleton
Jinsen
Corsack
```

Fail-fast design pattern implementation—console output without failure

In the next section, we will modify our `FailFastImplementation1` program and introduce an event that will cause the program to fail. We will use a `FailFastImplementation2` class to demonstrate this failure.

Introducing a fail event

Our `FailFastImplementation2` class is similar to our `FailFastImplementation1` class from the previous section. We start with the import statements, the class definition and, the `main()` method definition, and then output a blank line to the console. Here is that code:

```
package CH9FailFast;

import java.util.ConcurrentModificationException;
import java.util.HashMap;
import java.util.Iterator;
import java.util.Map;

public class FailFastImplementation2 {

    public static void main(String[] args) throws
ConcurrentModificationException {
        System.out.println();

        Map<String, String> firstLast = new HashMap<String, String>();
        firstLast.put("Kay", "Brentwood");
        firstLast.put("Daisy", "Jinsen");
        firstLast.put("Frank", "Corsack");
        firstLast.put("Hugo", "Trapleton");
```

In our next section of code, we create a `HashMap` containing first and last names.

The `Iterator` class `next()` method performs a check on the `modCount` flag. This is a part of the `Iterator` class. If the `modCount` flag was changed after the creation of the `Iterator`, then the `ConcurrentModificationException` will be thrown. As you can see with the modified code next, we added a `firstLast.put("Ingrid", "Lithingson");` statement after the `Iterator` instance was created. This will throw the aforementioned exception. Here is the rest of the `FailFastImplementation2` class:

```
Iterator iterator = firstLast.keySet().iterator();

while (iterator.hasNext()) {

  try {
      System.out.println(firstLast.get(iterator.next()));
  } catch (ConcurrentModificationException e) {
      System.out.println("Encountered Exception: Failing
Fast!");
      return;
  }
  firstLast.put("Ingrid", "Lithingson");
}
    }
}
```

As you can see from the next screenshot, the fail-fast output was provided quickly:

```
Brentwood
Encountered Exception: Failing Fast!
```

Fail-fast design pattern implementation—console output with failure

This section provided the source code and the console output for our implementation of the fail-fast reactive design pattern.

Understanding the failure-handling design pattern

When we consider the resilient characteristic of reactive systems, systems and component failures are of utmost concern. It is important to handle these failures in a manner that we determine, which suggests we need to take a purposeful approach to failure-handling. This design pattern has two major components:

- Failure isolation
- Controlled failure

We will look at each of these components next.

Failure isolation

Isolating failure is ensuring that one component's failure does not impact other components. As an example, assume that you are developing an information system for an auto dealer. There are a lot of departments and functions used by the auto dealer and they hope to have their system operational as close to 100% of the time as possible.

Consider the following diagram. There are several components that rely on others. For example, the **Parts Procurement** service cannot be used if the **Payment Gateway** is down, nor can **Service Orders** be processed. If the **Parts Procurement** and **Service Orders** services were not reliant on the **Payment Gateway**, they could still be used by the auto dealer. When the **Payment Gateway** is down, jobs will be queued from the **Parts Procurement** and **Service Order** services. Once the **Payment Gateway** is back online, these jobs will be processed:

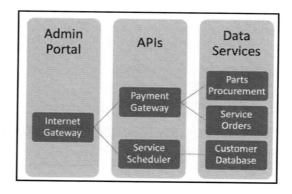

Failure-handling—poor isolation example

In the next section, we will continue the auto dealer scenario and focus on controlled failure.

Controlled failure

The next diagram shows a change to our auto dealer information system architecture. We moved the **Payment Gateway API** to be subordinate to **Parts Procurement** and **Service Orders** components, which are now labeled **Local Services**. Both of those services are no longer halted when the **Payment Gateway** is offline:

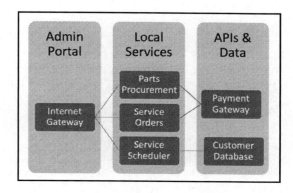

Failure-handling—good isolation example

Now that our structure is aligned for better isolation, we can control the failure. We will demonstrate this in a single `ControlledFailure` class. That class is provided next in three sections. The first section contains the `checkStatus()` method. This method checks to see whether a status is currently online. A divide-by-zero error is introduced to simulate a system being offline:

```
package CH9FailureHandling;

public class ControlledFailure {

    static int checkStatus(String component, int port){

        System.out.println("\n\tChecking status of : " + component);
        // artificial introduction of divide by zero error
        int result = (port / 0);

        return result;
    }
```

The second section of the `ControlledFailure` class contains the `processServiceOrder()` method. This method would be used as part of service order processing. Before submitting the information to the payment gateway, we can check to see whether it is offline. This will allow us to gracefully handle the error instead of the user receiving a harsh runtime error directly from JVM:

```java
static int processServiceOrder(String process, int serviceOrderNbr) {

    int gatewayStatus = 0;

    try
    {
        gatewayStatus = checkStatus(process, serviceOrderNbr);
    }
    catch(NumberFormatException ex)
    {
        System.out.println("Error detected: " + ex.getMessage());
    }
    return gatewayStatus;
}
```

The final section of the `ControlledFailure` class contains the `main()` method, which includes a `try-catch` block to catch and handle exceptions:

```java
public static void main(String args[]){
    String processToCheck = "Payment Gateway";
    int serviceOrderNumber = 319;

    try
    {
        System.out.println("\nService order processing . . . ");
        int serviceOrder = processServiceOrder(processToCheck,
serviceOrderNumber);

    }
    catch(ArithmeticException ex)
    {
        System.out.println("\n\tPayment Gateway is offline. Your orders
" +
                "\n\twill be automatically processed via batch "+
                "\n\twhen the gateway is back online.");

        System.out.println("\n. . . continue processing service
order.");
    }
}
}
```

Here is the output of our program. You can see that we inform the user that their service order is being processed and, when we receive an error, we provide information to the user. At that point, they can continue using the system despite the payment gateway's offline status:

```
Service order processing . . .

    Checking status of : Payment Gateway

    Payment Gateway is offline. Your orders
    will be automatically processed via batch
    when the gateway is back online.

. . . continue processing service order.
```

Failure-handling design pattern implementation—console output

This section provided the source code and the console output for our auto dealer information system implementation of the failure-handling reactive design pattern.

Understanding the fan-out and quickest-reply design pattern

The fan-out and quickest-reply reactive design pattern emphasizes rapid processing. Financial software that provides real-time, or near real-time, stock information uses this design pattern. The concept is to provide sufficient processing instances so requests can be processed without waiting in a queue.

To implement the fan-out and quickest-reply design pattern, we send each request to multiple processing modules. Each of those modules would process the request and send the results back to the requestor. The requestor would use the quickest reply, the first one received, and simply ignore the rest:

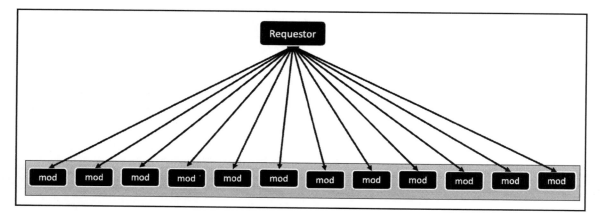

Fan-out and quickest-reply design pattern

As you would expect, the extra processing could make it a costly use of resources, so this approach should only be used when quick replies are of utmost importance.

This section provided an overview of the fan-out and quickest-reply design pattern.

Understanding the idempotency design pattern

In computer science, the term idempotent means an element whose value remains unchanged after repeated calculation. Consider the example of a hospital information system that adds one day to the length of stay for a patient record. It would be important that the system performs the addition the first time and ignore other requests within the calendar day.

To provide an example of this design pattern, we will create a hospital information system that maintains patient records. Each time an event occurs with a patient, a message is sent to update the number of days the patient has been in the hospital. It is important that we do not count the patient as being at the hospital more than once per day, to avoid overcharges.

The source code for the implementation of the idempotency design pattern is provided in the next section.

Programming the design pattern

Our hospital information system implementation of the idempotency reactive design pattern will consist of the `Patient` class and the `IdempotencyDriver` class. The `Patient` class is provided in three sections, with the first section appearing next.

In this first section of the `Patient` class, we define the three class variables and create the constructor method. The constructor only has one argument and that is for the `patientID` number. When a `Patient` instance is created, the `lengthOfStay` variable is set to 0 and `dayCounted` is set to `false`:

```
package CH9IdempotencyExample;

public class Patient {

    String patientID;
    int lengthOfStay;
    boolean dayCounted;

    // constructor
    public Patient (String patientID) {
        this.patientID = patientID;
        this.lengthOfStay = 0;
        this.dayCounted = false;
    }
```

The second part of the `Patient` class contains the three `accessor` methods. These methods are used to retrieve values of the class variable:

```
// accessor methods
public String getPatientID() {
    return this.patientID;
}

public int getLengthOfStay() {
    return this.lengthOfStay;
}

public boolean getDayCounted() {
    return this.dayCounted;
}
```

The final section of the `Patient` class contains the `mutator` methods. The `setPatientID()` and `setDayCounted()` `mutator` methods are straightforward. The `setLengthOfStay()` method has a logic check to see whether the current value of the `dayCounted` variable is true or false. If the day has already been counted, the value will be true; otherwise, it will be false. If the day has not been counted, the `lengthOfStay` will be incremented and the `dayCounted` value will be changed to true:

```java
    // mutator methods
    public void setPatientID(String patientID) {
        this.patientID = patientID;
    }

    public void setLengthOfStay(int lengthOfStay) {

        if (this.dayCounted) {
            System.out.println("\tIdempotency Implemented: Length of Stay
already computed.");
        } else {
            this.lengthOfStay += lengthOfStay;
            this.dayCounted = true;
        }
    }

    public void setDayCounted(boolean counted) {
        this.dayCounted = counted;
    }
}
```

The `IdempotencyDriver` class is the driver class for our hospital information system. The first section of that code is provided next and contains the `main()` method. That method contains a decorative header for console output and a local `tID String` variable:

```java
package CH9IdempotencyExample;

public class IdempotencyDriver {

    public static void main(String[] args) {

        System.out.println("\n = = = = = = = = = = = = = = = = = = = = = = = =
");
        System.out.println("\t\tHOSPITAL INFORMATION SYSTEM");
        System.out.println(" = = = = = = = = = = = = = = = = = = = = = = = =
");

        String tID = "XP330019";
```

The second and final portion of the `IdempotencyDriver` class is provided next. There are three sections of this code, each separated by inline comments. The first section, `Admission`, creates a `Patient` instance and makes a call to the `setLengthOfStay()` method. The second section, `Lab Work`, attempts to alter the `lengthOfStay` variable's value. The third section, `Next Day`, starts by setting the `dayCounted` value to false. It then makes a call to the `setLengthOfStay()` method:

```
        // Admission
        Patient patient = new Patient(tID);
        System.out.println("\nPatient " + patient.getPatientID() + "
admitted.");
        patient.setLengthOfStay(1);
        System.out.println("\tLength of stay : " +
patient.getLengthOfStay());

        // Lab Work
        System.out.println("\nPatient " + patient.getPatientID() + "
received lab work.");
        patient.setLengthOfStay(1);
        System.out.println("\tLength of stay : " +
patient.getLengthOfStay());

        // Next Day
        patient.setDayCounted(false);
        System.out.println("\nPatient " + patient.getPatientID() + "
received surgery.");
        patient.setLengthOfStay(1);
        System.out.println("\tLength of stay : " +
patient.getLengthOfStay());
    }

}
```

The console output for our program is provided next. As you can see, idempotency was implemented for the second attempt to update the patient's length of stay on their first day:

```
= = = = = = = = = = = = = = = = = = = = = = =
          HOSPITAL INFORMATION SYSTEM
= = = = = = = = = = = = = = = = = = = = = = =

Patient XP330019 admitted.
    Length of stay : 1

Patient XP330019 received lab work.
    Idempotency Implemented: Length of Stay already computed.
    Length of stay : 1

Patient XP330019 received surgery.
    Length of stay : 2
```

Idempotency design pattern implementation—console output

This section provided the source code and the console output for our hospital information system implementation of the idempotency reactive design pattern.

Understanding the monitoring design pattern

The monitoring design pattern is self-explanatory. In order to ensure our systems are reactive, specifically resilient, we need to monitor them. Modern large-scale systems are typically housed in a cloud-based system such as AWS, Google Compute, IBM Cloud, and Oracle Cloud. Each of these services provides graphical dashboards and an alert system.

The alerts can be customized based on the system administrator's determination and upper and lower thresholds for each service and system.

This section provided a brief overview of the monitoring reactive design pattern.

Understanding the publisher-subscriber design pattern

The publisher-subscriber design pattern establishes two entities: a publisher that sends messages based on events and a subscriber that subscribes to those events. With this design pattern, publishers transmit messages and subscribers listen for them and then take the appropriate action or inaction.

As illustrated next, the **Publisher** publishes events. The **Subscribers** subscribe to the events. Once an event is heard, the **Subscriber** provides the computation or processing as appropriate for the event:

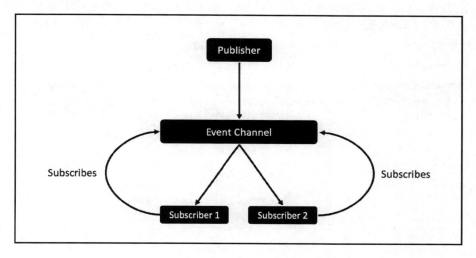

Publisher-subscriber design pattern—overview

This design pattern is event-driven and can be implemented by using the event-driven architecture, the observer pattern, and the message broker pattern, covered in previous chapters of this book.

This section provided a brief overview of the publisher-subscriber design pattern.

Understanding the self-containment design pattern

Systems that employ the self-containment reactive design pattern are not reliant on non-system components. This design pattern can also be applied at the system component level. In that instance, a system component would be self-contained and not rely on other system components.

To examine the self-containment reactive design pattern, let's first consider a system diagram depicting a lack of self-containment. As you can see from the next diagram, the **Financial Services API** is the only system component with access to the **Payment Gateway** and the related database. Both the **New Vehicle Sales** and service department sales shown by **Service Dept Sales** nodes, rely on the **Financial Services API** for access to its sub-components:

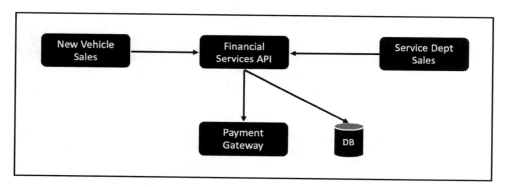

System in need of the self-containment design pattern

This architecture is not advised, as the reliance that the **New Vehicle Sales** and **Service Dept Sales** components have on the **Financial Services API** could result in bottlenecks, data collisions, and an interruption of service.

Next, let's examine a modified version of the same system, this time implementing the self-containment design pattern. In the following diagram, the **New Vehicle Sales** and **Service Dept Sales** components have direct access to the **Payment Gateway** and related database. This makes them self-contained and not reliant on other system components:

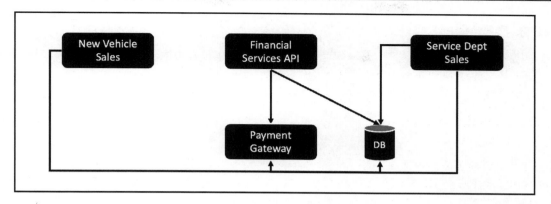

Modified system implementing the self-containment design pattern

This section provided an overview of the self-containment reactive design pattern.

Understanding the stateless design pattern

When we implement the stateless design pattern, we create classes and objects that do not retain state changes. In this approach, each use of the object, as an example, uses the object in its organic form. In our context, *state* refers to the values of the object's variables. So, there is no definitive list of states. The state of an object is specific to a moment in time.

Implementing the stateless design pattern is appropriate for the following cases:

- When we want to clone services
- When the current state of an object dictates that object's behavior
- When object behavior is a runtime decision and that behavior is state-dependent
- When you want to process the state of an object as if it were an object

In the next section, we will review the UML class diagram for an implementation of the stateless reactive design pattern.

Use case

We will create a CORGI STATELESS SYSTEM as an example implementation of the stateless reactive design pattern. Our system will comprise the following classes:

- CorgiState (interface)
- Corgi
- CorgiAwake
- CorgiEat
- CorgiPlay
- CorgiSit
- CorgiSleep
- CorgiWalk
- StatelessDriver

Our system will create a Corgi instance and permit the changing of states and demonstrating the stateless design pattern. We will prohibit changing from the Sleep state to any state other than the Awake state.

The next section will provide a UML class diagram to detail each of these classes.

UML class diagram

Our CORGI STATELESS SYSTEM example implementation of the stateless reactive design pattern will consist of eight classes. Those classes and their relationships are depicted in this UML class diagram:

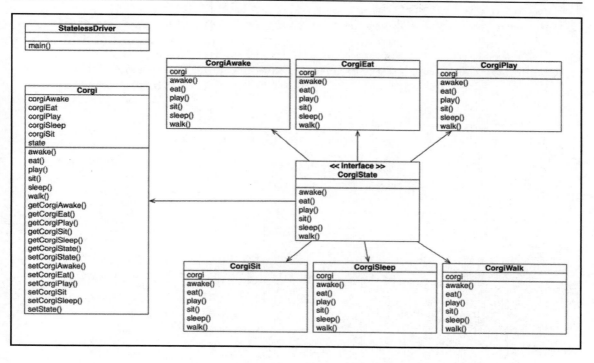

UML class diagram—stateless design pattern implementation

In the next section, we will program our implementation of the stateless design pattern.

Programming the design pattern

Our CORGI STATELESS SYSTEM consists of eight classes. Our first class is the CorgiState interface. As shown next, there are five interface methods—awake(), eat(), play(), sleep(), and walk(). Each of these methods represents a state for instances of the Corgi class:

```
package CH9Stateless;
public interface CorgiState {

    void awake();
    void eat();
    void play();
    void sit();
    void sleep();
    void walk();
}
```

Our primary object class for the application is the `Corgi` class, which implements the `CorgiState` interface. The class is provided in the next eight code sections:

1. The first section contains the class definition and the class variables. These class variables represent the possible states a `Corgi` object can have:

```
package CH9Stateless;

public class Corgi implements CorgiState {

    // class variables
    private CorgiState corgiAwake;
    private CorgiState corgiEat;
    private CorgiState corgiPlay;
    private CorgiState corgiSleep;
    private CorgiState corgiSit;
    private CorgiState state;
```

2. The second section of the `Corgi` class contains the `constructor` method. After `constructor`, the `Awake` state is set so that when a `Corgi` is instantiated, its default state will be `Awake`:

```
    // constructor
    public Corgi(){
        this.corgiAwake = new CorgiAwake(this);
        this.corgiEat = new CorgiEat(this);
        this.corgiPlay = new CorgiPlay(this);
        this.corgiSleep = new CorgiSleep(this);
        this.corgiSit = new CorgiSit(this);

        this.state = corgiAwake;
    }
```

3. The third section of our `Corgi` class contains the first three overridden methods from the `CorgiState` interface:

```
    // overriding interface methods
    @Override
    public void awake() {
        state.awake();
        setState(getCorgiSit());
    }

    @Override
    public void walk() {
        state.walk();
        setState(getCorgiSit());
```

```
}

@Override
public void sit() {
    state.sit();
    setState(getCorgiSit());
}
```

4. The fourth section of our `Corgi` class contains the remaining three overridden methods from the `CorgiState` interface:

```
@Override
public void eat() {
 state.eat();
 setState(getCorgiSit());
}

@Override
public void play() {
 state.play();
 setState(getCorgiSit());
}

@Override
public void sleep() {
 state.sleep();
}
```

5. The fifth section of the `Corgi` class contains the first three `accessor` methods for the class variables:

```
// accessor methods
public CorgiState getCorgiAwake() {
    return corgiAwake;
}

public CorgiState getCorgiEat() {
    return corgiEat;
}

public CorgiState getCorgiPlay() {
    return corgiPlay;
}
```

6. The sixth section of the `Corgi` class contains the remaining `accessor` methods for the class variables:

```
public CorgiState getCorgiSleep() {
```

```
        return corgiSleep;
    }

public CorgiState getState() {
    return state;
}

public CorgiState getCorgiSit() {
    return corgiSit;
}
```

7. The seventh section of the `Corgi` class contains the first three `mutator` methods for the class variables:

```
// mutator methods
    public void setCorgiState(CorgiState state){
        this.state = state;
    }

    public void setCorgiAwake(CorgiState corgiAwake) {
        this.corgiAwake = corgiAwake;
    }

    public void setCorgiEat(CorgiState corgiEat) {
        this.corgiEat = corgiEat;
    }
```

8. The eighth and final section of the `Corgi` class contains the remaining `mutator` methods for the class variables:

```
    public void setCorgiPlay(CorgiState corgiPlay) {
        this.corgiPlay = corgiPlay;
    }

    public void setCorgiSleep(CorgiState corgiSleep) {
        this.corgiSleep = corgiSleep;
    }

    public void setState(CorgiState state) {
        this.state = state;
    }

    public void setCorgiSit(CorgiState corgiSit) {
        this.corgiSit = corgiSit;
    }
}
```

Now that our `CorgiState` interface and `Corgi` class have been completed, we need a class for each of the four states (`awake`, `eat`, `play`, `sleep`, and `sit`). We will also need a `Driver` class. All of these six classes are provided next.

Our next class is the `CorgiAwake` class and is provided in the following two sections. The class implements the `CorgiState` interface and provides for the concrete state of `CorgiAwake`. The section that follows contains the `constructor` method and the first three overridden methods for the `CorgiState` interface:

```
package CH9Stateless;

public class CorgiAwake implements CorgiState{

    private final Corgi corgi;

    public CorgiAwake(Corgi corgi) {
        this.corgi = corgi;
    }

    @Override
    public void awake() {
        System.out.println("The Corgi is AWAKE.");
    }

    @Override
    public void walk() {
        System.out.println("The Corgi is WALKING.");
    }

    @Override
    public void sit() {
        System.out.println("The Corgi is SITTING.");
    }
```

The second half of the `CorgiAwake` class is provided next and contains the remaining overridden methods from the `CorgiState` interface:

```
    @Override
    public void eat() {
        System.out.println("The Corgi is EATING.");
        corgi.setCorgiState(corgi.getCorgiEat());
    }

    @Override
    public void play() {
        System.out.println("The Corgi is PLAYING.");
        corgi.setCorgiState(corgi.getCorgiPlay());
```

```
    }

    @Override
    public void sleep() {
        corgi.setState(corgi.getCorgiSleep());
        System.out.println("The Corgi is SLEEPING.");
    }
}
```

Our next class is the `CorgiEat` class and is provided next in two sections. The class implements the `CorgiState` interface and provides for the concrete state of `CorgiEat`. The next section contains the constructor method and the first three overridden methods for the `CorgiState` interface:

```
package CH9Stateless;

public class CorgiEat implements CorgiState{

    private final Corgi corgi;

    public CorgiEat(Corgi corgi){
        this.corgi = corgi;
    }

    @Override
    public void awake() {
        System.out.println("The Corgi is AWAKE.");
    }

    @Override
    public void walk() {
        System.out.println("The Corgi is WALKING.");
    }

    @Override
    public void sit() {
        System.out.println("The Corgi is SITTING.");
    }
```

The second half of the `CorgiEat` class is provided next and contains the remaining overridden methods from the `CorgiState` interface:

```
    @Override
    public void eat() {
        System.out.println("The Corgi is EATING");
        corgi.setCorgiState(corgi.getCorgiSleep());
    }
```

```
    @Override
    public void play() {
        System.out.println("The Corgi is PLAYING");
    }

    @Override
    public void sleep() {
        System.out.println("The Corgi is SLEEPING.");
    }
}
```

Our next class is the CorgiPlay class and is provided next in two sections. The class implements the CorgiState interface and provides for the concrete state of CorgiPlay. The following section contains the constructor method and the first three overridden methods for the CorgiState interface:

```
package CH9Stateless;

public class CorgiPlay implements CorgiState {

    private final Corgi corgi;

    public CorgiPlay(Corgi corgi){
        this.corgi = corgi;
    }

    @Override
    public void awake() {
        System.out.println("The Corgi is AWAKE.");
    }
    @Override
    public void walk() {
        System.out.println("The Corgi is WALKING.");
    }

    @Override
    public void sit() {
        System.out.println("The Corgi is SITTING.");
    }
```

The second half of the CorgiPlay class is provided next and contains the remaining overridden methods from the CorgiState interface:

```
@Override
    public void eat() {
        System.out.println("The Corgi is EATING.");
        corgi.setCorgiState(corgi.getCorgiSleep());
```

```
    }

    @Override
    public void play() {
        System.out.println("The Corgi is PLAYING.");
    }

    @Override
        public void sit() {
    System.out.println("The Corgi is SITTING and waiting for action...");
    }

    @Override
    public void sleep() {
        System.out.println("The Corgi is SLEEPING.");
    }
}
```

Our next class is the CorgiSleep class and is provided in the next two sections. The class implements the CorgiState interface and provides for the concrete state of CorgiSleep. The next section contains the constructor method and the first two overridden methods for the CorgiState interface:

```
package CH9Stateless;

public class CorgiSleep implements CorgiState{

    private final Corgi corgi;

    public CorgiSleep(Corgi corgi){
        this.corgi = corgi;
    }

    @Override
    public void awake() {
        System.out.println("The Corgi is AWAKE.");
    }

    @Override
    public void walk() {
        System.out.println("The Corgi cannot WALK when it is SLEEPING.");
    }
    @Override
    public void sit() {
        System.out.println("The Corgi is SITTING.");
    }
```

The second half of the `CorgiSleep` class is provided next and contains the remaining overridden methods from the `CorgiState` interface:

```java
@Override
public void eat() {
    System.out.println("The Corgi cannot EAT when it is SLEEPING.");
    corgi.setCorgiState(corgi.getCorgiSleep());
}

@Override
public void play() {
    System.out.println("The Corgi cannot PLAY when it is SLEEPING.");
}

@Override
public void sleep() {
    System.out.println("The Corgi is SLEEPING.");
}
}
```

Our next class is the `CorgiSit` class and is provided in the following two snippets. The class implements the `CorgiState` interface and provides for the concrete state of `CorgiSit`. The next section contains the constructor method and the first two overridden methods for the `CorgiState` interface:

```java
package CH9Stateless;
public class CorgiSit implements CorgiState{

    private final Corgi corgi;

    public CorgiSit(Corgi corgi){
        this.corgi = corgi;
    }

    @Override
    public void awake() {
        System.out.println("\tThe Corgi is now AWAKE.");
        corgi.setState(corgi.getCorgiAwake());
    }

    @Override
    public void walk() {
        System.out.println("The Corgi is SITTING and waiting for
action...");
        corgi.setState(corgi.getCorgiAwake());
        System.out.println("\tThe Corgi is now WALKING");
    }
```

The second half of the `CorgiSit` class is provided next and contains the remaining overridden methods from the `CorgiState` interface:

```
@Override
public void eat() {
    System.out.println("The Corgi is SITTING and waiting for
action...");
        corgi.setCorgiState(corgi.getCorgiEat());
    System.out.println("\tThe Corgi is now EATING.");
}

@Override
public void play() {
    System.out.println("The Corgi is SITTING and waiting for
action...");
        corgi.setCorgiState(corgi.getCorgiPlay());
    System.out.println("\tThe Corgi is now PLAYING.");
}

@Override
public void sleep() {
    System.out.println("Shhh; the Corgi is sleeping.");
    corgi.setState(corgi.getCorgiSleep());
    System.out.println("\tThe Corgi is now SLEEPING.");
}
}
```

Our next class is the `CorgiWalk` class and is provided in the following two sections. The class implements the `CorgiState` interface and provides for the concrete state of `CorgiWalk`. The next section contains the constructor method and the first three overridden methods for the `CorgiState` interface:

```
package CH9Stateless;

public class CorgiWalk  implements CorgiState {

    private final Corgi corgi;

    public CorgiWalk(Corgi corgi){
        this.corgi = corgi;
    }

    @Override
    public void awake() {
        System.out.println("The Corgi is AWAKE.");
    }
```

```
@Override
public void walk() {
    System.out.println("The Corgi is WALKING.");
}

@Override
public void sit() {
    System.out.println("The Corgi is SITTING.");
}
```

The second half of the `CorgiWalk` class is provided next and contains the remaining overridden methods from the `CorgiState` interface:

```
@Override
public void eat() {
    System.out.println("The Corgi is EATING.");
    corgi.setCorgiState(corgi.getCorgiSleep());
}

@Override
public void play() {
    System.out.println("The Corgi is PLAYING.");
}

@Override
public void sleep() {
    System.out.println("The Corgi is SLEEPING.");
}
}
```

Our last class for the CORGI STATELESS SYSTEM implementation of the stateless design pattern is the `StatelessDriver` class. This class contains the `main()` method and drives the application:

```
package CH9Stateless;

public class StatelessDriver {

    public static void main(String[] args) {

        System.out.println("\n = = = = = = = = = = = = = = =");
        System.out.println("\tCORGI STATELESS SYSTEM");
        System.out.println(" = = = = = = = = = = = = = = = =\n");

        Corgi corgi = new Corgi();

        corgi.awake();
        corgi.walk();
```

```
        corgi.play();
        corgi.eat();
        corgi.walk();
        corgi.sleep();

        corgi.play();
        corgi.sleep();
        corgi.eat();
    }
}
```

The output of our application is as follows. As you can see, we did not permit any action from the sleep state other than AWAKE:

```
= = = = = = = = = = = = = = =
    CORGI STATELESS SYSTEM
= = = = = = = = = = = = = = =

The Corgi is AWAKE.
The Corgi is SITTING and waiting for action...
    The Corgi is now WALKING
The Corgi is SITTING and waiting for action...
    The Corgi is now PLAYING.
The Corgi is SITTING and waiting for action...
    The Corgi is now EATING.
The Corgi is SITTING and waiting for action...
    The Corgi is now WALKING
Shhh; the Corgi is sleeping.
    The Corgi is now SLEEPING.
The Corgi cannot PLAY when it is SLEEPING.
Shhh; the Corgi is sleeping.
    The Corgi is now SLEEPING.
The Corgi cannot EAT when it is SLEEPING.
```

Stateless design pattern implementation—console output

This section provided the source code and the console output for our CORGI STATELESS SYSTEM implementation of the stateless reactive design pattern.

Summary

In this chapter, we explored the reactive design pattern category and its individual design patterns of asynchronous communication, autoscaling, bounded queue, bulkhead, caching, circuit breaker, event-driven communication, fail-fast, failure-handling, fan-out, quickest reply, idempotency, monitoring, publisher-subscriber, self-containment, and stateless. We also reviewed use cases for the design patterns and how they can contribute to well-designed and-developed systems that are reactive to internal and external changes.

You now have the necessary knowledge of the **Universal Modeling Language (UML)**, **Object-Oriented Programming (OOP)**, and over 60 design patterns to enhance your software design and development capabilities.

The design patterns in this book are not time-bound and will remain valid for several decades to come.

Questions

1. What are the main purposes of reactive design patterns?
2. What are the four characteristics of reactive design patterns?
3. Which design pattern allows the client to send multiple request messages to the server and not dedicate processing resources and anticipate a response message from the server?
4. What are the two types of autoscaling relevant to the autoscaling design pattern?
5. What type of queues have a fixed number of elements ?
6. Which design pattern uses open, closed, and half-open states?
7. Which design pattern includes failure isolation?
8. Which design pattern includes elements whose value remains unchanged after repeated calculation?
9. Which design pattern is event-based and relies on subscribers?
10. Which design pattern employs self-sufficiency?

Further reading

- *Java EE 8 Design Patterns and Best Practices* (https://www.packtpub.com/application-development/java-ee-8-design-patterns-and-best-practices)
- *Learning Design Patterns with Java [Video]* (https://www.packtpub.com/application-development/learn-design-patterns-java-video)
- *Design Patterns and Best Practices in Java* (https://www.packtpub.com/application-development/design-patterns-and-best-practices-java)
- *What is the Reactive Manifesto?* (https://hub.packtpub.com/what-is-the-reactive-manifesto/)

Assessments

Chapter 1

1. Behavioral and structural
2. UML was originally created to visually document object-oriented systems
3. Activity diagram, interaction diagram, state machine diagram, and use-case diagram
4. Activity diagrams illustrate the flow of processes in a system
5. Use-case diagrams document the interactions between users and the system
6. Actors are a system's users
7. Structural diagrams illustrate components of a system
8. Class diagram
9. The composite structure UML diagram shows the runtime structure of a system
10. The deployment diagram provides a visual representation of a system's hardware and software

Chapter 2

1. Portability, inheritance, encapsulation, and polymorphism
2. The class structure lends itself well to portability
3. Encapsulation
4. In OOP, polymorphism states that different types of objects can be accessed via a common interface
5. In Java, we can use the `this` keyword as a reference to the current object
6. Accessor methods are those that allow an object's data to be accessed
7. Mutator methods allow the object's instance variables to be changed
8. Constructors are a special kind of method that are run when an object is initialized
9. Their definition has a unique set of parameters
10. Left to right

Chapter 3

1. Memento design pattern
2. Behavioral design patterns
3. The purpose of the dependency is to update subscriber objects when a change is made to the publisher object's state
4. State design pattern
5. Strategy design pattern
6. Template method design pattern
7. Chain of Responsibility design pattern
8. Transaction or action design pattern
9. The interpreter design pattern is used to establish a grammatical representation and an interpreter that interprets language
10. The `Iterator` interface

Chapter 4

1. The purposes of creational design patterns are as follows:

   - Separate object creation from the system
   - Support reliance on object creation vice inheritance
   - Encapsulate information regarding which classes are used by a system
   - Protect object creation details

2. Abstract factory, builder, `factory` method, prototype, simple factory, and singleton
3. Object scope and class scope
4. In Java, abstract classes cannot be instantiated, but they can be inherited
5. Abstract factory design pattern
6. Builder design pattern
7. Factory method design pattern
8. Prototype design pattern
9. Simple factory design pattern
10. Singleton design pattern

Chapter 5

1. How objects and classes are combined to form a system
2. Adapter, Bridge, Composite, Decorator, Facade, Flyweight, Proxy
3. Adapter design pattern
4. Structural class design pattern
5. Adapter design pattern
6. Composite design pattern
7. Decorator design pattern
8. Facade design pattern
9. Flyweight design pattern
10. Proxy design pattern

Chapter 6

1. Architectural patterns take a holistic view of systems and group components
2. A non-prescriptive approach is taken for visually documenting architectural patterns
3. Blackboard pattern
4. Broker pattern
5. Client-server pattern
6. Event-driven pattern
7. Extract-transform-load pattern
8. Layered pattern
9. Master-slave pattern
10. Microkernel pattern

Chapter 7

1. Modularity, processing efficiency, and maintainable code
2. By splitting up both the processing and the storage between multiple servers
3. Microservices pattern
4. Model-view-controller pattern
5. Naked objects pattern
6. Peer-to-peer pattern
7. Pipe-filter pattern
8. Serverless pattern
9. Service-oriented pattern
10. Space-based pattern

Chapter 8

1. Functional rules:
   - They do not mutate any data
   - They provide consistent results, given the same set of arguments
   - They exist to provide a return value
2. Execute Around, Lambda, Loan, MapReduce, Memorization, Streams, Tail Call
3. Mathematical functions
4. Execute around
5. Lambda
6. Loan
7. MapReduce
8. Memoization
9. Streams
10. Tail call

Chapter 9

1. The purpose of reactive design patterns is to provide system architects, engineers, and developers with the ability to create systems that are, at their core, responsive and scalable
2. Responsive, resilient, elastic, and message-driven
3. Asynchronous communication design pattern
4. Vertical scaling and horizontal scaling
5. Bounded queues
6. Circuit-breaker design pattern
7. Failure-handling design pattern
8. Idempotency design pattern
9. Publisher–subscriber design pattern
10. Self-containment design pattern

Other Books You May Enjoy

If you enjoyed this book, you may be interested in these other books by Packt:

Java 11 Cookbook - Second Edition
Nick Samoylov , Mohamed Sanaulla

ISBN: 9781789132359

- Set up JDK and understand what's new in the JDK 11 installation
- Implement object-oriented designs using classes and interfaces
- Manage operating system processes
- Create a modular application with clear dependencies
- Build graphical user interfaces using JavaFX
- Use the new HTTP Client API
- Explore the new diagnostic features in Java 11
- Discover how to use the new JShell REPL tool

Mastering Java 11 - Second Edition
Dr. Edward Lavieri

ISBN: 9781789137613

- Write modular Java applications
- Migrate existing Java applications to modular ones
- Understand how the default G1 garbage collector works
- Leverage the possibilities provided by the newly introduced Java Shell
- Performance test your application effectively with the JVM harness
- Learn how Java supports the HTTP 2.0 standard
- Find out how to use the new Process API
- Explore the additional enhancements and features of Java 9, 10, and 11

Leave a review - let other readers know what you think

Please share your thoughts on this book with others by leaving a review on the site that you bought it from. If you purchased the book from Amazon, please leave us an honest review on this book's Amazon page. This is vital so that other potential readers can see and use your unbiased opinion to make purchasing decisions, we can understand what our customers think about our products, and our authors can see your feedback on the title that they have worked with Packt to create. It will only take a few minutes of your time, but is valuable to other potential customers, our authors, and Packt. Thank you!

Index